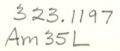

AMERICAN INDIAN POLICY

Self-Governance and Economic Development

Edited by LYMAN H. LEGTERS
and FREMONT J. LYDEN

Prepared under the auspices of the
Policy Studies Organization
Stuart S. Nagel, Publications Coordinator

Contributions in Political Science, Number 329

GREENWOOD PRESS
Westport, Connecticut • London

Library of Congress Cataloging-in-Publication Data

American Indian policy : self-governance and economic development /
   edited by Lyman H. Legters and Fremont J. Lyden.
      p.   cm. — (Contributions in political science, ISSN 0147–1066
 ; no. 329)
   Includes bibliographical references and index.
   ISBN 0–313–28992–1 (alk. paper)
   1. Indians of North America—Politics and government. 2. Self-
determination, National—United States. 3. Indians of North
America—Government relations. 4. Indians of North America—
Economic conditions.   I. Legters, Lyman Howard.
II. Lyden, Fremont J.   III. Series.
E93.A45   1994
323.1′197—dc20   93–9319

British Library Cataloguing in Publication Data is available.

Library of Congress Catalog Card Number: 93–9319
ISBN: 0–313–28992–1
ISSN: 0147–1066

First published in 1994

Greenwood Press, 88 Post Road West, Westport, CT 06881
An imprint of Greenwood Publishing Group, Inc.

Printed in the United States of America

∞™

The paper used in this book complies with the
Permanent Paper Standard issued by the National
Information Standards Organization (Z39.48–1984).

10 9 8 7 6 5 4 3 2 1

Contents

Figures and Tables

FIGURES

TABLES

Introduction

Lyman H. Legters and Fremont J. Lyden

Throughout the two hundred years of history of the U.S. government, American Indians have been battling to regain self-governance. As Felix Cohen observed, self-governance

> includes the power of an Indian tribe to adopt and operate under a form of government of the Indians' own choosing, to define conditions of tribal membership, to regulate domestic relations of members, to prescribe rules of inheritance, to levy taxes, to regulate property within the jurisdiction of the tribe, to control the conduct of members by meaningful legislation and to administer justice. (Cohen 1942, 122)

The history of these efforts is traced by Willard in chapter 1 of this volume. As he notes, these attempts to attain self-government have not proved very successful. In the fall of 1987, however, Ross Swimmer, assistant secretary of Indian affairs, proposed to the House Interior and Related Agencies Appropriations Subcommittee that a demonstration project be authorized to transfer the Bureau of Indian Affairs funds, which were presently controlling the operation of all Indian reservations, to those tribes seeking such a transfer. This proposal was based on recommendations made by the President's Commission on Reservation Economics in 1984.

Congressman Sidney Yates (D-Illinois), chairman of the subcommittee, asked Quinault president Joe DeLaCruz and Lummi tribal chairman Larry Kinley to meet with him to discuss the proposal. The tribal leaders were not supportive of the proposal, however, because it also contained a provision absolving the U.S. government of its trusteeship obligations to any tribes accepting the transfer. After this provision was removed from the proposal, the tribal leaders did express an interest.

A series of discussions followed, resulting in a tribal proposal for the establishment of a self-government demonstration project. Congressman Yates's subcommittee accepted this proposal and included funds for further consideration in the Appropriations Act of 1987. Five months later, ten Indian tribes volunteered to participate in planning a self-government project. In September 1988, Congress amended the Indian Self-Determination and Education Assistance Act (PL 100–472) authorizing a five-year demonstration project to determine whether such a self-governance effort would be feasible (see Appendix at end of the volume). The ten tribes entered into such an agreement, and later, other tribes were allowed to join in the effort.[1]

The Self-Government Demonstration Project is now well underway. It therefore seemed appropriate to assemble a collection of articles that deal with the circumstances related to such an effort. Self-government assumes that tribes will eventually be able to develop their own resources sufficiently to become independent of continued funding by the federal government. Economic development is, therefore, the key to realizing self-government. Without the possibility of self-sufficiency, no tribe can realistically contemplate self-government.

It is hoped that the chapters in this collection will provide a useful resource to individuals undertaking the task of evaluating the efficacy of self-government. Accordingly, in part I, the articles examine the concept of self-governance, the organizational implications of adopting self-governance, the politics associated with such efforts, and the relationship of self-governance to Indian education, religious freedom, and Indian employment in the Bureau of Indian Affairs.

In part II of the volume, self-governance is examined in relation to the likelihood of tribes securing economic independence. The chapters deal with a redefinition of property rights, a survey of economic development being practiced on reservations today, the subsidization of economic development, and the success of efforts by an Indian tribe and an Alaskan Native American corporation to utilize their timber resources effectively and appropriately.

It should not be imagined—and none of the contributors to this book supposes—that this pilot effort represents a simple undertaking. The relationship between American Indians and the surrounding white majority carries a heavy burden of remembered exploitation and frustration, so much so that a new initiative of this sort can hardly get underway before encountering deep and, unfortunately, well-founded mistrust. Recent policies and rulings of federal agencies and courts have done little to dispel skepticism among Indians that their historical oppressor could underwrite a good-faith program to promote genuine self-governance and economic development.

Assuming, however, that mistrust can be sufficiently overcome, or at least set aside, to allow for an authentic partnership to the benefit of the tribal government and the economy of Native Americans, the obstacles that remain are still formidable. Tribal government has suffered so much from manipulation and outright nullification by state and federal authority that, in its present condition, it may not speak authentically for its constituency. When it does, moreover, its habitual inclination is one of minimizing damage inflicted from outside, not acting autonomously for the enhancement of its community life. This is not to denigrate tribal government, of course, but only to underline the historical legacy of dependence.

Circumstances are no better in the economic sphere. The tutelary relationship has given low priority to measures that might have secured greater self-sufficiency on the reservation and, conversely, has found justifications for alienating tribal resources. The result is not merely a minimal basis for economic development, but also a very low level of investment in the human resources needed to capitalize on initiatives to promote economic improvement and self-sufficiency. Again, the only habits that could be cultivated under the prevailing conditions appear to have failed to serve the needs of a program focusing on fundamental change.

Nonetheless, if improvement is to be sought at all, it has to make a beginning somewhere. Just as political weakness and economic dependence reinforce each other, and have done so on the reservations for generations, so must any program of change address political and economic needs jointly. The encouragement of self-determination is as brave an attempt as it is overdue, but it will require sustained effort on both sides of the relationship over a long period of time if the legacy of a grim past is to be overcome. Underlying this collection of essays is the hope that severely critical analysis will prove helpful and the conviction that nothing short of that will suffice.

NOTE

1. Confederated Salish and Kootenai Tribes, Hoopa Tribe, Jamestown Band of Klallam, Lummi Indian Tribe, Mescalero Apache Tribe, Mille Lacs Chippewa Tribe, Quinault Indian Nation, Red Lake Chippewa Tribe, Rosebud Sioux Tribe and Tlingit and Haida Central Council.

REFERENCE

Cohen, Felix S. *Handbook of Federal Indian Law*. Washington, D.C.: U.S. Government Printing Office, 1942.

PART I

Self-Governance

I

Self-Government for Native Americans: The Case of the Pascua Yaqui Tribe

William Willard

American Indian self-government in the United States is a product of a historical heritage that resulted from the conquest of many small native governments with varying kinds of organization, the acquisition of the colonial claims and settlements of several European nations, and the acquisition of the northern quarter of Mexico through war and purchase.

Each time a war ended, a treaty was drawn up, which usually included land cessions. There was one feature of these treaties that was of little importance at the time but that eventually became very significant. This was the definition of a treaty as an agreement between sovereign nations. The original use of treaties was to cloak land acquisitions under a legal mantle, but in the process of land ownership transfer, the recognition by the American legal system of the sovereign status of the American Indian governments became a permanent part of U.S. law.

Three basic principles were established in what has been called the formative era:

1. An Indian tribe possesses, in the first instance, all the power of any sovereign state.

2. Conquest renders the tribes subject to the legislative power of the United States and, in substance, terminates the external powers of sovereignty of the tribe, particularly in reference to its power to enter into treaties with foreign nations. However, it does not, by itself, affect the internal sovereignty of the tribe in regard to its powers of local government.

3. These powers are subject to qualification by treaties and by express congressional legislation, but except as expressly qualified, full powers of internal sovereignty are vested in the Indian tribes and in their duly constituted organs of government.[1]

These three principles were clearly intended to end the possibilities of alliances by Indian governments with European nations and to establish control over Indian governments. The principles are articulated in the Cherokee cases that were decided by the U.S. Supreme Court.[2]

In the formative years, the United States followed a steady policy of forcing Indian communities into exile from their former homelands. This was descriptively called the Indian Removal Policy. After 1871, Congress halted further treaty making with American Indian governments, since no existing native government posed a serious threat to the United States.

By the mid-nineteenth century, the national boundaries of the United States had reached the Pacific Ocean to the west, Canada to the north, and Mexico to the south. No native government now held uncontested control over any land area within the three North American nations. Native groups did seek refuge from the coercions of one or another of these new nations within the territory of the others during the nineteenth and twentieth centuries. In the 1850s, the external exile system of the Indian Removal Policy was replaced by an internal exile system called the reservation system.

On the reservations, the federal Indian Service replaced whatever former Indian governments had existed. Indian Service officials appointed tribal court judges, hired the police force, and controlled the distribution of federally supplied food and clothing. Religion was mandated to Christian missionaries, while formal education was delegated to denominational mission schools and a national system of federal Indian schools.

Federal policy moved to a new phase on many reservations in 1887 under the terms of the congressionally legislated General Allotment (or Dawes Severalty) Act. The General Allotment Act provided for the survey of reservations, creation of tribal rolls, and allotment of land to individual enrolled members. Its goal was to abolish reservations, bring an end to tribal governments, and mandate the assimilation of American Indians. Land that was federally determined to be surplus was to be distributed to nonnative homesteaders.

Local self-government did exist under some unique circumstances. The southern Indian nations had been forced into external exile during the 1830s under the federal Indian Removal Policy. There, in new, trans-Mississippian homelands, the Cherokee, Choctaw, Creek, Chickasaw, and Seminole nations recreated their institutions on the model of the parliamentary democracies toward which they had been evolving before their deportation. Their sovereignty was recognized by the government of the United States in the 1890 act that established the territory of Oklahoma.

That sovereignty began to erode and then was removed by a bill to provide for the final disposition of the affairs of the Five Civilized Tribes in the Indian Territory, which became the Act of April 26, 1906 (34 Stat. 137). Under the act, the Five Tribes lost their courts (criminal and civil jurisdictions), and all fiscal, educational, and social functions were either ended or assumed by federal agencies. Public buildings were sold, and the structure of self-government was demolished. In a derisory concession, the governments of the Five Tribes were allowed to meet once a year only as puppet governments with the single parodic power to declare the annual close of the meetings.

There was another set of native governments in the Southwest. The southwestern region of the United States had been acquired through the events of the U.S.-Mexican War; the subsequent treaty of Guadalupe Hidalgo of 1848, which ended the state of war; and the Gadsden Purchase of 1856 (in the area south of the Gila River to the present U.S.-Mexican border). Under Mexican law, no legal distinction is made between indigenous and nonindigenous communities. In the United States, however, this distinction has always been made.

The Indian Pueblos of New Mexico were placed in an anomalous situation in which the legal status of the treaty existed but the federal Indian Service served in an administrative position over the Pueblos as if they were, in fact, part of the reservation system. Finally, as in all legal questions involving American Indians, a case, *U.S. v. Sandoval*, made its way to the U.S. Supreme Court. The case questioned whether the Pueblos of New Mexico were in "Indian Country" and, if so, whether the members of the Pueblos were therefore legally Indians. The Court ruled that the members of the Pueblos were Indians and that their communities were in "Indian Country."[3]

However, these communities had a long experience in maintaining their own self-governments under Spanish colonial administrations. In the process, they had evolved well-tried defense systems to buffer the control mechanisms of alien governments. Their governmental form was a theocratic city-state modified by the forced adoption of a Spanish colonial civil government of a governor, a lieutenant governor, and a council with officials in charge of community services (such as the police force and irrigation services). Generally, the imposed civil government was covertly controlled by Pueblo religious societies.

When the federal policies aimed at dispossessing the Indian Pueblos of their land base and resources came into play in 1921, the vehicle was the Bursum Bill. The bill was a piece of legislation introduced by a New Mexican senator, Holm O. Bursum. The incumbent secretary of interior, Albert B. Fall, a former senator from New Mexico, lobbied for the bill. The purpose of the Bursum Bill was to award squatters' rights involving land titles and water rights to nonnatives who had moved onto Pueblo lands. Heretofore, the transfer of titles and rights had been done without regard for the interests of native communities. Settlers, squatters, and the land speculators who frequently employed them or bought their claims had usually accomplished their goal of acquiring land and natural resources for no compensation in the regions east of the Mississippi.

As one historic example, in the 1830s the Cherokee Nation had sought the legal protection of their treaties with the United States to retain sovereignty in their southeastern homeland. The Cherokee national government made its defense through legal action and lobbying activities in Washington, D.C. It had achieved pyrrhic victories in the Supreme Court decisions of the "Cherokee Trilogy" of *Johnson v. McIntosh, Cherokee Nation v. Georgia,* and *Worcester v. Georgia,* but had lost the last remnant of their southeastern homeland.

In the 1920s, an All-Pueblo Council assembled to resist the impending loss. They were joined in alliance with a Santa Fe–based group of non-Indian artists, writers, and their wealthy patrons, along with the General Federation of Women's Clubs, and other groups that are less easily categorized.

The All-Pueblo Council, unlike the Cherokee national government, had no long history of existence and evolution from the pre-Columbian past. The council had come into existence once before in 1680 to stage the Pueblo Rebellion against the Spanish colonial government. After the Spanish colonials fled from the uprising, the council ceased to exist until 1922.

The General Federation of Women's Clubs established an Indian Welfare Committee in 1922, and two field representatives were hired to investigate Indian problems. One of the representatives was Gertrude (Zitkala Sa) Bonnin, a Yankton Dakota woman who had been active for a dozen years in the politics of Indian issues, and the second was John Collier, who was a novice in Indian issues. Gertrude Bonnin went to Oklahoma to investigate the scandals arising out of the disposition of oil income from Indian land in Oklahoma, while John Collier was sent to New Mexico to assist in the fight against the Bursum Bill.[4] Once in the Southwest, Collier emerged as the chief organizer of the resistance campaign. He went on to become a long-term figure in U.S.-Indian issues, first as a lobbyist and then as commissioner of Indian affairs. The Bursum bill was defeated, so in one sense, the alliance was successful. However, in 1924 Senator Bursum introduced new legislation, the Pueblo Lands Bill, which was passed. That act has been described as a compromise that tried to give something to everybody.

Federal policy shifted away from the policy articulated by Commissioner Thomas J. Morgan in 1888 when, in 1933, the sometime lobbyist John Collier was appointed commissioner. As commissioner, John Collier introduced major changes through departmental policies and through legislation embodied in the Indian Reorganization Act of 1934 (IRA). The Indian Reorganization Act affirmed the right of American Indians to self-government. It provided for voluntary adoption, through election, of a tribal council system, the establishment of a constitutional government, and the organization of tribes as business corporations to manage the development of Indian-owned resources. Acceptance of the Indian Reorganization Act was a voluntary action.

The legal basis for the federal-Indian governmental relationship that had been laid down in the treaties and Supreme Court decisions over the years now came to be interpreted as official recognition of the sovereign status of

American Indian governments, along with the recognition of the three basic principles that had developed out of the formative period of the treaty era.

The Collier administration, through the Indian Reorganization Act, produced legislation that was a compromise between assimilation and limited self-government. Nevertheless, whatever the defects of the IRA as a piece of compromise law, it provided a framework of self-government that allowed tribal governments to exist. Some tribal governments were weak and some existed only by legal fiction, but others were strong enough and sufficiently sustained by a consensus of their membership to continue to develop. The change in policy had the effect of renewing the government-to-government relationship between the federal and tribal governments that had existed before the end of the treaty-making era. The policy reestablished the concept of tribal sovereignty and provided for the possibility of Indian self-determination. Under the terms of section 16 of the act, any Indian tribe or tribes residing on the same reservation shall have the right to organize for their common welfare and may adopt an appropriate constitution and bylaws. The IRA presented a breakthrough in the reassertion of tribal sovereignty and created the possibility for tribal governments to become recognized legal entities in the American governmental system of local, state, and federal governments, as well as territories and commonwealths.

It was good that some tribal governments were well established with the consensus of support when the next federal-Indian policy change came, because their strength was to be severely tested. The next policy change was the termination era (1945–1961), a time when policy reverted to the intent of the nineteenth-century Dawes Act. The basic idea of termination was that the special relationship of the federal-tribal connection should come to an end. What did that mean? Land was to be appraised and then sold; all legal jurisdiction was to be transferred to state and county governments, the buffer of federal and tribal law was to come to an end; and all exemptions from state tax laws and all special federal programs were to be terminated.

The majority of the federally recognized tribal governments survived on into the present-day era of self-determination policy. The chief piece of legislation of this period is Public Law 93–638, the Indian Self-Determination Act of 1975 and its amendments. Under the act, authority was given to the secretaries of interior and of health, education, and welfare to enter into contracts with tribes and other Indian organizations for the delivery of federal services. The effect was that although tribal programs continued to be funded by the federal government, the responsibility for planning and administering the programs was assigned to the tribal governments that had entered into the contracts.

Self-rule within the rules of the legacy of legislation now became possible. How is that conducted in actuality? There is a southwestern tribal government that is, as are all Indian tribal governments, unique in much of its history, but that also shares a history with all other American Indian tribes. The particular tribe is the Pascua Yaqui Tribe of Arizona. It became a federally recognized tribe in 1978 (with all the positive and negative values involved in that status), a century after many others had been officially recognized.

The members of the tribe are descendants of people who moved to Arizona over the past two centuries, some in the time of the Spanish colonial frontier, and the majority as refugees from Yaqui Pueblos in the Mexican state of Sonora. The majority arrived in the years between 1905 and 1920. The refugees came north fleeing the fighting, executions, deportations, and imposed peasant status caused by the long Yaqui war against Mexican domination, a war that continued (with interruptions caused by Mexican independence) to the 1930s. They had the same legal status as the Metis who fled from Canada to the United States after the collapse of the Louis Riel Rebellion in 1876. Members of both groups were illegal refugees who could be sent back to probable imprisonment and possible execution.

The image of self-government that the refugees brought as part of their cultural baggage was derived from that of the Yaqui River towns as they had developed in the nineteenth century. These town governments were characterized by certain basic features dominated by a strong sacred orientation. One of the basic town components was the Church and its associated religious societies which carried out direct services for God.

Equal to the church organizations and not subservient to them, the households of the town formed a connection of kin and ritual kin groups that united for a variety of activities. Each household formed a social unit. A civil-military government functioned in each town. The civil officials held titles derived from Spanish colonial government, as did the civil officials of the New Mexican Pueblos. They were elected annually by everyone, both men and women. The idea of a council and general assembly was basic. The military organization was patterned on that of the Mexican army of the late nineteenth century. Each year, the two organizations participated in the major public sacred event, the Lenten-Easter ceremony.

In the United States, the refugees sought work wherever they could: on the railroads, in copper smelters, and on the irrigated farms. Work on the farms increased with the increased cultivation of cotton. The Yaquis gradually developed a group pattern of working on the farms during the growing season and in the off-season intervals, moving to one of the permanent Yaqui settlements which were established wherever circumstances allowed a community to be built.

The settlements were all constructed around a plaza with a church, a kitchen, and a *Pascola ramada* (an open-sided performance enclosure). The arrangement of the plaza and church was based on the pattern of the Yaqui river towns. Leadership for these settlements rested on the officers of the religious organization of the Yaqui community, because the civil and military organizations had no functions in Arizona without towns to govern or a military enemy to fight.

The plaza and church arrangement that was based on the pattern of the Yaqui River valley towns was revived in the more tolerant atmosphere of Arizona. Leadership for these settlements was lodged in a village council composed of the officers of the religious societies of the Yaqui community.

From their beginnings, these colonies existed on the brink of crisis because the payment of purchase prices for land and land taxes was always difficult for people who depended on seasonal farm work. One of the first of these colonies, the original Pascua, developed in 1921 near Tucson. While it was not the only permanent Yaqui settlement, it is the best described.[5]

The first attempt to find a way for the Yaqui refugees and their descendants to become federally recognized as American Indians was in 1934, after John Collier became commissioner of Indian affairs. In 1934, John Provinse, who was then a faculty member of the department of archaeology at the University of Arizona (and later, an official in the bureau during the Collier administration), worked with Thamar Richey, a public school teacher at Pascua, to prepare a plan to resettle the Pascua people on a farm colony under supervision by the Bureau of Indian Affairs (BIA). The plan failed because the Arizona congressional delegation had added a proviso to the 1935 BIA appropriation that prohibited the expenditure of funds for buying nonadjacent, off-reservation land in Arizona. If the land had been bought for the subsistence farm colony, the Pascua Yaquis would have become de facto American Indians in 1935.[6]

After 1935, the Yaqui communities continued on a cyclical pattern of work on the Arizona cotton farms for the next twenty years. Then, the use of more and larger machines, along with an increasing use of agricultural chemicals, gradually reduced the number of workers needed until, by 1960, the available work was no longer enough to sustain very many people.

During these years, the Pascua group functioned under a continuation of the traditional council, which was interested largely in religious matters. However, a shift toward other interests began to develop about 1950. The major new interest was in a movement to build new housing and improve existing houses.

During the 1930s, the original real estate company had ceased to collect payments for the lots and finally sold its interests to an agent of the Louise H. Marshall Charitable Foundation of Tucson. The foundation did not evict anyone for nonpayment, but nevertheless, there was the fear of eviction. When approached, foundation representatives refused to consider selling any of their lots in the subdivision. After a long negotiation with many delays, the foundation did agree to accept adverse possession rights from people living on some of their lots.

The end of the farm work cycle eliminated the economic base of the community and the Marshall Foundation began to reacquire the lots by paying the back taxes of delinquent landowners. The council joined with a group of non-Yaqui people with social conscience interests to form the Pascua Housing Committee. The committee accepted the task of searching for a secure land base for the small community. The committee found that the only way that seemed to be workable, given the deteriorating economic situation of the Pascua people, was to petition Congress for a land grant for some Bureau of Land Management (BLM) acreage in the Tucson area.

The council and the Housing Committee were both unofficial entities, and to receive a land grant there had to be some official organization to receive the grant. The Pascua group incorporated as the Pascua Yaqui Association, a nonprofit Arizona corporation, in order to become that official organization. The new association then petitioned, with the aid of southern Arizona Congressman Morris K. Udall, the federal government for a land grant. The congressman prepared a Congressional Land Grant Bill (H.R. 6233) to transfer 200 acres of BLM-controlled federal land to the Pascua Yaqui Association. On October 8, 1964, the land transfer of two hundred acres of federal land located southwest of Tucson was officially made.

Next, there was the problem of how to put houses, electricity, water lines, and streets on two hundred acres of desert. The Pascua Housing Committee approached the new federal Office of Economic Opportunity (OEO). Members of the committee had sufficient political influence to persuade the director of the OEO Research and Demonstration Division to send a representative to Tucson to advise the Committee on acceptable OEO proposal preparation.

The resulting proposal was a research and demonstration construction skills training program. The proposal requested a grant to train Yaqui men for construction work and, as by-products of the training process, new houses would be built for members of the Pascua Yaqui Association on the land grant acreage. In September 1966, the Office of Economic Opportunity approved and authorized expenditures for a Research and Demonstration program.[7]

In 1969, the program became a housing project; it continued with OEO and Ford Foundation financial support for the next six years. In 1972, the Pascua Yaqui Association began to lobby for federal recognition for the tribe. In order to gain political support, Yaqui representatives met with other Arizona tribal governments, the Arizona congressional delegation, and two national Indian organizations—the National Congress of American Indians and the National Tribal Chairmen's Association.

Official federal recognition of the Pascua Yaquis occurred in 1978, fifty-three years after John Collier and John Provinse had attempted to secure de facto recognition. The new status meant that there now existed a formally recognized American Indian tribe under the federal regulations, public laws, and court and administrative decisions that make up United States Federal Indian Policy. The Congressional Land Grant was now the Pascua Yaqui

Indian Reservation, established pursuant to the Act of Public Law 99–375 (992 Stat. 712).

The next step was to put an interim tribal council into place to serve as a government while a constitution was being written. That step occupied the next ten years. There had to be an official tribal roll of the membership of the new tribe in order to provide a tribal census. The federal recognition act provided that the new tribe had to prepare a constitution under the rules of the Indian Reorganization Act of 1934. Section 16 (25 U.S.C. 476) of the act provides that tribal members must ratify the constitution and that the secretary of the interior must approve the document. Originally, the writing of a constitution was to take two and a half years, but two problems interfered and caused it to take longer. The first problem involved preparing a document that would be acceptable to the Pascua Yaqui membership, and the second was to deliver a proposed constitution that would be acceptable to the Bureau of Indian Affairs before being sent to the secretary of interior for his signature. The first hurdle was in the BIA area office in Phoenix, which proved to be the most difficult. By the time the first proposed constitution had been forwarded to the area office (after several amendments), the time allotted for the development of the constitution was running out. In February 1981, the tribal attorney drafted a letter to the secretary of the interior to request guidance and assistance in making a final draft of the constitution. The letter was to accompany the February 16, 1981, revised version of the proposed constitution.

On January 27, 1983, the secretary of the interior approved the constitution and a Secretarial Election on the proposed constitution in April 1983. Three years later, there still was not a constitution. As of July 1986, a revised constitution had been received by the secretary but no action had been taken. Finally, after the intervention of the Arizona congressional delegation in August 1987, the tribal constitution was accepted by the secretary of the interior. Next, the approved constitution was presented to the voting members of the tribe for their approval, and it was approved on January 26, 1988. A first election of a tribal council, after ten years of interim councils, was held on June 11, 1988.

The Pascua Yaqui Tribe of Arizona includes the Pascua Pueblo Reservation (with a land area of 892 acres, near Tucson), the town of Vemela Pahkua/Pascua Pueblo on the reservation, and off-reservation membership in several communities: Yoem Pueblo in Marana; Guadalupe near Tempe; the 39th Street community in South Tucson; Se Chopoi, a few miles south of Guadalupe; Penhamo in Scottsdale; Siva Kovi near Somerton; and Pahkua/Old Pascua in Tucson. All the communities are in southern Arizona. The tribal enrollment was 8,200 at the time of the first election in June 1988.

Each tribal government exists within the framework of the federal government, current federal-Indian policy, any treaties or federal statutes that apply to particular tribes, and the cumulative effects of past historical experiences on the membership of the tribal group. There is always the danger for American Indian governments of being overwhelmed by the greater political and economic force of the federal government.

Each of these governments shares the commonalities of having passed through the process of receiving official recognition as a tribal entity from the federal government. These tribes, as are all other tribes, are forced to spend much time and energy either resisting negative federal policy or trying to obtain the benefits of favorable policy.

Under recent policy as formalized in the Indian Self-Determination Act (P.L. 93–638), tribal governments have moved from being puppet governments totally controlled by the federal government to official establishments as parts of the American governmental structure of states, tribal governments, territories, and commonwealths, under the supremacy of the federal government.[8] Some tribal governments have used this status pragmatically to gain control over their own internal affairs and to legislate their own policies.

The Pascua Yaqui Tribe of Arizona represents the Arizona Yaqui people who existed without a secure land base for most of the time that there have been Yaquis in the United States. Now, these people comprise a federally recognized tribe with a federal trust status reservation in southern Arizona. They are an indigenous group that has shown the will to maintain an ancient identity, in spite of the problems of surviving the twists and turns of the policies of colonial and postcolonial governments.

NOTES

1. These principles are discussed in Charles F. Wilkinson's *American Indians, Time, and the Law: Native Societies in a Modern Constitutional Democracy* (New Haven, Conn.: Yale University Press, 1987).

2. *Cherokee Nation v. Georgia*, 30 U.S. (5 Pet.) 1, 8 L. Ed. 483 (1831); *Worcester v. Georgia*, 31 U.S. (6) 515, 8 L. Ed. 483 (1832).

3. Supreme Court of the United States, 1913: 231 U.S. 28, 34 S. Ct. 1, 58 L. Ed. 107.

4. The book *Land, and Water, and Culture: New Perspectives on Hispanic Land Grants* edited by Charles L. Briggs and John P. Van Ness, (Albuquerque: University of New Mexico Press, 1987), presents an account of the intricacies of the ownership of land and water rights in New Mexico.

5. The circumstances of the land acquisition are described in detail in E. H. Spicer's classic ethnography, *Pascua: A Yaqui Village in Arizona* (Tucson: University of Arizona Press, 1984).

6. John H. Provinse Papers, 1935, Archives, Arizona State Museum, University of Arizona, Tucson.

7. H. Lawrence Huerta, "Memorandum to the Pascua Yaqui Tribal Council," December 5, 1986. Edward H. Spicer Archives, University of Arizona, Tucson.

8. Wilkinson, *American Indians*, p. 86.

REFERENCES

Friends of the Indians. *Proceedings of the Tenth Annual Meeting of the Lake Mohonk Conference of Friends of the Indians.* Lake Mohonk, N.Y. 1892.

Getches, David H., Daniel H. Rosenfelt, and Charles F. Wilkinson. *Cases and Materials on Federal Indian Law.* St. Paul: West Publishing Co., 1979.

Huerta, H. Lawrence. "Memorandum to the Pascua Yaqui Tribal Council." December 5, 1986. Edward H. Spicer Archives, University of Arizona, Tucson.

Lewis, John R., Edward H. Spicer, and William Willard. "The Pascua Yaqui Development Project, 1966–1969." Unpublished report on an OEO program in Pima County, Arizona.

Provinse, John H. Papers, 1934–1937. Archives, Arizona State Museum, University of Arizona, Tucson.

Spicer, Edward H. *Cycles of Conquest: The Impact of Spain, Mexico, and the United States on the Indians of the Southwest, 1533–1960.* Tucson: University of Arizona Press, 1962.

Spicer, Edward H. "Patrons of the Poor." *Human Organization,* 29, no. 1 (1970):12–19.

Spicer, Edward H. *The Yaquis: A Cultural History.* Tucson: University of Arizona Press, 1980.

Strickland, Rennard, ed. *Felix S. Cohen's Handbook of Federal Indian Law.* Charlottesville, Va.: Michie Bobbs-Merrill, 1982.

U.S. Congressional Record. H.R. 623, a bill to provide further conveyance of certain land of the United States to the Pascua Yaqui Association, Inc., May 9, 1963. 88th Cong. 1st sess. Washington, D.C.: U.S. Government Printing Office.

U.S. Department of the Interior. *Annual Report of the Commissioner of Indian Affairs.* Washington, D.C.: U.S. Government Printing Office, 1889.

U.S. House of Representatives. Report No. 1809, May 9, 1963. 88th Cong., 2d sess. Washington, D.C.: U.S. Government Printing Office.

Wilkinson, Charles F. *American Indians, Time, and the Law: Native Societies in a Modern Constitutional Democracy.* New Haven, Conn.: Yale University Press, 1987.

Willard, William. "Gertrude Bonnin and Indian Policy Reform, 1911–1936." In *Indian Leadership,* ed. Walter Williams. Manhattan, Kans.: Sunflower University Press, 1984.

Willard, William. "The Comparative Political History of Two Tribal Governments." *Wicazo Sa Review,* 6, no. 1 (Spring 1990): 56–62.

Willard, William. "The First Amendment, Anglo Conformity and American Indian Religious Freedom." *Wicazo Sa Review,* 7, no. 1 (Spring 1991): 1–8.

2

Designing a Tribal Organization for Self-Governance

Fremont J. Lyden and Ernest G. Miller

This chapter sets forth the recommendations of the authors to an Indian tribe on how the tribe could revise its administrative organization to allow the Tribal Business Council (the tribe's legislative body) to have better control over decision making and to demonstrate to Congress that the tribe is capable of governing itself without federal tutelage.[1]

Questions are first asked about whether this tribe's cultural values are consistent with the requirements of modern organizational decision making and whether the tribe has sufficient economic development potential to support self-government. The results of the study are then presented along with recommendations made to the tribe about self-government.

THE SELF-GOVERNANCE MOVEMENT

The United States government has struggled with the enigma of the American Indians for over two hundred years. Are they citizens of the United States or members of a foreign nation, or are they both? What of the Indian tribe? Is it a sovereign foreign nation existing within the boundaries of the United States, or is it a domestic dependent nation subject to the authority of the U.S. Congress?[2]

These questions have been debated throughout American history. At times, the United States has adopted a policy of assimilating the Indians into American society. At other times, the Indians have been encouraged to live on reservations with their lives governed by tribal customs and laws under the general tutelage of the federal government.[3] The Indians have stubbornly resisted attempts at assimilation, and they have never been given sufficient autonomy on their reservations to develop self-sufficient tribal governments.[4]

American policy now appears to be changing. In 1970, President Richard Nixon declared that termination policy had been a failure and called on Congress to develop a new policy that would permit Indian tribes to manage their own affairs with a maximum degree of autonomy (116 *Congressional Record* 23257). In 1975, Congress passed the Indian Self-Determination and Educational Assistance Act which allowed government agencies to enter into contracts with tribes. Such contracts allowed the tribes to assume responsibility for the administration of federal Indian programs (25 *USCA* p. 450 et seq.). Other laws followed that encouraged self-governance, culminating in the amendment of the Indian Self-Determination and Education Assistance Act in 1988 to authorize the development of self-governance plans by Indian tribes. Congressional appropriations were also provided for selected Indian tribes to finance the planning process involved in justifying self-governance. The Indian tribe that requested our assistance was one of these selected tribes.

One of the tasks involved in the development of such a plan was to decide how the existing tribal organization could be changed to make it more responsive to the direction of tribal leadership. We were contacted by the council to provide advice on how it could develop a more responsive decision-making process in the organization. A council retreat held in 1987 concluded that the following characteristics inhibited action: (1) undefined authority and responsibility relationships between the council, its members, and the general manager; (2) lack of or delayed action by the council in budgeting, leading to misguided spending or overspending; (3) lack of regular reviews of tribal departmental goals by the council or the general manager; (4) continual conflict with non-Indians over land, natural resources, and jurisdiction; and (5) inadequate communication among members of the council, on the one hand, and the general manager and his departmental heads, on the other.

CULTURAL VALUES AND ORGANIZATIONAL DESIGN

What kind of an organization would be able to solve these problems? In a recent survey of lawyers who specialize in Indian law, Linda Medcalf reported that the respondents said that "tribes must be able to *act*, and adequate action requires organization, efficiency and rationality. . . . Efficiency is concerned with organizing in order to be better able to transact business. Rationality involves 'better' procedures and an improved style of decision making."[5]

Our first question, then, was whether the tribe's cultural values would support the development of an efficient decision-making system in the organization. Some scholars have argued that the organizing principles of the

Iroquois Confederation provided one source for the development of the American form of government. Johansen and Grinde argued that the Albany Plan, the Articles of Confederation, and the U.S. Constitution all reflect some characteristics of the early Indian confederation.[6] If so, one might assume that a modern tribal government would find the decision-making principles on which the federal government is organized to be compatible with their own cultural values.

On the other hand, Elizabeth Hooker found that decisions made by the Iroquois Confederation were all based on the principle of unanimity: "All of the League . . . [representatives] were to be of 'one mind' to give efficacy to their legislation."[7] Decision making in modern American government is based on majority rule in legislation and the delegation of authority in administration. If modern Indian tribes require that all decisions be based on unanimity, real problems could be encountered in both the legislative and administrative operations of government.

While the tribe with which we were working does certainly observe some consensus requirements for decision making, we needed to inquire into the values that underlie this decision making to know whether these requirements would impede the introduction of modern decision-making practices into tribal government. Fortunately, the Kluckhohn Research Center had recently conducted a study of values on this reservation.[8] The Values Orientation Method (VOM) is a research instrument designed to elicit a pattern of values from respondents that reflect the different ways in which people think about life and the world around them.[9] It is assumed that values influence people's behavior and that different patterns of values will reveal something about the predispositions of respondents to make decisions in one way or another. VOM further assumes that there are four basic dimensions of value orientations that each of us develops, relating to:

—*Time*: Whether we prefer to base our behavior on "the way things were" (past—Pa), "the way things are" (present—Pr), or the "way things are likely to be " (future—Fu).

—*Activity*: Whether we are oriented to doing things (doing—Do), or to experiencing things as they are (being—Be).

—*Humanity/Nature*: Whether we think of ourselves as masters *over* nature (Ov), *subjected* to the whims of nature (Su), or in harmony *with* the operation of nature (Wi).

—*Relational*: Whether we look to our ancestors (lineal—Li), our contemporaries (collateral—Co), or to ourselves as individuals (individualism—In) as the most important basis for guiding behavior.

Each individual falls somewhere within each of the four modality scales. There may be little difference in where we classify our preferences on some of the scales but distinct differences on where we fall on others. For example, on the Activity scale, we may all be "doing"-oriented people who want to take positive action to solve a problem, or we may be "being"-oriented, more predisposed to wait and see whether the problem resolves itself without our intervention. Perhaps we do not differ on the Activity scale, while on the Time scale, some of us believe that the most appropriate solution to the problem should be consistent with past ways of solving the problem, while others believe we should solve the problem based on the circumstances as we perceive them to exist or as we assume they may exist in the future. If one looks at a profile of one's responses to all four scales, it may be possible to predict how one is predisposed to deal with life situations.

The Kluckhohn Values Orientation Method is based on a series of questions that pose decision situations related to each of the four scales and ask respondents to choose from the several alternate solutions indicated.[10] The scores of each respondent reveal a pattern of preferences on the four value scales. We know from previous research that persons who are oriented to the present rather than the past or future, to mastery over nature rather than subordination to or harmony with nature, to a doing rather than a being orientation, and to ourselves or our colleagues rather than our ancestors would be most likely to look favorably on developing an organization that could deal with decisions efficiently and expeditiously.[11]

When selected members of the Indian tribe were asked the VOM questions, their responses were as follows on each of the value scales:[12]

Time:	[Pr = Pa] > Fu
Humanity/Nature:	Ov >Su >Wi
Activity:	Do > Be
Relational:	Co > In > Li

We see that the Indians do stress doing over being, human mastery over nature, and a collateral relation with others rather than reliance on ancestral ways. All these responses appear consistent with the above-reported findings of persons who would find efficient decision making an acceptable basis for behavior. On the Time dimension, however, the Indians regard the past as equally important as the present as a reference for decision making. This obviously means that in decision making, they will be more constrained by past precedents than will governments and businesspeople with whom they deal. In addition, on the Activity dimension, while tribal respondents regard themselves as very doing-oriented, they perceive others in the tribe as very being-oriented. They also see themselves as results-oriented whereas they perceive other tribal members as preferring a more relaxed life-style.[13] This suggests that tribal members are caught in the cross pressures of traditional tribal life values and the values of the outside white society. Their values are, however, much more consistent with the values of governmental decision makers than our stereotypes about Indians would lead us to believe.

Nonetheless, they are not identical to those of governmental decision makers.[14] Consequently, recommendations to redesign the tribes' decision-making style in order to make self-governance successful must be carefully weighed against the effect of such changes on their cultural heritage.

The next question we asked was whether this Indian tribe had the economic development capacities to finance self-governance.

ECONOMIC DEVELOPMENT CAPACITIES

In an analysis of how a region grows, H. S. Perloff argued that every community has its economic development advantages and limitations. Some areas have greater advantages than others in terms of climate, amenities, labor skills, transportation facilities, markets, or resources.[15] In a note on American Indian economic development policies in the *Journal of Planning Literature*, additional advantages were strongly identified: entrepreneurial skills, attitudes toward economic development, availability of capital and financial assistance, stability, and commitment to tribal leadership.[16]

In examining the Indian tribal situation that we studied, it would seem that many, if not most, of these economic development strategies are strongly evident. Furthermore, these strengths are not of recent origin only but rather have evolved and been reinforced over many years of their history.

Before White Settlement

In his extensive study of this Indian community, Vine Deloria, Jr., observed that from their beginning, tribal members had been fishermen, and even after a century and a quarter, which included a number of disastrous experiments by the federal government to change their economic ways, they were fishermen still.[17] Their homeland base was on the Northwest coast, and they followed the natural cycle of fish life throughout the year, with the summer season being spent fishing in the islands and the other seasons spent on the mainland coast where the seasonal salmon runs, abundant shellfish, and berries and camas roots provided substantial sustenance.

White Settlement and Early Reservation Years

The tribe continued its fishing activities but also began to raise vegetables for sale to the white settlers, thus expanding its food production economy.[18] In the treaty of Point Elliott (1855), the tribe's "usual and accustomed" fishing patterns were affirmed.[19] In a report just two years after the treaty, U.S. agent E. C. Fitzhugh stated:

As a general thing their women are very industrious, and do most of the work, and procure the principal part of their sustenance; they cultivate potatoes, and generally have a superabundance, so that they dispose of a great many to the whites, by which means they procure the greater part of their clothing. They have an abundance of fish; salmon is the principal stand-by, also shell fish of all kinds; in fact I think I never saw a country so well adapted for the Indians to live in as this.[20]

In the late 1800s, farming was promoted by federal agents, and in 1872, a sawmill was built to clear reservation lands and provide lumber for houses. Some of the tribal men thus learned skills in the lumbering industry, and farm acreage was increased considerably. While these activities demonstrated tribal initiative, however, fishing continued to be the favored occupation.

The Poverty Years (1890–1968)

During this period, economic conditions declined: profitable timber stands were used up, farming was marginal, and even fishing declined in the face of struggles over fishing rights and competition with whites, who had the capital to finance new fishing technology that the tribe could not afford. The Bureau of Indian Affairs (BIA) promoted knitting, weaving, and crafts projects, but these proved to be of little value.

An Economic Breakthrough: The Aquaculture Project

The tribal members were approached in 1967 by a company that wanted to build a magnesium oxide plant at their bay. The loss of the bay to sea and shore life deeply concerned several tribal leaders, who began to search for a viable economic alternative that would preserve their tidelands. Word of the tribe's concerns reached a nearby college professor, Wallace Heath. Heath had studied Hawaiian aquaculture activities, and after visiting the bay, he asked the Indians if they had ever considered using it for commercial seafood production. They had not, but after hearing about aquacultural projects, a number of the tribal leaders decided that they wanted to give it a try. Discussion and arguments ensued within the tribe over the contending proposals, and as Deloria observed:

Advocates of aquaculture visualized the whole community participating in the transformation of fishing techniques into sea farming of the most sophisticated nature. [They] could continue to be fishermen, aquaculture proponents argued, and everyone could participate in all the decisions; with the magnesium oxide plant, however, [they] would once again be laborers for some outside group.[21]

Finally, at the tribal council meeting of April 1968, the tribe voted approval of the aquaculture project.

1968 to Present

In rapid succession, with the tribe itself functioning as the primary contractor, an experimental pond, a larger sea pond, a fish hatchery, and an oyster hatchery were constructed. By the end of 1972, these initial projects had been completed, and attention was next given to ensuring that the aquaculture project would be commercially profitable. Two facts about the construction and operation are especially important in regard to the strength of the project: (1) the extensive involvement of the Indians themselves in the true spirit of community development, and (2) the commitment to training the tribal members to handle all phases of aquaculture.[22]

Since 1972, hatchery facilities have been expanded and programs to enhance fish and shellfish production have been promoted. In 1978, a tribally owned seafood-processing plant was built. The revitalized tribal fishing fleet, employing six hundred people, is the largest fleet in the Northwest. There are over four hundred boats, and the total annual harvest value in 1990 was $9,667,343.

However, fishing is a limited-resource industry, a fact recognized by the Tribal Business Council when it declared a need to "achieve economic self-sufficiency for tribal members in areas other than fishing."[23] The economic ventures begun in recent years include a cold storage facility, a restaurant, and a boat and motor sales office. The importance of forestry to the tribe was recognized in 1979 with the adoption of the tribal Forest Development Program. Since that date, more than one thousand acres have been planted with Douglas fir and western red cedar seedlings.[24] Future plans call for expanding some of the current enterprises, namely the grocery store and gasoline facilities, and the opening of a gaming and entertainment facility that will feature varieties of card games. This facility is expected to employ from 150 to 200 persons, most of whom will be tribal members.[25]

Not all evaluators of the tribe's economic ventures have viewed their efforts positively. Daniel Boxberger argued that the tribe has little experience in the *organized*, as contrasted to the *individualized*, management of tribal resources:

Some scholars have noted that in fairly closed fishing communities the more prolific fishers use their success to create a political following.[26] By carefully selecting crew members and by helping others enter the fishery, they build a strong faction that helps them acquire political power through elected office and through support of the decision-making process. A parallel structure exists [with the tribe], where a small faction of the tribe, the purse seine operators, who take over 60 percent of the total [tribal] fish harvest, controls the tribe's decision-making body. Those in a position to restructure the fishery to benefit the maximum number of [members] are the ones least likely to benefit from doing so.[27]

Boxberger concluded that this trend has resulted in the development of fishing resources on a private, entrepreneurial scale rather than an organized, tribal basis. The tribal government itself has thus gained little experience in the actual management of the fishing industry. Table 2.1, showing the average earnings of the tribal fisheries for 1981 through 1984, would appear to support Boxberger's conclusions.

Table 2.1
Average Earnings of Salmon Fishers, 1981–1984

Gross Earnings($)	Number of Fishers	Approximate%*
0–5,000	458	74
5,000–10,000	70	11
10,000–15,000	36	6
15,000–20,000	15	3
20,000–25,000	12	2
25,000–50,000	18	3
50,000–100,000	6	1
100,000 +	7	1
Total	622	100

*Total has been rounded.

Source: Daniel Boxberger, To Fish in Common (Lincoln: University of Nebraska Press, 1989), p. 174.

Consequently, while this discussion has demonstrated that the tribe has cultural values and economic resources that are not inconsistent with the streamlined decision making required of bureaucratic organizations, it also has a distinct cultural and economic history suggesting that conversion to a modern decision-making system would not be automatic. With these concerns in mind, we began our study of tribal organization, hoping that organizational changes could be proposed that would solve the tribe's current decision-making problems without undercutting traditional tribal values.

METHODOLOGY

The existing organizational chart (Figure 2.1) was approved in May 1985. There are seven departments shown, including a Department of Parks and Recreation, which is not currently staffed. We found that the Water/Sewer Department is regarded as a separate department and not a part of the Department of Public Works. There is no director of public works. A part-time consultant signs the paychecks of the foreman of the maintenance crew but is not involved in work planning or direction. The foreman receives

Figure 2.1
Organizational Chart

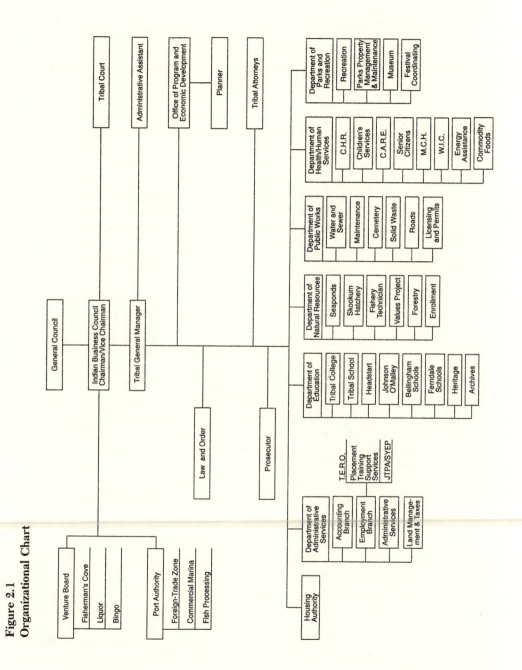

supervision from whatever department has maintenance work to be done. "Law and Order" is the police department, which is listed as a staff unit on the chart. The Department of Administrative Services is shown as a department but has no director. Instead, the various accounting, personnel and administrative service units report directly to the general manager.

It appears to us that the chart represents a paper organization with little resemblance to the actual working relations occurring in the organization. It did, however, provide us with a general basis for questioning organizational members on how the organization really operates. We interviewed each of the departmental heads (including the police chief) and the staff units (economic development, personnel, accounting, property management, etc.) and obtained similar information from their subordinates through a questionnaire. All respondents were asked what tasks they performed, whom they worked with, whom they worked for (and supervised, if applicable), what work problems they encountered, what backlogs resulted, and whom they regarded as "in charge" of their work. Sociometric charts were constructed to show respondents' work and supervisory relationships (Figures 2.2 and 2.3).

CONCEPTUAL APPROACH TO ORGANIZATIONAL STUDY

Most analyses of organizations are based on who is responsible for what, as depicted in an organizational chart. When proposals are subsequently made for reorganization, little change usually occurs. This, of course, is because organizations are social entities that respond to formal and informal requirements. A more realistic way of studying an organization is to regard it as a system wherein inputs (resources) are brought into a throughput, where they are converted from one form to another through the performance of tasks and activities. These activities then result in outputs of work, which eventually should contribute to the solution of some societal problem.

Inputs → Throughputs → Outputs → Impacts
(resources)   (activities)

Four different dimensions of the throughput contribute to the resource conversions. First, there must be some reason for performing the work. This may be regarded as the Mission of the organization, and the conversion process can be viewed as the accomplishment of goals, subgoals, objectives, and subobjectives. Next, the Work dimension identifies how work is performed, as organized by work procedures, task designs, work measurement, and so forth. Third, the Mission and the Work dimensions of the throughput are brought together by making persons responsible for the performance of specific duties, in the Authority dimension. Finally, interpersonal relations are developed by the employees themselves (informal organization) to enable them to work together. This is the Social dimension of the throughput. All these dimensions permeate everything that occurs in the throughput. Therefore, if one changes an element in one dimension, some effects will be felt in all of the three others. Consequently, when studying an organization, one must find out how each of the four dimensions of the organization operates. We explained to the tribe how we would use the four dimensions, as follows:

—*Mission dimension*: Every organization is created for a purpose, which is evidenced in legal mandates and other statements of a community as expressed through its plans, programs, citizen participation, and so on.

—*Work dimension*: (''What do you do and whom do you work with?''): These are the activities that people do in the organization, including writing or typing reports, compiling lists, and filing materials, as expressed by the organization as outputs (number of letters typed, reports written, lists compiled or letters filed) and inputs (person-hours or other resources required per output). Work is reflected in time reports, budget expenditures, and so forth.

—*Authority dimension*: (''Whom do you supervise and who supervises you?''): This dimension establishes individual responsibility for the work done by the organization, as expressed by job descriptions, hierarchy charts, and so on.

—*Social dimension*: These are the roles played by people in an organization, as defined by social interactions of persons rather than the formal requirements of the organization (and frequently referred to as the informal organization because it was not specifically created by the formal organization). This dimension can be observed by noting with whom in the organization employees associate when not specifically required to do so by their job or their work responsibilities.

THE ORGANIZATION OBSERVED

The results of the survey can be summarized in terms of the four organizational dimensions:

Work Dimension

Each person interviewed was asked with what three persons he or she worked most often in carrying out his or her duties. Figure 2.2, "Work Relationships," shows the results. It will be observed that not only department heads but also supervisors at the second and third levels of the organization work frequently with the general manager. This suggests a significant information overload coming to the general manager. Additionally, two out of the five second-level supervisors in the Health and Human Services Department do not indicate that they work closely with their own department head. This could indicate that some of the work in this department is not closely coordinated at the departmental level. There are many people outside the organization with whom these supervisors work.

Figure 2.2
Work Relationships

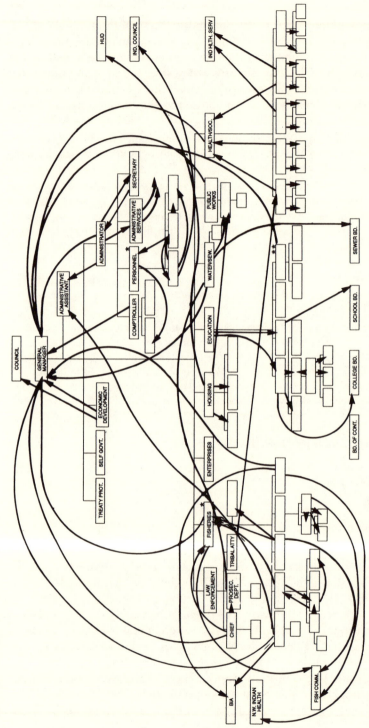

→ Indicates person with whom the individual works.
* Indicates that the individual works with all employees.

A great amount of detail work in addition to much complained-about paperwork appears to be created by the many contracts and grants that each department has with different federal and state agencies. Rules and regulations stemming from many different statutes make it necessary to work with outside agencies, not only on questions of policy interpretation, but also on a case-by-case implementation of such policies. This tends to cause departmental personnel to be preoccupied with detail, and in fact, in some cases to be swamped with detail. This preoccupation with work detail prevents departments from spending time on the overall coordination of work. Consequently, as noted in the chart on work relationships, such within-department coordination appears to be done by the department heads or second-level supervisors working directly with the general manager rather than each other. The result is to spread the attention of the general manager over too many within-department problems and to diminish the responsibilities of the department heads for their own departments.

Mission Dimension

The work relationships, as described, appear to occupy so much time of so many people in the organization that little attention is given to organizational planning, except in specialized ways such as venture planning and economic development. Since the venture boards and port authority are run as autonomous operations, we have not included them in the study.

The council holds retreats that appear to give much attention to goal development and planning, but the results of such work never appear to be passed on to the departments in ways that relate to their ongoing work responsibilities. Only one person who was interviewed indicated any knowledge of these efforts, even though the results of the 1987 retreat were formally approved by the council. None of the department heads interviewed presented us with their own departmental plans except for the police chief.

These findings indicate that departmental work is not, in most instances, unified by the use of program-based work plans. Goals appear to be thought through in terms of those required by individual contracts rather than as a goal structure that reflects the total responsibilities of a department. The goal-setting process of the council has not been passed on to the department heads to provide a basis for their work planning.

Authority Dimension

One of the concerns expressed to us by the general manager was the desire to see clear patterns of responsibilities established so that departmental expenditures could be related to departmental goals. Figure 2.3 shows the organization's perceptions of its supervisory responsibilities. It

Figure 2.3
Supervision

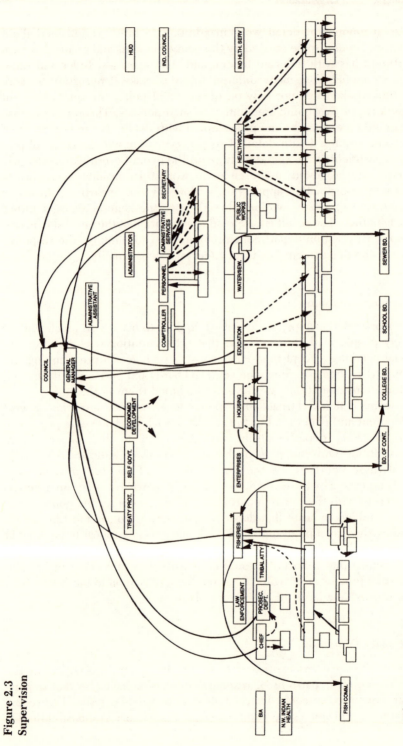

→ Who supervises you?

---→ Whom do you supervise?

* Supervises ten subordinates.

indicates who each person interviewed viewed as his or her supervisor and whom they felt they themselves supervised.

Again one may observe the large number of people reporting that they are supervised directly by the general manager. Moreover, three major department heads perceived that they were supervised by their boards and not by the general manager. The fact that each of these boards includes one council member further confuses the general manager's responsibilities. It appears to indicate that *many* people perceive that the general manager is their boss, while three of the major department heads look more toward their board, and, consequently, to the council, for direction. Finally, the Public Works Department exists only on paper, with the work of this function actually being split between the Water/Sewer Department and a floating maintenance crew. Obviously, all public works activities should be integrated into a single department.

At present, the boards and commissions shortcut the establishment of any clear line of responsibility between department heads and the general manager. In addition, the general manager is also a member of the council. As long as he tries to act as a council member and a general manager as well, his responsibilities will be confusing to everyone.

Social Dimension

Perhaps the most difficult dimension of the organization to analyze is the social one. The tribe is concerned about preserving traditional cultural values which center around family responsibilities. Frequently, organizational responsibilities (which should be based on performance) and family responsibilities (based on family loyalties) become intertwined, causing a weakening of both when compromises are attempted. The challenge here to the tribe is to develop an organization that will preserve cultural values but also demonstrate to the federal government that it can act responsibly in terms of the bureaucratic values (performance) intrinsic to the federal government.

At present, the active role played by boards and commissions, with each having one council member, contributes to the mixing of organizational and family responsibilities in the departments. It would appear that only by removing council members from these boards and commissions and turning these bodies into true policy-advisory boards to the council will this situation be remedied. By taking this type of action, tribal members would still have a means of ensuring that organizational decisions take traditional cultural values into consideration without interfering with administrative efficiency.

STREAM ANALYSIS

The problems discussed here are, of course, interrelated. Stream analysis is a technique that can be used to trace the possible origins of such problems

Figure 2.4
Stream Flow Chart

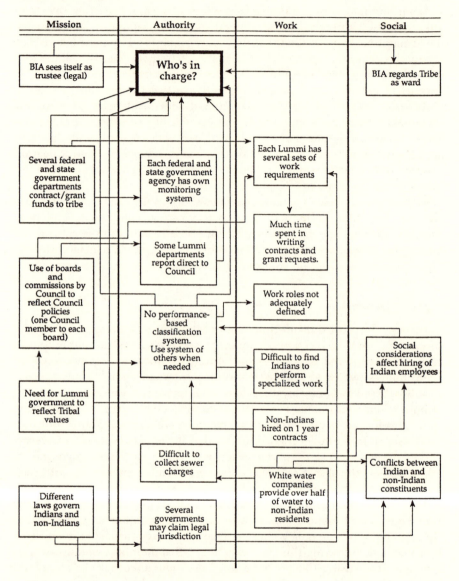

and show how each problem is related to the others.[28] It also allows one to identify the core problem and see which dimensions of organizational behavior can explain its origins. In Figure 2.4, a stream analysis is presented, based on the responses provided in the interviews and questionnaires. It is clear that the core problem is determining who's in charge. The stream analysis shows that this situation exists because of problems in the other three dimensions of the organization (Mission, Work, and Social) as well as other problems in the Authority dimension. The primary cause of the core problem (of who's in charge) stems from the Mission dimension. Here we see that the Bureau of Indian Affairs tends to view itself as the tribe's trustee. In the Social dimension, this also causes the bureau to view the tribe as a ward, calling for a paternalistic relationship. The bureau consequently hesitates to treat the tribe as a mature, responsible entity able to make its own decisions.

A problem in the second Mission dimension arises because several federal and state government departments provide funds to the tribal government via contracts. This affects the tribe's Authority dimension, since each federal and state government department or agency has its own legal mandates and its own monitoring system for enforcing them. This, in turn, affects the operation of the Work dimension, since each tribal department has several sets of work requirements to meet in order to fulfill its contract responsibilities. This, in turn, means that too much time is spent writing contract and grant requests, thus impeding effective coordination of the work force.

Another problem in the Authority dimension contributes to the core problem: The tribe feels the need for its government to aggressively reflect tribal cultural values. This affects the Social dimension of the organization by requiring that social (family) considerations be considered when hiring policies are employed. This, in turn, discourages the Authority dimension of the organization from developing its own performance-based classification system. The tribe tends to borrow characteristics of other governmental classification systems when it feels they are needed (i.e., in making specific decisions). The Work dimension of the organization is affected by the lack of a career-based job classification system. According to the departmental employees interviewed, it is frequently difficult to find Indians to perform specialized work, except in the aquaculture area. Therefore, non-Indians are hired on a one-year contract basis. These short-term contractual relationships hardly encourage such employees to develop a long-term career identification with the organization. The lack of a career-based classification system, of course, also tends to discourage long-term professional identification with the tribe.

One final problem in the Authority dimension that affects the core problem is seen in the fact that different laws frequently govern Indians and non-Indians on the reservation. This results in several governments claiming jurisdiction, as in law enforcement situations, and conflict arising between Indian and non-Indian clients, as in the provision of water service on the reservation. The latter conflict also affects the Work dimension in cases where white-owned water companies provide water for most of the non-Indians on the reservation. The tribal water/sewer district has difficulty collecting sewer charges from these non-Indian customers since they have no means of enforcing payment.

All of these Mission, Work, and Social dimension problems, therefore, contribute to bring about the core problem (concerning who's in charge).

Trying to make changes in the Authority dimension alone (by proposals for reorganization) will not resolve the core problem. Only by freeing itself from a dependency relationship with the Bureau of Indian Affairs and other federal and state agencies will the tribe be able to gain complete control over the operation of its administrative organization. Some interim steps can be taken, however, to strengthen the general manager's control over administration.

CONCLUSIONS

This study has demonstrated that the tribe that we studied could stream-line its decision-making system without violating its basic cultural values, although not without some members experiencing some strains in the ways in which they deal with their tribal government. The tribe also has economic resources to support itself as a self-governing entity, though again, some members will undoubtedly feel caught between conflicting societal values if the tribe begins to actively manage such resources on an organized tribal basis.

To accomplish organizational change, the tribe must do the following:

1. Remove the general manager from membership on the council. The division of responsibilities proposed by the International City Managers Association for city manager cities would appear appropriate for the tribe, with the general manager acting as the professional manager and the council as the policy-making body (see Figure 2.5).
2. Remove the administrative functions of boards and commissions, instead making them advisory policy boards that work directly with, and report to, the council. The existing boards and commissions have served to ensure that traditional cultural values of the tribe continue to be reflected in policy-making. By turning such bodies into policy boards working directly with the council, they would still serve as watchdogs to ensure the preservation of cultural values but will cease bogging down the operation of administrative work.
3. Develop a departmental planning system with department heads responsible to the general manager for results. Each departmental head would be responsible for developing operational (measurable) departmental goals, to be submitted to the general manager each year and to provide the basis for the development of the annual departmental budget.
4. Develop a program budget system by which performance can be measured. Such budgets would be constructed to accomplish the goals set forth in each department's plans.
5. Develop a job classification system that will define duties on a performance basis that can then be used to relate work duties to performance budget requirements.

These recommendations will also allow the council and the tribe to continue the practice of requiring consensus in decision making when policy issues are involved. However, it will also allow administrative decisions to

Figure 2.5
Proposed Organization

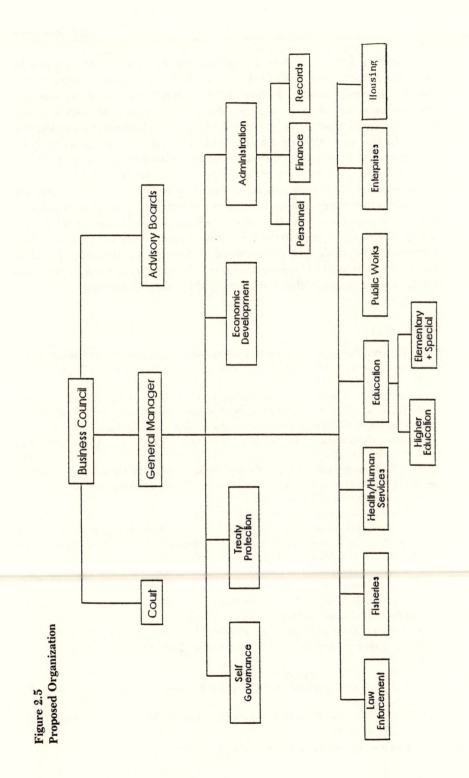

be made on a delegation-of-authority basis by the general manager and by his or her subordinates, going from the council to the general manager and from the general manager, in turn, to the subordinates. If at any time the council disagrees with the way in which an administrative decision is made, it merely has to change the policy on which the administrative action was based. In this way, the tribe will be able to retain its consensus basis for making policy decisions, while allowing administrative decisions to follow the more efficient delegation-of-authority basis for implementing decisions.

Our general conclusion, then, is that this Indian tribe does have the capacity for becoming a self-governing entity but that effecting such a change will not be possible unless the tribe is willing to accept some modification in how it presently relates to the tribal government. By developing a modern organizational system, as recommended in this chapter, the tribe should be able to demonstrate to Congress that it has the capacity to exercise the same self-governing status as that now exercised by American states.

NOTES

1. The tribe is located on a coastal reservation consisting of 12,500 acres of upland area and 5,000 acres of tideland, and with an Indian population of approximately 3,000.

2. William C. Canby, *American Indian Law* (St. Paul, Minn.: West Publishing, 1988); Linda Medcalf, *Law and Identity* (Newbury Park, Calif.: Sage Publications, 1979); Charles F. Wilkinson, *American Indians, Time, and the Law: Native Societies in a Modern Constitutional Democracy* (New Haven, Conn.: Yale University Press, 1988).

3. U.S. Commission on Civil Rights, *Indian Tribes: A Continuing Quest for Survival* (Washington, D.C.: U.S. Government Printing Office, June 1981).

4. Canby, *American Indian Law.*

5. Medcalf, *Law and Identity*, p. 68.

6. Bruce E. Johansen and Donald Grinde, "The Debate Regarding Native American Precedents for Democracy: A Recent Historiography," *American Indian Culture and Research Journal, 14*, no. 1 (Summer 1990): 61–88.

7. Elizabeth Hooker, "The United States Constitution and the Iroquois League," *Ethnohistory, 35*, no. 4 (Fall 1988): 315.

8. Fremont J. Lyden, "Value Orientations in Public Decision-Making," *Policy Studies Journal, 16*, no. 4 (Summer 1988): 843–56.

9. Florence Kluckhohn and Fred Strodtbeck, *Variations in Value Orientations: A Theory Tested in Five Cultures* (Evanston, Ill.: Row, Peterson, 1961).

10. Ibid.

11. Lyden, "Value Orientations."

12. See ibid. for methodology. The symbol = means equal to; the symbol > means greater than.

13. Kurt Russo, *The Price of Recovery* (Bellingham, Wash.: Lummi Indian Business Council, June 1981).

14. Lyden, "Value Orientations."

15. Harvey Perloff, *How a Region Grows: Area Development in the U.S. Economy* (New York: Committee on Economic Development, 1963).

16. Lorrie Kirst, "American Indian Economic Development Policies," *Journal of Planning Literature*, 2, no. 1 (Winter 1987).

17. Vine Deloria, Jr., "The Lummi Indian Community: The Fisherman of the Pacific," in Sam Stanley, ed., *American Indian Economic Development* (The Hague, Holland: Mouton Publishers, 1987), p. 89.

18. Ibid., pp. 94–95.

19. Ibid., p. 98.

20. Ibid., p. 101.

21. Ibid., p. 127.

22. Ibid.

23. Tribal Fact Sheet (undated; author's files).

24. M. H. Simonson, interview by author, Summer 1989.

25. Marc Russell, interview by author, Summer 1991.

26. Paul Alexander, *Sri Lankan Fisherman: Rural Capitalism and Peasant Society* (Canberra: Australian National University, Monographs on South Asia, 1982).

27. Daniel Boxberger, *To Fish in Common* (Lincoln: University of Nebraska Press, 1989), p. 174.

28. Jerry Porras, *Stream Analysis* (Reading, Mass.: Addison-Wesley, 1987).

3

American Indian Self-Governance: Fact, Fantasy, and Prospects for the Future

· *Ward Churchill* ·

I did a two year study on ratified and unratified treaties and agreements of all tribes with the white man.... I can think of nothing from the studies I've done nor from [American Indian] oral history that would suggest that [Indians] ever gave, or ever intended to give, civil and criminal jurisdiction to the United States.

—Vine Deloria, Jr., 1974

The question of self-governance among the American Indian nations encapsulated within what is now the United States of America is one of the more confused issues in modern politics. While there is a general understanding that the indigenous nations of North America once existed as fully self-governing entities, those concerned with the matter have proven spectacularly unable to arrive at even a common definition of what constitutes (or might constitute) contemporary Indian self-governance and whether it presently exists, or, if it does not, how it might be achieved. This chapter is an effort to examine both the proper meanings (facts) and misunderstandings (fantasies) of self-governance, apply these observations to the situation in which Indian nations presently find themselves vis-à-vis the United States, and advance a prospectus for Indian self-governance over the coming decades. Insofar as the space available for the pursuit of these themes is quite limited, only the briefest sort of overview will be possible.

FACT

The various American Indian peoples resident to the territory now known as the United States are nations within even the strictest legal definition.

Further, they have been formally, and in many cases repeatedly, recognized as such by the U.S. government. Article 1 of the U.S. Constitution affirms quite clearly that subordinate sovereignties such as states, counties, municipalities and individuals or groups of individuals are prohibited from entering into treaty agreements. Only the federal government itself is allowed to engage in treaty making, and then, *only* with other fully sovereign national entities (never with states, counties, etc.). In advancing these principles within its own domestic law, the United States was, and is, reflecting the terms, understandings, and requirements of international law, custom, and convention. Each of the at least 371 ratified treaties between the federal government and an American Indian people or peoples thus represents the de facto formal recognition by the United States of the fully sovereign national status of the people or peoples, in accordance with both the laws of the United States and the laws of nations.[1] From this, we may readily discern that American Indian nations possess every legal and moral right to conduct themselves as such, unless they themselves have knowingly, willingly, and formally given up such rights.

Today, representatives of the federal government contend that while all this may be true in principle, and may have actually been true in practice in certain historical instances, the contemporary circumstance is rather different. They point to a series of federal court decisions and statutes holding that, rather than comprising nations in the fullest sense of the term, American Indian peoples constitute "domestic dependent nations" over which the federal government exercises superior sovereign prerogatives, as well as a "fiduciary" or "trust" responsibility involving jurisdictional and administrative control.[2] Further, they argue, while American Indians within the United States are acknowledged as still belonging to their various indigenous polities, they are also citizens of the United States under provision of the 1887 General Allotment Act and the 1924 Indian Citizenship Act, and are thus doubly subordinate to the federal system of authority.[3] From the federal perspective, the bottom line is, therefore, that American Indian nations enjoy a "limited sovereignty." This is to say that they retain all their original national rights other than those specifically restricted or taken away by "Acts of Congress."[4] That there are presently more than 5,000 federal statutes designed to effect precisely this usurpation of sovereign native rights speaks amply to the latitude of national self-governance with which Indians have been left by the 1990s.

Advocates of the federal view purposefully neglect to mention that each of these elements of "law" was unilaterally extended (imposed) by the United States in direct contradiction to the treaty understandings that were already (and, in most cases, are still) in effect with North America's indigenous nations. There is no record of these nations having willingly accepted the notion that they were either domestic to or particularly dependent on the United States. To the contrary, these same nations are well documented as having spent the latter part of the eighteenth and the bulk of the nineteenth centuries engaged in armed resistance—incurring truly horrendous suffering all the while—in concerted efforts to avoid being accorded exactly this status. Similarly, there has never been anyone, even a federal bureaucrat, recorded as being brazen enough to suggest that Indians were somehow mutual participants in bringing about passage of the Allotment and Citizenship acts, that they requested the extension of federal criminal and civil jurisdiction over their homelands, or that they in any way desired the rest of the measures on which the idea of a superior U.S. sovereignty has come to rest.

What is avoided in elaborations of the federal posture is any acknowledgement that, minus the willing consent of Indian nations to the diminishment of their sovereign status, such measures on the part of the federal government can be viewed only as abridgements (violations) of the treaties into which it entered with native people. The implications of this are readily apparent in Article 6 of the U.S. Constitution, in which it is stated unequivocally that treaties represent the "Supreme Law of the Land," on par with the law embodied in the Constitution itself. The terms and provisions of a ratified and unabrogated treaty cannot be *constitutionally* contradicted or impugned by the passage of any subordinate legislation such as local ordinances, state laws, or subsequent federal statutes.[5] The same principles, of course, cover the regulations effected by the host of governmental agencies operating within the modern sociopolitical and economic contexts.

Proponents of the official view also omit mentioning (quite willfully, it appears, insofar as such matters have been repeatedly pointed out to them), that this unilateral reduction of American Indian nations to federally subordinate or "quasi-sovereign" status—similar to that occupied by the states of the union or, increasingly, to that of counties or municipalities, subject to even state jurisdiction and control—was, and is, quite illegal in terms of the constitutional requirements pertaining to entities with which the U.S. government is authorized and empowered to treat. This is no mere academic point of order. For the government to hold that Indian peoples are anything less than fully sovereign nations is to necessarily argue a concomitant: that the entire treaty-making process undertaken by the United States with those peoples is, and always was, legally invalid. This, of course, would serve to void the treaties *en toto*. In turn, given that these same treaties include the land cession clauses by which the United States acquired what it contends is its "legal title" to upwards of 70 percent of its present domestic territoriality, the basis by which the United States has always claimed a right to its own land base would be obliterated.[6]

Absent its Indian treaties, the only options open to the United States by which it could attempt to explain the legitimacy of its occupancy in North America would be resort to the Doctrine of Discovery and its notorious subpart, the Rights of Conquest.[7] Such resort obviously presents no small doctrinal problem to a nation-state that—even in the wildest revisions of its history—can make no claim to having "discovered" its land base (that dubious assertion instead accrues to various European powers).[8] Moreover, the United States carefully foreswore conquest—both in its Articles of Confederation and again, specifically with regard to American Indian nations, in the Northwest Ordinance of 1794—in order to attain a posture of supposed moral enlightenment, on which it has traded ever since.[9]

Federally oriented legal theorists and policymakers are thus forced to advance and insist on the validity of a sheer logical impossibility: that Indian nations are simultaneously fully sovereign (in the abstract sense) for purposes of treaty making and transferring land title to the United States, but less than sovereign (in the practical sense) for purposes of allowing "legitimate" federal control ("exercise of trust") over Indian land, water, and other resources; regulation of trade and diplomatic relations; form of governance; recognition of citizenry; jurisprudence; and virtually anything else striking the federal fancy. Such a convoluted and absurd "doctrine" must also be maintained in order for the United States to be able to assert in the international arena that it has always comported itself on the basis of humane, treaty-anchored (that is, nation-to-nation) understandings with "its" indigenous populations) while at the same time insisting that "Indian Affairs" are a purely "internal" concern of the United States, and are thereby not subject to international consideration, scrutiny, or intervention (as would be the case in any true nation-to-nation relationship, under international law).[10]

In a number of important ways, it is not difficult to discover recent parallels to the U.S. attitude toward American Indian nations. The French, for example, offered similar arguments to "justify" their relationship to Indochina and Algeria during the 1950s. The Belgians advanced similar rationales in an attempt to retain their hold on the Congo during the same decade. Portugal offered the same arguments concerning Mozambique and Angola during the 1960s and 1970s, and, of course, the list could go on at great length. The point, however, is that the common denominator of every example that could be mustered is that the relationship is one of colonialism.[11] The matter can be framed clearly: American Indian nations within the United States are held as colonies—internal colonies—of the United States. Viewed in this light, all the apparent inconsistencies and contradictions of U.S. Indian policy disappear; the policy is quite simply illegal under international law, every step along the way. Federal "Indian law" is not, and was never, so much a matter of law as it is, and always was, an exercise in rationalizing the extension and maintenance of U.S. colonial domination over every indigenous nation it has ever encountered.

Many points can be made from this understanding, but what is of primary importance here is that, as is the case in *any* colonial setting, the notion of self-governance among the colonized—while its illusion is often deliberately fostered as a tactical expedient by the colonizer—is a cruel hoax. Often, in advanced colonial settings such as that evidenced within the United States, the colonized peoples are convinced to administer and impose on themselves the policies and regulations set forth by their colonizers. This self-*administration* is what is so often cynically touted by the colonizers and their puppets among the colonized as being self-governance. In sum, it is both fair and accurate to state that American Indian self-governance does not currently exist within the United States, and that in fact, it *cannot* exist until such time as the fundamental structural relationship between the United States and Indian nations is radically altered. American Indian nations, if they are ever to exercise self-governance, must confront the necessity of a decolonization struggle in the truest sense of the term.

FANTASY

The origin of what is typically passed off as the "model of modern American Indian self-governance" can probably be dated from 1919, when Standard Oil sent a group of geologists to the northern portion of the Navajo Reservation to investigate the possibility that there were petroleum deposits in the area. The explorers' reports being highly favorable, Standard next (in 1921) dispatched a group of representatives to negotiate—in cooperation with the federal Bureau of Indian Affairs—a leasing arrangement by which the corporation could begin drilling and extraction operations. By provision of the 1868 treaty between the Diné (Navajo) Nation and the United States, it was necessary for Standard to secure both an agreement from the Diné government and the approval of the secretary of interior in order for any such contract to be legal and binding. As it turned out, secretarial approval posed no problem, but the traditional Diné Council of Elders voted unanimously to reject the idea of allowing the corporation to exploit their land and resources.[12]

This outcome was obviously unacceptable to Standard, and to the Department of Interior, under which responsibility for virtually all development of "government" lands and resources is lodged. Consequently, in 1923, the Interior Department unilaterally appointed what it called the "Navajo Grand Council," a small group of handpicked and "educated" Indians (namely, individuals who had been indoctrinated in the values and mores of Euro-America), from which representatives of the traditional Diné government (with which the United States had entered into a solemn treaty) were entirely excluded. Washington then announced that this new council, devoid as it was of any sort of *Navajo* support, would henceforth be recognized as the sole "legitimate" governmental representative body of the Navajo Nation; thus, the traditional Diné form of governance was, at the stroke of the federal pen and with no popular Diné agreement whatsoever, totally disenfranchised and supplanted. One of the very first acts of the Washington-appointed replacement group was, of course, to sign the federally and corporately desired leasing instruments, setting in motion and "legitimizing" a sustained process of mineral expropriation on the Navajo Reservation which has quite mightily profited a range of non-Diné businesses and individuals.[13] Correspondingly, the Diné people have been forced into truly abject poverty, their traditional subsistence economy has been ruined, and their land base has been destroyed to the extent that it has been seriously considered for official designation as a U.S. "National Sacrifice Area."[14]

Throughout the entire period since 1923, the *forms* of democratic governance among the Navajo—the inculcation of voting rather than consensus as a means of governmental selection; subdivision of the reservation into electoral districts; expansion of the council to include representatives from each district; the hypothetical division of governmental structure into executive, legislative, and judicial spheres; and so on—have been carefully polished. Moreover, the rhetoric of self-governance—supposedly evidenced in the fact that leaders of the tribal council always affix their signatures to business agreements made "on behalf of" their people, through the maintenance of a Navajo lobbying office in Washington, and via similar tokens—has been consistently advanced by Navajo and federal politicos alike. It is even possible that at least some of the actors on both sides of the equation actually believe what they are saying.[15]

However, reality is dramatically different from rhetoric. During the entire half-century in which the Navajo council has been functioning in its mature form, it has never been allowed to negotiate a single business agreement on its own initiative. It has continued to be totally restricted from entering into *any* agreement with a "foreign government" other than that of the United States, whether for purposes of trade or for any other reason. Consequently, it has never been able to negotiate mineral extraction royalty rates on anything resembling favorable terms, to establish or enforce even minimal standards of cleanup and land reclamation upon transient extractive corporations doing business upon its land, or even to determine the number of livestock that can be grazed within its borders.[16] For that matter, the Navajo council has never—as the ongoing "Navajo-Hopi Land Disputes" readily attest—been able to exert any particular influence in the determination of the exact borders of the Navajo Nation.[17] Even the citizenry of the Navajo Nation has been defined by the federal government, through imposition of a formal eugenices code termed "blood quantum" and nearly a century of direct control over tribal rolls; these federal "methods" of manipulating and arithmetically constricting the indigenous population have become so imbedded in the Indian consciousness and psyche that Washington can rely on the "self-governance" mechanisms of the Native Americans to abandon their own traditions and concern with sovereignty, instead adhering to federal definitions of Indian identity and thus imposing the burden of stark racism upon *themselves*.[18]

Council members like to point out that they have a court system, police force, and jails operating on the reservation, and they submit that this is evidence of self-governance, but the fact of the matter is that the Navajos possess no jurisdictional authority at all over non-Navajos committing crimes within the Navajo Nation.[19] For that matter, they have equally little jurisdiction over their own citizenry when it comes to felony and serious misdemeanor crimes, as well as in a number of important civil areas.[20] In order to resolve issues between themselves and any of their corporate lessees, they have no recourse but to pursue matters in U.S. courts rather than their own.[21] In order to resolve issues with the federal government, they must secure permission from that same government to litigate in that government's own courts.[22] In order even to impose a severance tax on their own mineral resources as these are extracted by transnational corporations—the uncontested right of every state of the union—they must secure permission from the federal government to seek (and, in a limited way, secure) a federal court opinion allowing them to do so.[23] Things are, at this point, so confused that one can hear Navajo "tribal leaders," in all apparent seriousness and in the context of the same speech, spouting rhetoric about being part of a "sovereign, self-governing nation," *and* proposing that the Navajo Nation be *elevated* to the status of a state within the United States.[24]

Is this national self-governance? The fact is that, fantasies to the contrary, the Navajo council and its chair have absolutely no control over any aspect of Navajo affairs. Every shred of their policy is, and always has been, utterly contingent on the approval of the U.S. secretary of the interior, the federal courts, and, often enough, corporate executives and the governments of the three states (Arizona, New Mexico, and Utah) within which the Navajo Reservation technically lies.

The same situation presently prevails on almost all reservations in the United States. The reason is that the model of the Navajo Grand Council had, by the early 1930s, proven itself so successful in serving U.S. interests, while offering useful illusions to the contrary, that it was imposed across the face of Indian country through the 1934 Indian Reorganization Act (IRA).[25] *Imposed* is the correct word because, although each American Indian nation that was "reorganized" under the statute—having its traditional governmental structure usurped and replaced by a council patterned directly after a corporate board—allegedly voted in a referendum to do so, the reality is, as always, rather different.[26] At the Pine Ridge Reservation (Oglala Lakota Nation), for example, a number of dead people somehow managed to vote for reorganization; even after this was documented, the referendum results were allowed to stand and reorganization to proceed.[27] In the Hopi Nation, to take another example, more than 85 percent of all eligible voters (federally defined) opposed and actively boycotted the referendum; however, their abstentions were counted as "affirmative" votes by the Bureau of Indian Affairs and reorganization proceeded.[28] The list of such examples might be extended, in one or another degree of virulence, to every Indian nation that was reorganized in accordance with the federal prescription.[29]

All fantasies of self-governing characteristics aside, the absolute predicate of any IRA government is its acceptance—indeed, reinforcement—of the emphatically subnational status accorded American Indian nations by the United States, to legitimize their people's subordination through their public endorsement of it, to toe the line of limitations decreed by the federal government, and ultimately to barter the genuine interests of their people in exchange for the petty position and essentially minor material compensation that serving as puppets of a foreign power affords them. This is advanced colonial administration in its very purest form, whether one wishes to draw one's parallel to the leadership of Vichy France or to the Thieu regime in what was once called the Republic of South Vietnam.[30]

Self-evidently, such governments will not, and in fact structurally cannot, pursue actual self-determination, self-governance, and sovereignty. They will never, and can never, attempt to consolidate real control over their remaining land bases, physically recover lands illegally taken from their people, throw the federal bureaucrats and supporting police off their reservations, try to physically bar the corporate rape of their territories, or enter into diplomatic and trade relations with other nations. They will not, and they cannot, because in the final analysis they owe their fealty and their allegiance, not to their own people (or even themselves), but to their colonizers. It is the colonizer, after all, and not their people, who provides the positions they occupy, whatever claim to legitimacy that colonizer really carries and whatever the means for its continuation. The relationship is one of symbiosis and mutual perpetuation in an unbalanced sort of way.[31]

From here it is but a short step to viewing IRA governments, not as champions of American Indian self-governance, but as literal barriers to it. This is true in the mere fact of the existence of such bodies and the confusion this inherently engenders in determining the *real* representatives of Indian people. Moreover, it has become true in the sense that these self-proclaimed and federally validated "responsible" (To whom? To what?) representatives of Native America have increasingly taken to lending their energies and their voices to discrediting any Indian or group of Indians audacious enough to address the questions attending a true resumption of national prerogatives by American Indian peoples.[32] We see this classically in the example of former Rosebud Sioux Tribal Chairman Webster Two Hawk, who wandered around on the federal dole like a clown, wearing a crew cut and "war bonnet" and parroting the views of the Nixon administration vis-à-vis the American Indian Movement. Finally, however, in 1972, he called upon the BIA to account for its colonial arrogance and at least a few of its more blatant transgressions at the expense of the Indian people.[33]

More grimly, we see former Pine Ridge Tribal President Dick Wilson forming a cabal of thugs known as the "Goons" to act as surrogates for the Federal Bureau of Investigation (FBI) and engaging in outright mass murder to prevent an insurgent grass-roots movement of traditional Oglalas pursuing their rights under the 1868 Fort Laramie Treaty from "spoiling" a planned secret expropriation of uranium deposits in the northwest quadrant of the reservation.[34] There is no shortage of examples comparable to the performances of Two Hawk and Wilson. Rather than serving, at any level, as models for the resumption and development of American Indian self-governance, the present IRA "governments" represent the exact opposite: institutionalized capitulation on virtually every significant issue of Indian rights. By and large, they are, in simplest terms, problems to be overcome as part of any genuine decolonization struggle and—if examples such as Wilson are any indication—they may be predicted to exact a nasty toll of their own ostensible constituents in a counterstruggle to avert any real dismantling of the colonial structure on which they have come to depend for income and a sort of prestige.

PROSPECTS FOR THE FUTURE

Native America is at a crossroads. If the present hegemony of IRA-style governance is maintained and allowed to continue its giveaway program in terms of American Indian resources and national rights, the future looks bleak indeed. Remaining on the course sketched above can result only in the permanent reduction of American Indian sovereignty and self-governance to, at best, the level of very minor components within the overall U.S. governmental/political apparatus. In the case of many, or even most, of the smaller Indian nations, eventual termination—*autotermination* may be a better term—and absorption directly into the "melting pot" seems the most likely outcome. In other words, the final liquidation of Native America is a distinct possibility over the next half-century or less.

Fortunately, alternatives have emerged since 1970. These have related, to a considerable degree, to the momentum created by the actions and activities of the American Indian Movement (AIM) and related "militant" organizations, particularly during the period of 1972 through 1978. In retrospect, there can be no serious question that the 1972 Trail of Broken Treaties occupation of the Bureau of Indian Affairs Building in Washington, D.C., for example, did more to bring Indians into the BIA than all the petitions and letters of "more responsible" and "legitimate" tribal officials over the preceding fifty years. The Twenty Point Program advanced by Trail participants as a cohesive American Indian sociopolitical agenda still represents a benchmark expression of indigenous sovereignty in North America.[35] Ironically, those Indians hired as result—during the major BIA "integration" period lasting from 1973 through 1976—seemed to take it as a matter of faith that they should comport themselves in a manner that can only be described as anti-AIM.[36]

Similarly, AIM's actions at Gordon, Nebraska, in 1972, and Custer, South Dakota, in 1973—demanding that the Euro-American murderers of Indian people be charged with their actual crimes rather than manslaughter—yielded an incalculable impact on the concept of Indian rights and the value of Indian life among non-Indians throughout the United States. In a tangible way, these AIM undertakings brought to a screeching halt a nationwide rash of ritual or "thrill" killings of Indian people which had been mounting for some time.[37] By any estimation, this was vastly more than had been accomplished by a decade of "polite" discussions about the "problem" by the federally approved Indian leadership with state, local, and national U.S. law enforcement officials. Predictably, however, so-called official Native America did little in response but criticize and condemn AIM's "violent tactics." (One is forced to ask here exactly how diminishing a wave of homicides through methods involving no loss of life could ever have been reasonably construed as violence?)

Again, AIM's stand on the Pine Ridge Reservation from 1973 through 1976, refusing to swerve from its support of Oglala national rights under terms of the 1868 Fort Laramie Treaty—in the face of a hideously lethal federal repression—can only be viewed as a tremendously important point of departure for the general rebirth of American Indian pride in the United States and an increasing Indian willingness to stand and attempt to assert (or reassert) their broader rights to genuine self-determination.[38] As always, "duly elected" tribal officials tended overwhelmingly to attack AIM, while defending the federal "right" to maintain "order" on the reservation, regardless of the cost and consequences of such order to Indians. It is now a sublime paradox that many tribal council members have themselves begun to mimic AIM viewpoints and AIM pronouncements of a decade ago, while never having abandoned their clever descriptor of those who showed them the way as being "Assholes In Moccasins."

What the AIM "radicals" were, and in many cases still are, demonstrating is that in order for Indians to make gains, to self-determine and self-govern, it is absolutely essential to proceed by something other than the self-serving "rules of the game" laid down by the U.S. government. Put another way, those who claim sovereignty must endeavor to exercise it; to rely on their own sense of legality and morality, and to act accordingly. By the 1980s, this dynamic had become clearly consolidated in the occupation of Yellow Thunder Camp near Rapid City, in the Black Hills, as part of an overt program of reclaiming Lakota territory guaranteed under the Fort Laramie Treaty but expropriated during the 1870s by the United States.[39] The same may be said of the ongoing resistance to federally imposed relocation of traditional Diné people from their land in the Big Mountain area of the Navajo and Hopi reservations in northeastern Arizona, and there are many other examples, ranging from the continuing struggles over fishing rights in the Pacific Northwest to the stands taken by the Haudenosaunee (Iroquois Six Nations Confederacy) along the U.S.-Canadian border in the Northeast, to similar positions adopted by the O'Otam (Papago) along the U.S.-Mexican border in the Southwest, and the refusal of nearly half of all the Seminole people of Florida to accept federal recognition as a "validation" of their personal and national existence.[40,41] Again, one might perceive the emergence of an American Indian presence in the international arena, through the United Nations Working Group on Indigenous Populations (a subpart of the UN Commission on Human Rights), to have come from the same impetus and to be following the same general trajectory.[42]

Perhaps the purest articulation of the AIM alternative to IRA colonialism may be found in the platform assembled under the title TREATY, for use by Russell Means in his candidacy for the Pine Ridge tribal presidency in 1984. Here, for the first time, or at least the first time during the twentieth century, was offered a truly comprehensive program by which a given American Indian nation could undertake to recover control over its own affairs, abolishing the IRA system and restoring political power to the traditional Councils of Elders. Further, the program would allow the nation to open up diplomatic and trade relations with nations other than the United States, begin a systematic effort at restoring its own land base and revitalizing a traditionally oriented economy thereon, assert jurisdictional prerogatives and control over the definition of its own membership/citizenry, and convert its educational system to its own rather than its opponents' uses. All this was conceived by way of using the IRA structure against itself in a sort of exercise in political jujitsu.[43]

The TREATY concept was seen as so effective and threatening by federal authorities and by those Indians on Pine Ridge who owe their allegiance to that government rather than to their own ostensible constituents that they conspired to disqualify Means from the reservation ballot, not on the basis of any alleged offense against the Lakota people or Lakota law, but because he had been convicted of expressing contempt—by way of engaging in "criminal syndicalism"—toward an alien *South Dakota* court some years previously. Despite the fact that it was never actualized on Pine Ridge, the point should be made that insofar as the IRA establishment was prepared to go to such lengths to suppress the TREATY, it obviously bears extensive study, adaptation, and implementation by other Indians in other places.

Indeed, this appears to be occurring, in both literal and more diffused fashions. The Haida Draft Constitution, which was generated by a people whose territory is split between the United States and Canada in the Alaska region, incorporates much of the same thinking that was brought forth in the TREATY Platform. Many of the gains posted by Pacific Northwest nations such as the Quinault and Lummi in recent years also proceed in accordance with liberatory principles similar to those expressed in TREATY.[44] Moreover, to a certain extent at least, most of the ideas concerning Lakota land recovery and self-governance contained in the present Bradley Bill (S. 705), are drawn from the TREATY framework.[45] These are all encouraging signs, and there are a number of others that might be cited.

It is time, if American Indian tribal self-governance in any real sense—as *nations* rather than as integral components of the Euro-American empire—is to once again become a functioning reality, to begin to consciously destroy the IRA system, to discard "leaders" who profess loyalty to it, to renounce the "federal trust relationship" and reject *all* interaction with the BIA, and to begin to assert (or reassert) actual *Indian* alternatives. It will not be a quick or pleasant process: There will no doubt be severe costs and consequences associated with such a line of action and development. The adversaries of Native America have shown themselves consistently, and for more than two centuries now, to embody the epitome of ruthlessness. The fact is, however, that the costs and consequences attending subordination to the federal will are, and have always been, far higher. The choice is really between extinction and resurgence. Viewed in this way, there is simply no real choice at all.

NOTES

1. The texts of 371 ratified treaty instruments appear in Charles J. Kappler, *Indian Treaties, 1778–1883* (New York: Interland Publishing Co., 1973). The Lakota scholar Vine Deloria, Jr., has uncovered several other texts of ratified treaties that are omitted in the Kappler compilation. Additionally, Deloria has collected more than 600 unratified treaties and agreements of various sorts, which the federal government considers to lack the same legal force as ratified instruments but on which it nonetheless predicates various portions of its aggregate land title. Concerning the recognition of sovereignty inherent to U.S. treaties with American Indian peoples, see Felix S. Cohen, *Handbook of American Indian Law* (Albuquerque: University of New Mexico Press, 1942; repr. 1971), pp. 33–36.

2. The concept of "domestic dependent nation" was first articulated by Chief Justice of the Supreme Court John Marshall in *Worcester v. Georgia* (6 Pet. 515 [1832]). It set in motion the emergence of a legal doctrine wherein in the United States contended that it held "plenary [full] power" over indigenous nations, a notion elaborated most fully in *Cherokee Nation v. Hitchcock* (187 U.S. 294 [1902]) and *Lonewolf v. Hitchcock* (187 U.S. 553 [1903]). The idea that the federal government, as the superior sovereignty in U.S.-Indian relations, is obligated to exercise a "trust responsibility" over the affairs of its native "wards" stems from the plenary power doctrine. It was framed most clearly in *U.S. v. Kagama* (118 U.S. 375 [1886]) and *U.S. v. Thomas* (151 U.S. 557, 585 [1894]). Tellingly, there was never a shred of Indian consent involved. For an excellent overview, see C. Harvey, "Constitutional Law: Congressional Plenary Power over Indian Affairs—A Doctrine Rooted in Prejudice," *American Indian Law Review*, no. 5 (1977): 117–50.

3. The 1887 General Allotment Act (25 U.S.C.A. § 331) was primarily aimed at destroying traditional patterns of indigenous land tenure and transferring some two-thirds of all reservation acreage into the "public domain." It contained a clause, however, stipulating a quid pro quo by which each Indian seeking to retain a portion of his or her reservation through acceptance of a land parcel would concomitantly have to accept U.S. citizenship. In 1924, all native people who remained "unallotted"

were decreed to be U.S. citizens under provision of the Indian Citizenship Act (8 U.S.C.A. 140 [a] [2]).

4. Incongruously, the supposed "source" of congressional authority to strip away the sovereign prerogatives of indigenous nations by legislative fiat is the "commerce clause" of the U.S. Constitution, a passage clearly intended by the framers to regulate the behavior of their own citizenry—*not* Indians—in their dealings with native people. This is readily borne out in the series of federal "Trade and Intercourse Acts" beginning in 1790 and extending through 1834. The principle became inverted, as is evidenced in *United States v. Forty-Three Gallons of Whiskey* (93 U.S. 188 [1876]) and, ultimately, in *In re Mayfield, Petitioner* (141 U.S. 107, 115, 116 [1891]). As the matter was put in *United States v. McGowan* (302 U.S. 535 [1938]): "Congress alone has the right to determine the manner in which the country's guardianship [of Indians and their affairs] shall be carried out."

5. Although in *Lonewolf v. Hitchcock* (1903), the Supreme Court determined that it was and is allowable for subsequent federal statutes to contravene treaty provisions, the original constitutional prohibition against such an "interpretation" had long been clear: "It [is] not competent for an act of Congress to alter the stipulations of [an Indian] treaty or to change the character of the agents appointed under it." (Commission on Indian Affairs, *House Report No. 447*, 23d Congress, 1st sess., Washington, D.C., May 20, 1834).

6. In effect, the United States holds title of other sorts only to the area of the original thirteen British colonies of the Atlantic seaboard, quit-claimed by King George III in the Treaty of Ghent, and to portions of northern Mexico quit-claimed by that republic through the 1848 Treaty of Guadalupe Hidalgo. In each case, the nation-state in question based its own title to the territory ceded on earlier arrangements made with native inhabitants, usually through treaties and/or direct purchase. With such transactions as the Louisiana Purchase, the United States acquired not territory, but the right to negotiate land cessions from native inhabitants within given areas. Hence, it entered into scores of treaties with Indian nations within the Louisiana Purchase territory. It is on these treaties, most of which involved land cessions, that actual U.S. title rests. See Charles C. Royce, *Indian Land Cessions in the United States* (Washington, D.C.: U.S. Bureau of Ethnology, Smithsonian Institution, 1899), for the most comprehensive delineation of the specific territoriality involved.

7. Under the so-called "Rights of Conquest," a subpart of the Doctrine of Discovery, European Crowns were constrained to pursue territorial acquisition by force of arms only under the conditions required for the waging of a "just war." The latter doctrine was initially elaborated by St. Augustine during the early fifth century (see James A. Brundage, *Medieval Canon Law and the Crusader*, Madison: University of Wisconsin Press, 1969; also see Herbert Andrew Deane, *The Political and Social Ideas of St. Augustine*, New York: Columbia University Press, 1963), and then codified by Thomas Aquinas during the thirteenth century (see Lloyd Weinreb, *Natural Law and Justice*, Cambridge, Mass.: Harvard University Press, 1987). Under the law, Crowns could exercise conquest rights only when indigenous populations (1) refused to accept Christian missionaries among them, (2) refused to trade with representatives of the Crown, or (3) engaged in unprovoked attacks upon subjects of the Crown. None of these conditions applied in the U.S. portion of North America, either before or after decolonization occurred. This was plainly recognized by George III in his Proclamation of 1763, barring territorial expansion by his subjects into areas

west of the Allegheny Mountains (see K. Knorr, *British Colonial Theories, 1570–1850*, Toronto: University of Toronto Press, 1944; also see Alden T. Vaughan, *Early American Indian Documents: Treaties and Laws, 1607–1789*, Washington, D.C.: University Publications of America, 1979). Hence, conquest rights would not apply to U.S. legal standing in North America, even if discovery rights somehow did.

8. The Doctrine of Discovery is poorly understood in this country, having been horribly garbled in Chief Justice John Marshall's attempted appropriation of it in 1823 to rationalize U.S. legal standing in North America (*Johnson v. McIntosh*, 21 U.S. 8 [Wheat.] 543). In actuality, the doctrine, from the time when it first began to emerge in the letters of Pope Innocent IV in 1271—and in the form in which it was ultimately codified by Franciscus de Victoria in his 1541 tract *De Indis et de Ivre Belli Reflectiones* (contained in James Brown Scott, *The Spanish Origins of International Law*, Oxford: Clarendon Press, 1934), and adopted from that source by Great Britain (see Edward Arber, ed., *The First Three English Books on America: Being Chiefly Translations, Compilations, etc., by Richard Eden*, Westminster, England: Constable Publishers, 1895)—holds clearly that discovery rights accrue *solely* to European *Crowns*. Invocation of the doctrine did not convey land title to the monarch invoking it. Rather, it vested the given Crown only with a monopoly (excluding other European Crowns) within the area claimed to acquire title, via purchase agreements or other arrangements, from the indigenous populations already holding the territory at issue (see Mark Frank Lindley, *The Acquisition and Government of Backward Territory in International Law*, London: Longmans, Green Publishers, 1926). Of course, a Crown could, and often did, vest title to certain areas in its subjects (usually individual aristocrats or corporate entities), once legitimate acquisition from the natives had occurred. However, George III made no such transfer of title to his former subjects in the Treaty of Ghent, the instrument by which he quit-claimed his thirteen colonies along the present U.S. Atlantic seaboard at the end of the American Revolution. To the contrary, the revolutionists had deliberately created a complete legal rupture between themselves and the Crown, to which discovery rights in their area of interest might be said to have accrued. Hence, the Doctrine of Discovery never applied to the legal standing of the United States, even if its content were what Justice Marshall claimed it was (see Bernard Bailyn, *The Ideological Origins of the American Revolution*, Cambridge, Mass.: Harvard University Press, 1967).

9. See Merrill Jensen, *The Articles of Confederation: An Interpretation of the Social-Constitutional History of the American Revolution, 1774–1778* (Madison: University of Wisconsin Press, 1940). Also see Reginald Horsman, *Expansion and American Indian Policy, 1783–1812* (East Lansing: Michigan State University Press, 1967) and Francis Paul Prucha, *American Indian Policy in the Formative Years: the Trade and Intercourse Acts, 1790–1834* (Cambridge, Mass.: Harvard University Press, 1962).

10. For one of the more influential attempts to forge this mutually exclusive set of elements into a single, cohesive whole, see Charles F. Wilkinson, *American Indians, Time, and the Law* (New Haven, Conn.: Yale University Press, 1987).

11. For a treatment tying all these apparently disparate settings together in terms of their conceptualization, see Charles Verlinden, *The Beginnings of Modern Colonization* (Ithaca, N.Y.: Cornell University Press, 1970).

12. This is covered very well in the first chapter of Jerry Kammer's *The Second*

Long Walk: The Navajo-Hopi Land Dispute (Albuquerque: University of New Mexico Press, 1980). Concerning the source of the present Navajo government's source of authority, this was spelled out quite clearly by the Supreme Court of the Navajo Nation in a finding (A-CV–13–89) in response to certified questions (WR-CV–99–89) raised in a case, *Navajo Nation, et al. v. Peter McDonald, et al.*, on April 13, 1989. In the opinion of the Honorable Robert Yazzie, writing for the court, "There is nothing in either the history of the present Navajo government or in the Tribal Code to support the argument that the source of the Chairman's and Vice Chairman's governmental authority is the voting public."

13. Kammer, *The Second Long Walk.* Also see Anita Parlow, *Cry, Sacred Land: Big Mountain U.S.A.*, (Washington, D.C.: Christic Institute, 1988).

14. The term accrues from the U.S. Energy Administration, *Project Independence: A Summary* (Washington, D.C., November 1, 1974).

15. Much of this is brought out in U.S. Senate, Select Committee on Indian Affairs, *The Federal Government's Relationship with American Indians: Hearings before the Special Committee on Investigations of the Select Committee on Indian Affairs, United States Senate, January 30, 31, 1989 and February 1, 1990*, 101st Congress, 1st sess. (Washington, D.C.: U.S. Government Printing Office, 1990). Also see R. Allan, "The Navajo Tribal Council: A Study of the American Indian Assimilation Process," unpublished report available from the *Arizona Law Review* (n.d.).

16. U.S. Commission on Civil Rights, *The Navajo Nation: An American Colony* (Washington, D.C.: U.S. Government Printing Office, 1975).

17. U.S. Senate, *Relocation of Certain Hopi and Navajo Indians*, 96th Congress, 1st sess. (Washington, D.C.: U.S. Government Printing Office, May 15, 1979). Also see U.S. Department of Interior Surveys and Investigations Staff, *A Report to the Committee on Appropriations, U.S. House of Representatives, on the Navajo and Hopi Relocation Commission* (Washington, D.C.: U.S. Government Printing Office, January 22, 1985).

18. For detailed elaboration on this theme, see M. Annette Jaimes, "Federal Indian Identification Policy: A Usurpation of Indigenous Sovereignty in North America," in *Critical Issues in Native North America*, vol. 1, ed. Ward Churchill (Copenhagen: International Work Group on Indigenous Affairs, 1989), pp. 15–36.

19. That Indians have no authority to dispense justice to non-Indians committing crimes against them, even in Indian country, has been a touchstone of U.S. jurisprudence since the passage of the first of the Trade and Intercourse Acts (1 *Stat.* 137) on July 22, 1790. Crimes by non-Indians against non-Indians in Indian country were left "a matter of common sense" for nearly a century, with native jurisdiction in such matters not being formally negated until *United States v. McBratney*, 104 U.S. 621 (1881).

20. This is pursuant to the "Seven Major Crimes Act" (23 *Stat.* 362, 385, 18 U.S.C. 548) of March 3, 1885, which was tested and affirmed in *Gon-Hay-Ee, Petitioner*, 130 U.S. 343 (1889). The original seven felonies covered in the act were expanded to ten by amendment to the legislation (25 U.S.C. 217–218) in 1910. Crimes committed by Indians against non-Indians in Indian country had been covered— with the United States preemptively assuming jurisdiction—since passage of an act on March 3, 1817 (3 *Stat.* 383), which was subsequently incorporated into the last of the Trade and Intercourse Acts (4 *Stat.* 729, 733) on June 30, 1834.

21. As a federal court put it:

If the United States is entitled [within its self-defined "trust capacity"] to institute an action on its own behalf and on behalf of the Indians, the Indians cannot determine the course of the suit or settle it contrary to the position of the government. The Indians, being represented by the government, are not necessary parties [to their own litigation]. *Heckman v. United States*, 224 U.S. 413 [1912]

Also see *Pueblo of Picuris in State of New Mexico v. Abeyta*, 50 F.2d (C.C.A. 10, 1931).

22. "Sovereign immunity" has always been a juridical principle of the United States and was first brought formally to bear against Indians in *Hy-yu-tse-mil-kin v. Smith*, 205 U.S. 458 (1907).

23. *Morris v. Hitchcock*, 21 App. D.C. 565, 593 (1903), aff'd, 194 U.S. 384 (1904).

24. Speech by Navajo Tribal Chairman Peter McDonald at the University of Colorado at Boulder, October 9, 1988 (tape on file).

25. 25 U.S.C.A. 461 (1934). For the original federal intent underlying the act, see Jay B. Nash, Oliver LaFarge, and W. Carson Ryan, *New Day for the Indians: A Survey of the Workings of the Indian Reorganization Act* (New York: Academy Press, 1938).

26. Extensive analysis of IRA governmental structure may be found in Vine Deloria, Jr., and Clifford M. Lytle, *The Nations Within: The Past and Future of American Indian Sovereignty* (New York: Pantheon Books, 1984).

27. Concerning Lakota referenda and "the vote of the dead," see Lawrence H. Kelly, ed., *Indian Affairs and the Indian Reorganization Act: The Twenty Year Record* (Tucson: University of Arizona Press, 1954).

28. On the Hopi referendum and its outcome, see Charles Lummis, *Bullying the Hopi* (Prescott, Ariz.: Prescott College Press, 1968). Also see Indian Law Resource Center, *Report to the Kikmongwe and Other Traditional Hopi Leaders on Docket 196 and Other Threats to Hopi Land and Sovereignty* (Washington, D.C., 1979).

29. See Kelly, *Indian Affairs*.

30. For a superb examination of contemporary analogies, see Edward S. Herman, and Frank Brodhead, *Demonstration Elections: U.S.-Staged Elections in the Dominican Republic, Vietnam and El Salvador* (Boston: South End Press, 1984).

31. This is precisely the phenomenon addressed by Frantz Fanon in his *Black Skin/White Masks* (New York: Grove Press, 1965). Another view may be found in Albert Memmi, *Domination* (Boston: Beacon Press, 1971).

32. For an analysis of the psychology of this circumstance, see Albert Memmi, *Colonizer and Colonized* (Boston: Beacon Press, 1967). Also see Frantz Fanon, *The Wretched of the Earth* (Boston: Grove Press, 1964).

33. See Editors, *BIA, I'm Not Your Indian Anymore* (Rooseveltown, N.Y.: Akwesasne Notes, 1973). Also see Vine Deloria, Jr., *Behind the Trail of Broken Treaties* (New York: Delta Books, 1974) and Robert Burnette, with John Koster, *The Road to Wounded Knee* (New York: Bantam Books, 1974).

34. See Editors, *Voices from Wounded Knee, 1973* (Rooseveltown, N.Y.: Akwesasne Notes, 1974). Also see Peter Matthiessen, *In the Spirit of Crazy Horse* (New York: Viking Press, 1984).

35. The complete 20 Point Program, and official federal responses to each point, are included as an appendix to *BIA, I'm Not Your Indian Anymore*.

36. This tendency is discussed to a certain extent in Deloria, *Behind the Trail of Broken Treaties*.

37. The AIM actions were focused on the brothers Melvin and Leslie Hare, non-Indians who had ritually murdered an Oglala Lakota named Raymond Yellow Thunder in Gordon, Nebraska, in January 1972, and Darld Schmitz, a non-Indian who had knifed to death another Oglala, Wesley Bad Heart Bull, in Buffalo Gap, South Dakota, in January 1973. The Hares were charged with nothing at all until AIM's intervention. Schmitz was charged with only "second degree manslaughter." Other major cases addressed by the movement during this period were the shooting death of an unarmed Papago youth named Philip Celay by a non-Indian sheriff's deputy, David Bosman, in Ajo, Arizona, in July 1972 (ruled "justifiable homicide"); the shooting death of the unarmed Mohawk political leader Richard Oaks by Michael Morgan in September 1972 ("self-defense"); and the shooting death of the unarmed Onondaga Special Forces veteran Leroy Shenandoah by non-Indian police in Philadelphia during November 1972 (another "justifiable homicide"). See Alvin M. Josephy, Jr., *Now That the Buffalo's Gone: A Study of Today's Indians* (New York: Knopf, 1982).

38. See Matthiessen, *In the Spirit of Crazy Horse*. Also see Bruce Johansen and Robert Maestas, *Wasi'chu: The Continuing Indian Wars* (New York: Monthly Review Press, 1979); and Ward Churchill and Jim Vander Wall, *Agents of Repression: The FBI's Secret Wars against the Black Panther Party and the American Indian Movement* (Boston: South End Press, 1988).

39. On Yellow Thunder Camp, see Rex Weyler, *Blood of the Land: The U.S. Government and Corporate War against the American Indian Movement* (New York: Everest House Publishers, 1983), pp. 251–64.

40. With regard to the Haudenosaunee, see ibid., pp. 245–50.

41. On O'Otam see *Akwesasne Notes*, late Summer 1973. Also see Milton Moskowitz, Michael Katz, and Robert Levering, eds., *Everybody's Business: An Irreverent Guide to Corporate America* (San Francisco: Harper and Row Publishers, 1980).

42. Independent Commission on International Humanitarian Issues, *Indigenous Peoples: A Global Quest for Justice* (London: Zed Press, 1987).

43. Russell Means and Ward Churchill, *TREATY: A Platform for Nationhood* (Fourth World Center for Study of Indigenous Law and Politics, University of Colorado at Denver, forthcoming).

44. In general, see Carol J. Minugh, Glenn T. Morris, and Rudolph C. Ryser, eds., *Indian Self-Governance: Perspectives on the Political Status of Indian Nations in the United States of America* (Kenmore, Wash.: Center for World Indigenous Studies, 1989).

45. The complete text of S. 705 may be found in *Wicazo Sa Review*, 4, no. 1 (Spring 1988): 3–17.

4

Indian Policy at the Beginning of the 1990s: The Trivialization of Struggle

Russel Lawrence Barsh

As we begin the last decade of the twentieth century, American Indian policy presents a paradox of big words and small gains. Our neighbors to the north are engaged in a struggle over constitutional power, with the fate of the entire country hanging in the balance. Here in the United States, lawyers and tribal leaders are preoccupied with annual appropriations and the revision of financial regulations. Is this because the real struggle is already behind us, or is it symptomatic of an insidious defeat? A case can be made that U.S. tribal governments have grown so integrated into the general institutional structure of the country that they are no longer able or willing to oppose it. If true, this means that the Indian Reorganization Act and liberal social programs have achieved in less than fifty years what a century of war and "forced assimilation" failed to do: mainstream the Indians.

A brief review of major Indian legislation and policy statements from 1990–91 reinforces this pessimistic conclusion. It also reveals the emergence of a new legal standard of "Indianness," which gives the administration a loaded gun to point at recalcitrant tribal leaders. While in limited respects the federal government is relinquishing its traditional day-to-day control over Indians' lives and lands and boasting of its commitment to "self-determination," it has claimed instead a far more powerful disciplinary weapon: the authority to decree tribes nonexistent.

WHERE HAS TRIBAL SOVEREIGNTY GONE?

By any objective standard, the doctrine of tribal sovereignty is a badly leaking ship in need of urgent repairs. The first major "leak" was *Oliphant*, the 1978 Supreme Court decision stripping tribes of any criminal jurisdiction over non-Indians.[1] Then, following a succession of increasingly confused and inconsistent rulings allowing the states to exercise limited jurisdiction on reservations, the Court announced in *Brendale* that tribes lack regulatory power over white settlements, and in *Duro* that tribes lack criminal jurisdiction over nonmember Indians.[2,3] What remained, then, was power over the tribes' own members and tribally owned land. I have called this the "country club" doctrine of tribal jurisdiction out of respect for Chief Justice Rehnquist, who agreed that tribes were *not* merely country clubs in *United States v. Mazurie* a number of years ago, yet went on to preside over the rulings that deprived tribes of the general territorial jurisdiction that all other divisions of federal, state, and local government enjoy.[4] The authority of a private club is *personal*; that of a government, *territorial*.

The problem has not been limited to the Court's specific rulings on the scope and extent of tribal authority but has extended to the way in which the Court has gone about reaching its conclusions, which could be characterized as a style of, "Look Ma, no rules!" As early as 1973, in its deceptively upbeat *McClanahan* decision, the Court asserted that the principle of tribal sovereignty is merely a "backdrop" against which it examines the specific facts in each case.[5] During the 1980s, tribes lost their few defenders on the Court and the backdrop faded into a mere shadow. The Court now seems to be deciding each Indian case on its own merits, with the principal considerations, other than the presence or absence of relevant federal legislation, being the race of the parties and the judges' own ad hoc ideas about federal Indian policy.[6] This not only leaves tribes without legal guidance, it reminds them that, when all is said and done, what matters is skin color.

THE POLITICS OF "PORK"

Since the 1970s, there has been a marked shift in federal Indian legislation from substance to money, and from problems of political power to disputes over dividing up the cash. While federal courts continue to chip away at tribal jurisdiction, tribal leaders concentrate their efforts at the Capitol on fund-raising for tribal administration. It is not that all the basic problems of jurisdiction or power were solved in the 1970s, but that tribal politics has given up on basic problems as too unrewarding and gone for the "pork." In the deficit-conscious 1990s, however, this will pit tribes increasingly against each other, as the federal trough shrinks, and it will strengthen the administration plan to divide tribes over the question of which is more deservingly "Indian."

The legislative override of the Supreme Court's decision in the *Duro* case is the exception that proves the rule.[7] While the Congress buckled up its courage sufficiently to chastise the Court and reaffirm the tribes' "inherent" criminal jurisdiction over all Indians, it left intact two earlier Court rulings to the effect that tribes lack criminal or (in "open" areas of reservations) civil jurisdiction over non-Indians. It is not just that this piecemeal legislative approach to basic problems mirrors the Court's disposal of general principles of Indian law. The deeper message is that tribal leaders have lacked the courage, and the power, to redress the more sensitive issue of jurisdiction over *whites*. Raking in grants and contracts comprises only the mere appearance of having power on the Hill. Money is cheap there, and tribes get less than .1 percent of it anyway. Getting whites to obey Indian law on the reservations is a *real* test of who has the power, and we failed it.

If that were not evidence enough, consider the fact that the tribes' major legislative "victory" on jurisdiction of the past few years was a provision allowing them to operate gambling casinos on Indian lands with only limited state regulation.[8] Each year, Indian children still slip through the cracks in the 1978 Indian Child Welfare Act and the non-Indians who live or work on reservations are shielded from tribal laws, but casino gambling is condoned. Money is more important than life or dignity. What tribal lobbyists did not recognize, perhaps, is that Congress is only too pleased to find "cheap" ways like this of getting tribes to pay for their own programs and services. In the 1970s, the government tried to reduce its share of service costs by encouraging reservation mining: that is, making Indians pay for the programs from environmental quality.[9] Now, Congress has tried to shift the costs to non-Indians through casino gambling, which is arguably more friendly to the ecosystem. In either case, reducing the federal deficit is the real agenda, not Indian self-determination or development.

THE SELF-GOVERNANCE SCAM

I do not wish to belittle the importance of social programs. The recent enactment of authorizations to address Indian family violence, substance abuse, and related social and health problems is justified in the broad sense of recognizing these problems as real and pressing.[10] It is not clear, however, that the *solution* to social problems, whether Indian or non-Indian, can emerge from a piecemeal scattering of loose change, like the small coins with which the British queen showers well-wishers from the steps of her palace each year on Maundy Thursday. Violence, alcoholism, and family breakups are diseases of despair more than of poverty, and symptomatic relief merely deadens the pain. In the long term, Indians' despair can only be conquered by their gaining power—and by this, I do not mean more powerful and authoritarian tribal governments, but more power of individual Indians over the conditions of their life and the future of their families.

The present situation began with a particularly odious form of discrimination in federal fiscal policy. State and municipal governments rely on the taxpayers for the bulk of their revenue, and most of what they receive from Washington is based on legislative formulas weighted by estimates of their service populations and need. Local finance is, consequently, relatively stable and predictable, while uncertainty comes from oscillations in the national economy, which affect tax collections. Indian tribes, on the other hand, have little tax base and depend heavily on federal funding for basic services.[11] Indian funding is nearly all competitive and discretionary rather than formula-based, so tribes devote a great deal of their time and effort in competing with each other for funds and trying to juggle appropriations and regulations in their favor.

This brings us to the "self-governance" demonstration program and a number of proposals on the drawing boards in the Senate Select Committee on Indian Affairs for overhauling the fiscal relationships between Washington and the reservations. Peeling layers of misleading rhetoric from "self-governance," what emerges is simply a block-grant arrangement.[12] Participating tribes have entered into contracts for annual lump-sum payments of their "Indian" funding with the objective, in principle, of setting their own priorities for program spending. A preliminary point to be made, then, is that this is not a recognition of greater tribal power over reservations; it only affects what tribes do with federal aid. The real key to understanding "self-governance" is to be found in the small print of the contracts: The United States makes no promises about maintaining current funding levels, but tribes assume full responsibility for the delivery of adequate services. The only legally binding result of this process, then, is to shift legal liability for Indian poverty to Indian governments.[13]

Where is this effort heading? Senator John McCain introduced legislation with the inspiring title "New Federalism," during the second session of the 101st Congress, in 1989.[14] Although it never left the Senate Select Committee on Indian Affairs, New Federalism marks the direction in which the committee's Republicans intend to take "self-governance" in the future. Under McCain's proposal, the secretary of the interior would be required to make a list of tribes that met certain political conditions: chiefly that their councils were elected, accountable, and fiscally responsible. Only these tribes would be eligible to receive lump-sum federal funding—subject to disclaimers as to liability for funding levels and services. Other tribes would still have to compete for discretionary grants. This is not only a poor imitation of self-government, it offers the tribes a very meager "carrot" in exchange for passing their political systems in review before the critical eyes of the secretary (who is presumably an expert on democratic design). The tribes not only waive federal liability for social services under this New Colonialism–type scheme, they also lose the right to scuttle the majority-rule electoral systems imposed on them by the Indian Reorganization Act in favor of relatively more participatory, consensus-based, and democratic forms of decision making.

It is clear that Congress is not prepared to yield any real power to tribal councils, except in exchange for budgetary relief. In other words, Congress is willing to allow tribes to make more decisions for themselves as long as they are prepared to pay for them. This makes a great deal of sense inside the Washington Beltway as a deficit-reduction measure. It makes no sense at all on the reservations, however, where tribes have no visible means of support—other than gambling and resource liquidation. Hence, the congressional cost-shifting strategy, cleverly cloaked behind warm phrases such as "self-governance" and "New Federalism," is in fact a guarantee of growing social problems and discontent in Indian country.

THE RIDDLE OF RECOGNITION

While Congress is considering ways of conditioning tribal funding on political correctness, the Interior Department is seeking the authority to review the legal status of individual tribes and decertify those it deems "insufficiently Indian." The department argued in its proposed rules that treaties, acts of Congress, and other forms of historical recognition of individual tribes as distinct governments were only good on the day when they were originally written. To retain its special legal status thereafter, the tribe must continue to "exist as an Indian tribe" to the satisfaction of the secretary. Evidence of an anthropological and sociological character is suggested, since the key test is whether there is "sustained interaction and significant social relationships which differentiate members from nonmembers."[15] In the words of California Indian Legal Services attorney Allogan Slagle, the United States has passed from the era of "Indian self-determination," to an era of "redetermination" of tribal status.

This all began fifteen years ago, when the American Indian Policy Review Commission highlighted the problem of non–federally recognized tribes, which it estimated to be possibly one-eighth of all U.S. Indians. As chairman of the newly established Senate Select Committee on Indian Affairs, former commission chairman James Abourezk drafted legislation to review these cases and confer full legal benefits on any group that could show *either* previous federal recognition by treaty or otherwise *or* demonstrate its historical existence as a distinct Indian society. The Interior Department told Congress that it could do the job efficiently without any further legislative guidance and published guidelines for the "acknowledgment" of Indian tribes in 1978. About 110 applications were filed; however, more than a decade later, fewer than one-fourth have been processed, most of which have been denied, including at least one involving a treaty.[16] The original regulations appeared to be *prospective* only: that is, designed to add more tribes to the list. However, the department now interprets its regulations as *retrospective* as well. Everyone must be able to pass the test, whether to get on the list or to stay there.[17]

Federal "recognition" was never an issue before the 1930s, when the Indian New Deal introduced a menu of social programs administered through tribal agencies rather than provided by federal agencies to individual Indians.

The Interior Department needed some standard to decide which Indian entities to fund, given the fact that many tribes had dispersed, disbanded, or recombined with others during the period of warfare, the establishment of reservations, and the allotment of Indian lands. Initially, recognition was associated with the approval of a tribal constitution under the Indian Reorganization Act, but Interior Department Solicitor Felix Cohen wrote in his 1942 *Handbook of Federal Indian Law* that recognition also includes tribes that made treaties, or were beneficiaries of federal legislation or executive orders; that is, any formal course of dealings with the federal government. Why is the same department now arguing that "Indianness" (or "tribalness") is the real test of tribal rights?

The answer is readily found in history: In periods of budgetary constraints, the Interior Department has typically protected itself by jettisoning Indians instead of bureaucrats when cutting costs. During World War I, the department forced fee patents and citizenship on allottees, while recruiting more bureaucrats to help this work go faster. Thirty years later, the department responded to postwar austerity measures by giving Congress a list of "progressive" tribes to be "terminated"—and increasing its staffing to help Congress do it. During the recession of the early 1980s, the administration proposed a blood-quantum test for individual eligibility for federal services, but basing Indian rights explicitly on race rather than political or historical tests was very clearly unconstitutional.[18] The same department lawyers found a better way to trim the federal caseload, however: eliminating whole tribes on the pretense that they have ceased to "behave like Indians."

INSTITUTIONALIZING INDIANNESS

As competition for dwindling federal dollars intensifies, both between bureaucrats and Indians and among the tribes themselves, there will be increased demands from both sides for a stricter definition of "tribe" and "Indian." This will not only affect which tribes are recognized by the Interior Department, but who may belong to a tribe as well. Steps have already been taken, on many reservations, to make membership criteria "tighter"; this generally means higher, or more strictly applied blood-quantum requirements rather than cultural or residency tests. Indeed, although tribes have jealously guarded their right to determine their own membership in the past, they have become increasingly critical of groups with low or zero blood-quantum thresholds. The bottom line is a resurgence of racism in Indian country: racism to the effect that Indianness is in your bloodstream, not in your heart, your spirit, your conduct, your upbringing, or even in the language you speak.[19]

The Interior Department itself encourages this in its rulings on tribal recognition (or "acknowledgment"). Repeatedly, its researchers have maintained that the children of mixed marriages are less "Indian" than their

Indian relatives and have judged a groups "tribalness" from the average Indian blood quantum of its members. Apart from the fact that race and culture overlap but are not equivalent, it is disturbing that Interior Department anthropologists have never thought to compare the purity of "blood" of federally recognized and non-recognized tribes; they merely have assumed that the ancestry of the recognized tribes is less mixed. What has evolved, then, is not only a linkage of tribal rights with "Indianness," but a rigid equation of Indianness with race. This may help the secretary of the interior balance the departmental budget in a way that satisfies the leaders of the larger recognized tribes, but in the long term it will demolish the pretense that Indian rights flow from political status, not race—without which Indian programs and services are unconstitutional. Even a segregated "country club" such as this is ineligible to receive federal aid. The tribes that feel smug and safe today should think about this fact.

Institutionalizing a "tighter" (more narrow) definition of Indianness may have its basis in fiscal competition, but it has had pernicious, and presumably unintended, side effects on other aspects of Indian life. Consider the two important pieces of cultural legislation that Congress enacted in 1990, the Native American Graves Protection and Repatriation Act (NAGPRA) and the Indian Arts and Crafts Act.[20,21] Both were designed with the best of intentions, to help Indians protect their arts and cultural heritage. NAGPRA confirms tribal ownership of human remains, sacred objects, and "cultural patrimony" (historically or culturally "important" objects). Tribes can demand from federal agencies and federally subsidized public museums the return of any remains or objects with which they have a "cultural affiliation" (or historical "shared group identity"). Moreover, buying and selling of these objects is a federal crime. The Indian Arts and Crafts Act applies to contemporary works, making it a federal crime to "misrepresent" their Indian origin at the time of sale. Both these new laws define "Indian" as members of federally recognized tribes.

What this means, in practice, is that a nonrecognized tribe has no cultural rights. It has no right to reclaim the bones of its ancestors (even if they are unquestionably the remains of tribal members' kin), no right to repatriate contemporary ceremonial materials from museums, and no right to sell the products of its own artists and craftspeople as "Indian." If any of its members are artists and sell works as "Indian" under the tribe's name, they can be imprisoned for up to five years. Surely this is taking "recognition" much too far. A group of people does not cease to be Indian culturally because some federal agency says there are too many white people in their families or they no longer live in a sufficiently "tribal" community. The ancestors do not care whether the great-grandchildren collecting their bones are "recognized as eligible for services by the Secretary of the Interior."[22]

The sum total of these policies is rather chilling. The Department of the Interior decides that a tribe is not "Indian" enough, depriving it of "recognition." By operation of this new cultural legislation, the tribe is stripped of its cultural property, and even the right to use its tribal name. Its artists can be jailed for daring to call themselves Indians. Could all this happen if the Indian movement was a genuine grass-roots struggle rather than a cooperative financial game between two tiny elites, namely, federally funded tribal technocrats and federal bureaucrats?

TRUST RESPONSIBILITY AND IRRESPONSIBILITY

When the Reagan administration floated the idea of abolishing the Bureau of Indian Affairs, tribal leaders all across the country cried foul. To be sure, the president had not chosen a very credible messenger for this proposal: James Watt, his conservative and bombastic secretary of the interior. Nevertheless, the message should have brought joy to Indian country. Why did tribes defend their longtime oppressor? I asked a number of my tribal colleagues at the time, and they had the same answer: "It would mean giving away Federal Trust Responsibility." Anywhere else in the world, such an answer would be met with chagrin. Try to imagine Namibia, a few years ago, rejecting independence and pleading to remain a UN trust territory.

Where did this idea of Trust Responsibility originate? Historically, it was a euphemistic way of referring to colonialism, while attempting to justify it in the same breath. "Nasty" governments such as Spain and Portugal (in the context of Victorian Great Britain and America) colonize, whereas democracies accept, with deep humility and a sense of God-given duty, the burden of trusteeship over the planet's many "ignorant" peoples. Admittedly, trusteeship implies responsibility as well as supervisory power. When U.S. Chief Justice John Marshall wanted to find a word to describe the relationship of the United States with its Indian tribes, his obvious sympathies for the Indians led him to choose *tutelage*, which was the term for trusteeship in Imperial Roman law. The *tutela* had rights in relationship to the *tutor* state, but not very many. As long as *tutelae* paid their taxes, praised the emperor, and put up with the daily aggravations of imperial bureaucracy, they could count on protection, the rule of law, and economic aid.

Trust Responsibility became solidly entrenched in the rhetoric of U.S. Indian policy as a result of Felix Cohen's 1942 *Handbook*. Cohen was trying, cleverly, to make the best of the old tutelage doctrine by transforming a benign power into a pure responsibility. Unfortunately, he outsmarted himself. You may fool Congress, but you cannot fool the civil service. Interior Department officials have reminded Indians for generations that the price they must pay for the "responsibility" (read, federal Indian programs) is putting up with the power. Tribal leaders who complain much too often discover—frequently in the middle of a recall election—that federal officials have denounced them to their own constituents as troublemakers who have alienated the department and will jeopardize their reservation programs. As it has been applied to Indian country, then, Trust Responsibility is an oxymoron: a contradiction in terms.

To be sure, tribal governments have been patiently chipping away at the power side of this two-edged doctrine since 1975, when the Indian Self-Determination and Education Assistance Act offered tribes an opportunity to assume some of the day-to-day management of federal Indian programs.[23] Subsequent legislation has largely reinforced this two-tiered arrangement, with general policy and guidelines designed inside the Beltway and routine decisions taken at the tribal level under year-to-year renewable contracts. The supervisory power of the Department of the Interior is not limited to program delivery, however; the true heart and soul of Trust Responsibility is the power to supervise land management and natural resources. Under legislation adopted from the 1880s to the 1950s, the Interior Department was the landlord, for all practical purposes, of the Indian reservations. Tribal governments faced a painful dilemma when trying to assert their independence. To become independent of federal aid, they had to produce income from their own resources. However, that also had to be on Washington's terms.

The most valuable reservation resources, in current export terms, are minerals (chiefly petroleum and coal) and timber. Greater tribal control of these sectors was the stated aim of two reforms: the 1982 Indian Mineral Development Act, and the 1990 National Indian Forest Resources Management Act.[24,25] Neither act involves any significant transfer of management authority, however. The first simply lists factors that the Interior Department must consider before approving mineral leases: these concern determining the "best interest" of the tribe, including the project's rate of economic return and its environmental, social, and cultural impacts. The second requires the department to develop a management plan for each Indian forest "with the full and active consultation and participation" of the tribe. The department is required to manage Indian forests for maximum sustainable commercial yield unless the tribe opts for leaving the land in its "natural state." The tribe has the final word in only one decision: whether to use the forest commercially.

Is this trusteeship or is it neocolonialism? Africans enjoyed a brief euphoria of nominal independence in the 1960s, before they fully appreciated how much power the Europeans could exercise through their aid programs and their banks. The recolonization of Africa has parallels in the illusory "self-determination" of American Indians. Reliance on external finance builds a welfare bureaucracy (bureaucrats on welfare) that straddles both countries. Bureaucrats in the donor and recipient countries have a common interest in justifying continued and increased aid flows. They defend one another and excuse one another's faults. Neither is necessarily concerned about the wishes of their respective countries' electorates, as long as they can continue to agree publicly on the need for spending and can obscure the results behind paperwork. The solution to every problem is another program, reshuffling a finite number of dollars behind an ever-larger web of rules and regulations. The donor bureaucracy pays the bills and therefore calls the tune; the words and music are chosen to sound sweet in the ears of the donor country's leading politicians.

There admittedly are some differences between neocolonialism in Africa and Trust Responsibility. International financial institutions and aid donors do not have formal authority to veto mineral leases and timber sales. Instead, they must influence resource-exploitation decisions by more indirect means. Nor can they discipline a recalcitrant national leader by declaring his or her country nonexistent and its people extinct. Only the U.S. Interior Department can do that.

MEANWHILE, NORTH OF THE BORDER...

The trivialization of the American Indian struggle into an elite game of fiscal redistribution is all the more striking and disturbing in comparison with events in Canada, where so-called aboriginal peoples have been engaged in a confrontational, and sometimes violent, struggle for constitutional power since 1978.[26] The first stage brought hundreds of tribal leaders to London, where they blocked parliamentary approval of Canada's new constitution until a section was added that "recognized and affirmed" aboriginal and treaty rights. For the next five years, negotiations between aboriginal coalitions, the prime minister, and the provincial premiers failed to produce a constitutional amendment clarifying the "rights" in question, in particular the right to self-government. Aboriginal leaders then blocked the ratification of a separate constitutional agreement (the "Meech Lake Accord") that would have granted special status only to Quebec.[27] Armed clashes on two Quebec Mohawk reserves in August 1990 forced the Canadian government to promise a new round of talks and to establish a Royal Commission on Aboriginal Peoples with both aboriginal and nonaboriginal members. Meanwhile, indigenous groups have upped the ante: They are demanding not only internal self-government, but seats in Parliament.

Two aspects of the Canadian aboriginal struggle are particularly significant. Tactically, the struggle has focused on constitutional amendments, rather than litigation. Strategically, it has been moving from a focus on internal self-government, or tribal autonomy, toward demands for a role in all national decision making. Indeed, aboriginal leaders have become key actors in the larger issue of national unity. Like Quebec, they are calling for a restructuring of Canadian society as a whole, rather than merely creating enclaves for themselves within the Canada that now exists. By comparison, U.S. tribes seem content with internal self-government, allowing Congress and the Department of the Interior to continue to legislate for them and supervise them. In Washington, U.S. tribal leaders are suppliants, not decision makers or partners in power. Moreover, when things go wrong, U.S. tribes scramble for the courts (as if justice must be found in the minds of Euro-American lawyers), while in Canada, tribes force the government to negotiate.

Are these differences explained by numbers? Canada's aboriginal peoples certainly have superior numerical leverage: They make up nearly 10 percent of the national population, compared with less than 1 percent in the United States plus they comprise a majority in the northern half of the country. I think there is more to it, though. Indigenous North Americans have been bombarded with mainstream national culture, on television and in the public schools, for at least a generation. Aboriginal Canadians are "Canadian" in the sense that they believe in the queen but not in Canada; they live in a country that is already formally divided on linguistic grounds and cannot conceive of why they should not have at least as powerful a constitutional status as Quebec. American Indians are "American" in the sense that they think of money as a solution for social problems—and cannot conceive of publicly disavowing allegiance to the flag. As a result, U.S. tribes are far more vulnerable to neocolonialism.

CONCLUSION: UNDER THE BED

Most of the Indian legislation of the 1980s was pork, and pork is elitist. It builds federal and tribal bureaucracies at the expense of building real power and self-sufficiency at the grass roots. More pork also means more insider deals and corruption at the interface between tribal governments, their lobbyists, Congress, and the administration. There may be a real need for an Institute of American Indian, Alaska Native, and Native Hawaiian Culture and Arts, which cost $5.5 million in 1990, or for a feasibility study on the establishment of a National Center for Native American Studies and Policy Development, which cost another $1 million.[28,29] We can hope that these and similar programs do not merely become golden parachutes for Select Committee staffers and Indian lobbyists. In any event, the Indian business today supports an average of about one administrator (federal and tribal) for every ten "recognized" Indians, while reservation conditions continue to be poor. As tribal leaders get closer to Congress, Indian policy looks more and more like the rest of what happens on the Hill: slicing bacon.

Tribal leaders and their lobbyists are increasingly side stepping the real issues of power in America. Fundamental problems of control of resources and territory are dissolved into technical and procedural disputes or bypassed altogether by appeasing tribes with new grant or contract programs. Consider the fact that a much-heralded "reform" of the Indian Reorganization Act in 1988 failed to strip the secretary of power to veto amendments to tribal constitutions; instead, it requires the secretary to give notice to the tribe of any defects therein, with a fixed time line for revisions and a final decision.[30]

The secretary's power to override tribal electorates was not questioned, only the procedures used in doing it. A similar effect has been had by the Indian Environmental Regulatory Enhancement Act of 1990, which does not, in fact, increase the tribes' authority to protect their territories from harm. Instead, it is another grant program, designed for building technocratic "capacity."[31]

The trivialization of the Indian struggle will weaken tribes both internally and externally. Within and among the tribes themselves, we will see increasing attention paid to bickering over who is an Indian and which individuals and tribes will get each slice of the dwindling supply of fiscal bacon. This situation will be rendered even more implosive by a growing reliance on racial distinctions, which have become more acceptable in tribal political rhetoric as the cultural and linguistic distinctions among Indians have disappeared. To be sure, in form at least, tribal governments have looked very much like state and municipal governments for years. Intensifying the fiscal and technocratic preoccupation of tribal governments will only exacerbate their transformation from kin groups with cultures into closed corporations with racially exclusive membership policies. Tribes are at risk of becoming "country clubs" in fact as well as law.

Trivialization also jeopardizes the tribes' ability to build external political support among non-Indians. Instead, they are becoming increasingly isolationist in their national political tactics, playing the Hill as if it were a zero-sum game, not only against other tribes, but against other marginalized social groups as well. Congress may flatter tribal leaders by using words like *sovereignty*, but who, ultimately, is making the decisions? It is a mistake to think that a political system that can continue to be unresponsive to blacks, the poor, the aged, and most of the rest of the world is generously making an exception in the case of Indians. This is the most dangerous kind of self-delusion, because it leads to a kind of smug superiority that will make future alliances with other social sectors much more difficult.

What should be the agenda for the 1990s? The fairness of the tribes' own institutions should top the list, I believe, along with the confidence of Indians (and the growing number of reservation non-Indians) in tribal governments. Achieving internal solidarity will depend on the extent to which tribal governments can offer an alternative to Euro-American life that is more humane, culturally rich, and genuinely democratic. Externally, political security must come from an effort to go beyond the issue of reservation autonomy by demanding a share in decision making at the national level. This was the Indians' country to begin with, after all, and who would be better than the Indians to take the lead in building an alliance aimed at making it a qualitatively better place to live?

That is my question for the next generation of American Indians. It took the passing of an old generation to make real reform possible in the (former) Soviet Union, and the same will undoubtedly be true in China a decade or so from now. Tribal governments in the 1990s will still be rooted in the pork-barrel thinking of the Great Society era, but tribal youth in this decade will be looking for something that is more substantive, that gives them more to believe in as Indians, than a white-collar tribal job. Is there a real Indian movement out there, somewhere? Watch the youth.

NOTES

1. *Oliphant v. Suquamish Indian Tribe*, 435 U.S. 191 (1978).

2. *Brendale v. Yakima Indian Nation*, 492 U.S. 408 (1989). Earlier, in *Montana v. United States*, 450 U.S. 544 (1981), the Court upheld state regulation of hunting and fishing on state-owned land within an Indian reservation. See also *Moe v. Confederated Salish & Kootenai Tribes*, 425 U.S. 463 (1976), concerning state taxation of reservation sales to non-Indians.

3. *Duro v. Reina*, 110 S.Ct. 2053 (1991).

4. *United States v. Mazurie*, 419 U.S. 544 (1975), discussed in Russel Barsh and James Y. Henderson, *The Road: Indian Tribes and Political Liberty* (Berkeley: University of California Press, 1980), pp. 176–78.

5. *McClanahan v. Arizona Tax Commission*, 411 U.S. 164, 172 (1973).

6. See my analysis in "Is There Any Indian 'Law' Left? A Review of the Supreme Court's 1982 Term," *Washington Law Review*, 59 (1984): 863–93.

7. P.L. 101–511, section 8077, 104 Stat. 1892 (November 5, 1990), made permanent by P.L. 102–137, 105 Stat. 646 (October 28, 1991).

8. Indian Gaming Regulatory Act, P.L. 100–497, 102 Stat. 2467 (October 17, 1988).

9. See Russel L. Barsh, "Indian Resources and the National Economy: Business Cycles and Policy Cycles," *Policy Studies Journal 16*, no. 4 (1988): 799–825.

10. For example, Indian Child Protection and Family Violence Prevention Act, P.L. 101–630, Title IV, 1104 Stat. 4544 (November 28, 1990); Indian Old-Age Assistance Claims Act, P.L. 98–500, 98 Stat. 2317 (October 19, 1984); and Indian Alcohol and Substance Abuse Prevention and Treatment Act, P.L. 99–570, Title IV, 100 Stat. 3207 (October 27, 1986).

11. Russel L. Barsh and Katherine Diaz-Knauf, "The Structure of Federal Aid in the Decade of Prosperity, 1970–1980," *American Indian Quarterly*, 8, no. 1 (1984): 1–32.

12. The authorization can be found in P.L. 100–472, section 209, 102 Stat. 2296 (October 5, 1988), amended by P.L. 102–184, 105 Stat. 1278 (December 4, 1991). The amendment simply enlarges the number of tribes involved from twenty to thirty and makes technical corrections.

13. Total funding for the "self-governance" project is only $5 million, which adds up to less than $200,000 per tribe, or about $100 per tribal member. Department of the Interior Appropriations, P.L. 102–154, 105 Stat. 1004 (November 13, 1991).

14. S.2325, 101st Congress, 2d sess. (1989). Senator Dennis DeConcini is expected to reintroduce this bill, or a revised version, in the 102nd Congress.

15. "Procedures for Establishing That an American Indian Group Exists as an Indian Tribe," *Federal Register, 56*, no. 181 (September 18, 1991): 47320–30. See

especially the discussion of proposed section 83.6 on pp. 47321–22, and section 83.1 on p. 47324.

16. The Samish Indian Tribe, which has challenged the denial in federal court. *Greene v. Lujan*, No. C89–6452, Western District of Washington. See "Final Determination That the Samish Indian Tribe Does Not Exist as an Indian Tribe," *Federal Register* 52 (February 5, 1987): 3709–10.

17. The department has tested this several times in the past few years, most notably when it advised the Burns Paiute Tribal Council that, as a "community of adult Indians" rather than a historical "Indian tribe," they had no inherent right to self-government on their reservation. A vigorous chastisement from Oregon Senator Mark Hatfield persuaded the department that it had been in error—this time, at least.

18. *Morton v. Mancari*, 417 U.S. 535 (1974), is the source of this test for the constitutionality of special Indian legislation.

19. Another small, but poignant, example of how fiscal constraint, rather than cultural reality, drives current legislation is the Aroostook band of Micmacs Settlement Act, P.L. 102–171, 105 Stat. 1143 (November 26, 1991). Although Congress acknowledges the Aroostook community to be a part of the Micmac Nation, which is located mostly in Canada, it restricts the right of Canadians to become band members in the future. Section 7(b).

20. Native American Graves Protection and Repatriation Act: P. L. 101–601, 104 Stat. 3048 (November 16, 1990).

21. Indian Arts and Crafts Act: P.L. 101–644, 104 Stat. 4662 (November 29, 1990).

22. Strictly construed, NAGPRA would even permit a "recognized" tribe to demand the return of cultural materials from a nonrecognized one, where both tribes shared ties with the same ancestral culture. So, too, the National Museum of the American Indian Act, P.L. 101–185, 103 Stat. 1336 (November 28, 1989), section 16(8), limits participation in the museum's management to "recognized" tribes, although "non-recognized" tribes will be included in the collections. Only the Native American Languages Act, P.L. 101–477, 104 Stat. 1153 (October 30, 1990), departs from this pattern—perhaps because no money is involved.

23. P.L. 93–638, 88 Stat. 2203 (January 4, 1975); 25 U.S.C. 450 *et seq.*

24. Indian Mineral Development Act: P.L. 97–382, 96 Stat. 1938 (December 22, 1982); 25 U.S.C. 2106 *et seq.* See *Quantum Exploration Inc. v. Clark*, 780 F.2d 1457 (9th Cir. 1986), for a discussion of the continuing federal supervisory role.

25. National Indian Forest Resources Management Act: P.L. 101–630, Title III, 104 Stat. 4532 (November 28, 1990).

26. See generally Menno Boldt and Anthony Long, eds., *The Quest for Justice: Aboriginal Peoples and Aboriginal Rights* (Toronto: University of Toronto Press, 1985).

27. The Meech Lake Accord would have effectively closed the door to a later constitutional entrenchment of aboriginal self-government, since it would have required the unanimous consent of the provinces to any future revision of the political boundaries of Canada.

28. Institute of American Indian, Alaska Native and Native Hawaiian Culture and Arts: P.L. 99–498, Title XV, 100 Stat. 1600 (October 17, 1986). The project was originally supposed to cost $1 million annually, but $4.4 million was appropriated in 1989, and $5.5 million in 1990.

29. National Center for Native American Studies and Policy Development: P.L. 101–301, section 11, 104 Stat. 211 (May 24, 1990).

30. P.L. 100–581, Title I, 102 Stat. 2938 (November 1, 1988) ("Indian Reorganization Act Amendments").

31. P.L. 101–408, 104 Stat. 883 (October 4, 1990).

5

Indian Self-Determination and the Tribal College Movement: A Good Idea That Not Even Government Can Kill

C. Patrick Morris

Historically, Indian education in the United States has been viewed by the Indian community, thoughtful educators, and many public officials as one of the most egregious and continuing failures in American education. Despite annual federal budgets now reaching in the hundreds of millions of dollars and more than a century of control by the federal government, churches, and now the states, the measured results of these educational efforts are dismal. Today, Indian students as a group continue to occupy a solid hold on the bottom of nearly every educational measurement, from language skills to math and from history to science (see U.S. Senate 1969; Fuchs and Havighurst 1972; Astin 1982; Fries 1987).

What these sad statistics and numerous critical studies tell us is that something continues to be fundamentally wrong with the way in which the federal, state, and local schools educate Indian children and adults. The obvious and most frequently asked questions are why, and what is being done to change this endemic failure into a measurable success? One remarkable response coming from Indian country has been the emergence of the tribally controlled college (TCC) movement.

In 1992 there were twenty-seven tribal colleges located in Indian country from Michigan to the state of Washington, with a combined enrollment of over 4,500 students. Since their inception barely a decade ago, Indian-controlled and -chartered tribal colleges have graduated thousands of Indian students in a variety of science, technology, humanities, human service and other vocational and academic areas, an accomplishment that has revolutionized the educational attainment of reservation Indian youth and adults (see Senate Select Committee on Indian Affairs 1990, 10).[1] Even for the most ardent critics it is becoming increasingly apparent that the tribal college movement is one of the few successes in the history of Indian education.

Until very recently, the almost unknown local heroes who brought about this educational revolution have had little time and few opportunities to articulate in writing the growing impact that the tribal college movement continues to have on Indian education programs and policies and on Indian reservation communities.[2]

This chapter explores some of the prominent educational policy issues that have emerged from the tribally controlled college movement and some of the unique educational efforts that tribal colleges have made to become on-reservation Indian-directed academies dedicated to tribal cultural, social, and economic preservation and development. Because the tribal college movement continues to be a creature of federal Indian policy, the chapter also highlights some of the prominent political, financial, and cultural hurdles overcome by those Indian and non-Indian educators and leaders who created the Indian tribal college movement.

FOUNDING OF THE TRIBAL COLLEGE MOVEMENT

In 1968, a radically new approach to Indian higher education was undertaken on the Navajo reservation in a small, rural community called Many Farms. Initially guided by a white educator and local tribal supporters, an effort was made to develop a tribally controlled on-reservation two-year college. To provide financial assistance for this unique educational endeavor, Navajo tribal educators and leaders successfully lobbied Congress in 1971–72 to pass the Navajo Community College Bill to provide federal dollars to support the college's development and operation. What resulted was the Navajo Community College, the first Indian tribally controlled institution of higher education in the United States (Fuchs and Havighurst 1972, 264–72).

As the Navajo Tribal College emerged from its incubation period at Many Farms, a new campus was built at Tsali and branch campuses were organized at other locations across the more remote areas of the more than 14 million acre Navajo reservation (Fuchs and Havighurst 1972, 271). Soon, other Indian educators from other tribes began to see in the Navajo effort an opportunity for the development of a tribal college on their own reservations. As a result, Indian leaders and educators used existing personnel and education structures, such as local OEO (Office of Economic Opportunity) programs, Title III, and Adult Education programs, to form an administrative and faculty core that could take the first tentative steps toward developing other tribally controlled colleges, should adequate funds be found.

Encouragement for the tribal college movement came from several federal initiatives that encouraged greater Indian participation in Indian education. In 1975, the Indian Self-Determination and Education Assistance Act of

1975, PL 93–638, passed Congress. As originally envisioned by presidential supporters and the tribes, the policy of Indian self-determination was interpreted to mean the eventual transference to the tribes of a broad range of federal services once administered by the Bureau of Indian Affairs (BIA) and other federal agencies. In the words of President Richard Nixon, self-determination meant "to break decisively with the past and to create the conditions for a new era in which the Indian future is determined by Indian acts and Indian decisions" (President Nixon's Message to Congress, July 8, 1970).

Since the passage of PL 93–638, Indian self-determination has emerged as the cornerstone of U.S. Indian policy (Fuchs and Havighurst 1972, 265). Indian tribes themselves could now administer federal programs, thereby eliminating unwanted and unwarranted bureaucratic oversight and political interference in local tribal affairs; at least, that was what many Indian people believed self-determination to mean.

Following the thinking, and hopefully the intent, of the 1975 Indian Self-Determination Act, in 1978, approximately ten years after the founding of the Navajo Community College, tribal leaders and educators from several reservations successfully lobbied Congress to pass Public Law 95–471, the Tribally Controlled Community College Assistance Act of 1978 (hereafter referred to as the Tribal College Act or TCA). Like the earlier Navajo bill, this new legislation provided federal dollars to assist the development of on-reservation tribal colleges (Dupris 1980, 41). What had started at Many Farms on the Navajo reservation had now become a national movement in Indian higher education.

The passage of the Tribal College Act was viewed by most Indian educators as a logical federal step toward increasing Indian self-determination in education. Through the TCA, the Indian tribes could assert institutional control over higher education through the chartering of on-reservation tribal colleges. Unfortunately, this overly optimistic interpretation of Indian self-determination was no sooner expressed than it was shattered by Washington politics, much of it related to the arrival of Reagan's political philosophy of "New Federalism," which reinterpreted Indian self-determination to mean "a smaller federal role in Indian affairs and a smaller investment in Indian self-determination." According to the administration, "Indian education was not a trust responsibility, not even a federal concern," a policy statement that surprised the tribes, the Congress, and even the BIA (Morris 1988, 733).

This new and historically unprecedented reinterpretation of the federal role in Indian education quickly found one of its clearest expressions in the annual struggle over budget appropriations for the Tribal College Act. Indeed, to understand the struggling development of the tribal college movement, it is essential to understand the Washington "money game" surrounding the TCA annual authorization and appropriation process which made it clear that if Indians were going to develop tribal colleges, they would have to do it with greatly reduced federal support.

THE POLITICS OF POLICY: TRIBAL COLLEGE DEVELOPMENT AND THE WASHINGTON MONEY GAME

Following the election of Ronald Reagan in 1980, a series of unprecedented federal budget cuts were proposed for a wide range of social service and education projects and programs, including Indian programs (see Morris 1988). Beginning with the first Indian budget hearings, the Reagan administration and its loyal congressional allies used every conceivable stratagem to implement their own definition of Indian "self-determination," one that flourished in the media but proved fatally undernourished in content (see U.S. Senate Select Committee on Indian Affairs 1981).[3]

Along with attacks on Indian program budgets, the Reagan administration shocked Indian country with the announcement that federal support for Indian education was not a "trust" responsibility, that is, not a federal obligation arising from a treaty, executive action, or act of the Congress. According to the administration, Indian education is not a federal task but rather belongs to the individual states (Morris 1981–82). This was a remarkable policy position given the fact that treaties, acts of Congress, and other presumably legal guarantees had been cited and used by the federal government for over a century to forcibly educate Indian children.[4]

Armed with the New Federalism policy of transferring federal responsibilities to the states, the Reagan and, later, the Bush administrations immediately took steps to use the Bureau of Indian Affairs to unilaterally close federally funded Indian schools and to curtail federal support for Indian programs in general, including a proposal to totally eliminate the vital Johnson O'Malley program, which earmarked federal funds for state allocation to Indian education (see Morris 1988).

Unfortunately for the tribal college leaders, it would be within this highly charged political atmosphere of denied and reduced federal support that they must wage a battle over budget appropriations authorized by the 1978 Tribal College Act. In fact, for the entire decade of the 1980s and into the 1990s, the tribal colleges found themselves in an annual political battle with the Reagan and Bush administrations over federal support for the tribal colleges.

The funds authorized by the Tribal College Act were extremely modest, even pecuniary, given the task of starting a new kind of institution of higher education on an Indian reservation. The original 1978 Tribal College Act authorized $4,000 per Full-Time Equivalent (FTE) student, a sum still $1,300 per student *less* than that used to educate a student in a non-Indian public community college at that time. However, shortly after the budget committee convened, it quickly became apparent that not even this low level of funding would be appropriated. In fact, since its passage in 1978 (now 14 years), the tribal colleges have never received full authorized funding (see Comtec 1986, 3–4). Instead, the tribal colleges continue to struggle against an unrelenting fiscal crisis, much of it precipitated by administration political issues promoted in the guise of financial ones. Here is how the tribal college Washington money game is played.

To determine the Tribal College Act or TCA annual budget allocations, officials from the tribal colleges, the BIA (representing the administration), and the Congress present their annual tribal college student FTE enrollment projections. Once the figures have been presented, a purported debate ensues to determine which projection will be used. The number selected is critical—even a life-and-death decision for some of the colleges—as the figure that is selected will be used to determine the annual appropriations. The higher the Indian student FTE, the greater the appropriations. However, each year there are always differences between the tribal college's own FTE projection and those made by the BIA and the Congress. Invariably, the BIA (administration's) and congressional projections are much lower than those given by the tribal colleges, and the real fight begins in the budget appropriation meetings over whose projections are to be used to determine the final appropriations. The obvious question asked each year is, "Whose FTE projections are the most accurate?" Moreover, each year, without fail, the FTE projections by the administration and BIA are low: significantly below what later is found to be the actual enrollments. In contrast, the tribal college annual projections are higher and more accurate. However, despite this proven record, the tribal college's projections are not used. Instead, the lower and less accurate administration/BIA or congressional projections are used to determine the annual TCA appropriations for the tribal colleges. As a result, each year tribal college leadership must return to Washington and plead for supplemental appropriations for unfunded FTE. Every year the tribal colleges must scramble to cover funds already expended on those FTE enrolled but not funded because of the administration/BIA's or Congress's inaccurate projections and low appropriations. For example, in 1981, per-FTE funding appropriated for the tribal colleges was $3,100, or $900 per student below that authorized by the TCA. Nine years later, in 1990, the per-FTE funding dropped to $1,965 or "less than 50 percent of what a small state institution would receive" (see Senator Kent Conrad's [D-N.D.] comments in U.S. Senate Select Committee Hearing on Indian Affairs 1990).

This precipitous decline in real dollars created by the annual underfunding of the TCA has occurred during the tribal colleges' greatest period of institutional development and enrollment growth. Between 1978 and 1986 there was an annual average increase in tribal college enrollments of 11 percent, resulting in a 78 percent increase over this five-year period. Nonetheless,

TCA funding actually declined during these years of explosive enrollments. The federal government has, in effect, implemented a fiscal strategy of less money for more Indian students.

For the struggling tribal colleges, the lack of adequate and predictable TCA funding has created serious administrative and programmatic difficulties for college administrators, faculty, and students at a time when these unique educational institutions are engaged in a life-or-death struggle to meet local educational needs and regional accreditation standards. One can only conclude that the Reagan and Bush administrations, through the BIA and their congressional allies, have used the federal budget process to deliberately and systematically undermine the tribal college movement, and even to threaten its very existence. Apparently, the tribal colleges are expected to not only survive but to flourish without adequate funding, despite the fact that most are located on Indian reservations with a financial environment that includes between 25 and 90 percent unemployment, complex language and cultural issues, and an almost nonexistent access to private, state, or other nonfederal sources of financial support.

What is particularly galling about these annual budget battles is that throughout the 1980s, presidents Reagan and Bush made salutary public pronouncements reaffirming the nation's moral obligations to the Indian, while at the same time behind the scenes they deliberately provoked a never-ending, no-holds-barred war to financially dismantle Indian education, and with it, the tribal colleges. As a result of these annual budget fights, a climate of financial uncertainty continues to surround every tribal college and nearly all Indian education programs.

Besides the budget appropriations process, the federal government also used its regulatory powers to curtail growth in tribal college enrollments, thereby limiting TCA appropriations. It is this use of federal regulations to curtail student counts that I will examine next.

ABUSE OF REGULATORY POWERS: RULES AND REGULATIONS

In addition to the wholesale attack on Indian tribal college appropriations through the FTE count, the Reagan years saw an orchestrated campaign through the BIA, Congress, and other federal agencies to undermine the legislative intent of the Tribal College Act. This attack took the form of newly authored and highly discriminatory federal rules and regulations designed to prevent the tribal colleges from using those funds that managed to survive the annual FTE battles. During the Reagan years, the administration's use of federal rules and regulations to curtail access of Indian college students to federal assistance programs suggested a deliberate attempt to contravene the intent of Congress, an effort that verged on lawlessness on the part of the executive branch (see Morris 1988).

An example of these highly irregular efforts by the Reagan administration occurred in the fall of 1986 when the BIA, on instructions from the administration, proposed new federal regulations that would not allow the tribal colleges to count several categories of students, thereby reducing the FTE student count used to determine federal support. Students not to be counted included those who did not possess a high school diploma or those pursuing degrees or certificates that did not lead to a B.A. degree at a four-year institution. In other words, the administration sought to deny federal support to those students who needed the tribal colleges the most: high school dropouts, those with general equivalency diplomas (GEDs), or those Indian students pursuing vocational-educational technical training to become gainfully employed (see U.S. Federal Register 1987, 6482–87).

This stupid and mean effort to cut student eligibility requirements, if successful, would have destroyed a key mission of the tribal college movement, namely, to enable on-reservation Indians with little education, lacking much-needed coping skills or with limited or no employment to have access to educational programs so that they could then reach out for new human and vocational alternatives. To stop the threat posed by these new and openly discriminatory federal regulations, it became necessary for numerous tribal college leaders and supporters to spend several days in Washington, D.C., convincing congressional leaders and the BIA not to adopt the administration's proposed rules. The BIA listened impatiently, and then refused to change its position. Fortunately, congressional supporters of the tribal college movement overrode the administration and the BIA and successfully tabled the proposed rules (see Morris 1982–83).

Such politically motivated fiscal attacks on the TCA have meant that tribal college leaders and their allies have had to use their limited time and financial resources to rush to Washington to prevent various efforts to derail TCA funding, thus leaving less time and effort for the education of deserving Indian students. Despite a change in administration with the Bush election in 1988, BIA fiscal attacks continue to pose enormous obstacles and costs to the tribal college movement. However, some good has come out of these money wars.

Because of the clear need to maintain constant vigilance over federal policies and appropriations, the tribal colleges organized themselves into a national consortium called the American Indian Higher Education Consortium or AIHEC and hired a full-time Washington, D.C., lobbyist to prevent precipitous "overnight" federal actions that might damage or destroy the tribal college movement. So far, AIHEC has become an invaluable source of information, new policies, and an intercollegiate coordinating group representing tribal colleges throughout Indian country. Through AIHEC, intertribal higher education leadership has been strengthened, and the consortium is becoming a formidable national body for the creation and implementation of Indian education policies. AIHEC members have proven themselves to be highly skilled in the political infighting that is characteristic of Washington, D.C., politics.

However, one must not forget the administration and BIA fiscal attacks on the tribal colleges have extracted a high personal and professional price from tribal college leaders, faculty, and staff, as well as the students and communities that they are intended to serve. Instability in tribal college administration precipitated by budget crises and personnel changes in faculty, staff, and programs at some tribal colleges is directly related to the uncertain fiscal climate created by more than a decade of organized federal obstructionism.

Nevertheless, something wonderful is happening in Indian higher education, which is not clearly measurable nor the result of prior planning. Some of the most remarkable results have emerged from the struggle concerning human issues, the forging of new institutional and community relationships, and the role of culture and traditions. It is a story about how college and community came together, and it is the most important story to be told about the tribal college movement.

TRIBAL COLLEGE AND TRIBAL COMMUNITY

The creation of a tribal college raises a number of important issues involving the relationship of the college to the Indian reservation community that it is intended to serve. Until the rise of the tribal college movement, no Indian tribe had had the opportunity to be responsible for its own institution of higher education. Previous so-called Indian colleges were either BIA-, or church-, or privately run. Therefore, it was not immediately clear what kind of impact a tribally controlled college might have on the unique, but highly complex, culture of the modern Indian reservation.[5]

Many of the brave souls who initially sought to establish a tribal college had acted more out of their faith in Indian people than in a studied assurance that institutions of higher education would work on Indian reservations. In this new educational arena, there were no historical precedents or assurances, only the realization that a change in how Indians were being educated was desperately needed.

Beyond the obvious educational role of any college, for many tribal college advocates there remained the larger unanswered questions of how the reservation community itself would interpret the new formal institutional roles that the college would bring to Indian country and whether such a white institution could adjust to the unique communal character of an Indian reservation. Could the tribal colleges accommodate themselves to the unique cultural realities of the Indian reservation?

To the non-Indian outsider, the typical expectations associated with collegiate culture, such as lectures, class attendance, and the student's maintenance of a personal budget, appears culturally neutral. However, to significant segments of the Indian community, this regime is anything but. No one was sure if Indian people wanted to support and adjust to a collegiate cultural regime, at least to the extent that effective and competitive levels of academic performance could be attained. Although motivated by faith in their own reservation communities, those who started the tribal colleges had no assurance about what would happen.

Besides the collegiate question, there were other cultural issues still to be discovered, defined, and resolved if a new tribal college was to avoid alienating itself from the very people whom it wanted to serve. The most immediate (and, some would say, permanent) challenge facing all the tribal colleges is their untested ability to respond effectively and consistently to the ever-present and competing forces confronting them: (1) internal community expectations that the new tribal college fairly and accurately reflect the most fundamental and important values of the local Indian culture(s), and (2) external community demands from white colleges, accreditation associations, and academic peers that the Indian colleges fairly and accurately reflect the standards and values of the non-Indian "culture" of higher education. Essentially, every tribal college is expected to simultaneously conform to two competing sets of cultural and educational standards.

Most of those involved in the development of the tribal colleges are fully aware than the long history of failures in Indian education has no more prominent cause than the failure to find a link between the dominant culture's ideas about education and those of the Indian community. However, the discovery and forging of just such an educational link is expected of the new tribal colleges. Vociferous critics of the tribal college movement are quick to recognize that an inability to satisfy the expectations of both cultures, white and Indian, will mean certain failure.

To add to the difficulties posed by competing intercultural educational standards and expectations, the job of creating a tribal college is made even more difficult by the fact that every Indian reservation and culture is different. In some cases, different tribes live on the same reservation, each having languages as different as English and Chinese and different, or even competing, social, political, religious, and educational traditions (historically, in many instances the BIA placed warring tribes on the same reservation). Efforts by administrators to impose external national or even state educational standards eventually ran into the continuing diversity, and even intense rivalry, among Indian tribes—even those living on the same reservation.

Given the complex and often competing realities of contemporary Indian reservation life it became obvious to Indian educational and community leaders (but apparently not to the federal government) that what might work for one college on one reservation might fail, or even cause open revolt, if tried on another.

Consequently, those involved in starting a tribal college shared ideas, information, and experiences, but eventually, the founding leadership of each tribal college had to address the uniqueness of its own Indian reservation community and culture—and that of the white educational establishment surrounding it. To find the right balance between the demands of external federal and state educational and governmental agencies and the complex and different needs and expectations of the local reservation means that every tribal college desperately needs sufficient time and resources to make adjustments to such vastly different and competing cultural and educational interests and jurisdictions. Unfortunately, the continuing federal battles over TCA appropriations and other political wars over Indian education policies reduced the amount of time and money tribal college administrators could devote to such long-term structural issues. However, despite what can only be described as an ambiguous mandate from the federal government, one by one, tribal colleges began to appear across Indian country. In retrospect, for many of the builders of these new institutions the idea was to do it first, and then adjust to the various institutional and community political, financial, and other circumstances as they arose. It was an Indian version of "management by crisis," with the future of Indian-controlled higher education hanging in the balance. No single comprehensive vision of what a tribal college should or must be emerged beforehand; instead, educational reality and vision were often shaped and merged by the same act: with action becoming a form of thought, and then, if successful, college policy.

For those who led, and continue to lead, the tribal college movement, the constant financial constraints have shaped an agile but firm pragmatism. Underlying and guiding tribal college leadership is the common conviction that all educational standards could and would be met—but that this time, it would be on Indian terms.

The Indian Reservation Community as Cultural Curriculum

As the tribal colleges began to gain a foothold in Indian country, issues other than meeting competing state and federal educational standards began to emerge, many of them related to the new colleges' potential for precipitating change, and particularly unanticipated or uncontrolled change, on the reservation. Indian community members wondered what impact a tribal college might have on existing local socioeconomic and cultural patterns: "Would the college change who had jobs and who could legitimately act as cultural teachers and leaders?" "What role would the tribal past have in the future of the tribal college?"

Tribal College and Tribal Culture

According to Indian people, the heart of the tribal college movement is the Native Americans' unbroken commitment to reclaiming their cultural heritage. Such devotion to communal identity has provided the Indian with the courage to try to change educational failure into self-directed success. However, such change is not easy. The words *tribal college* themselves invoke an image of an institution divided in culture and purpose. All tribal colleges are institutions that are pulled in at least two academic and cultural directions, with a need to look and be like other non-Indian colleges. At the same time they are struggling to look and be responsive to unique local community needs and cultures. To a remarkable extent, the tribal colleges have succeeded. One important element in this success is the curriculum.

Regardless of size, location, or local circumstances, all the tribal colleges provide uniquely broad curriculums that set them apart from non-Indian public or community-based colleges. Presently, all twenty-four tribal colleges have Native American or Indian Studies programs, with each providing students with an opportunity to study their own tribe's history, culture, and language in a formal academic setting. In several of the colleges, Native American Studies has developed into a comprehensive reintegration of tribal culture through a reassessment and redesign of the whole academic curriculum (see Salish Kootenai College 1989, 14–15). At Sinte Gleska, for example, the Lakota Studies program has developed a major summer institute program for all people, whether Indian or non-Indian, that attracts students from as far away as Europe (Stein 1986, 31).

However, the incorporation of culture-oriented and relevant classes in the tribal colleges has not been without concern and controversy. On some reservations the emergence of a tribal college has posed a special kind of threat to traditional forms of cultural leadership. For cultural leaders (e.g., "medicine" or "holy" men and women and other practitioners of the local culture), there was a concern that a new tribal college might undermine their role as the recognized "traditional" educators and cultural leaders. The issue involved not only who would teach but what would be taught and where was the most appropriate place to learn the culture. Would the teaching of traditional dances, music, religion, and other aspects of tribal culture be removed from their natural cultural settings and placed in a classroom, thereby making tribal culture a curriculum rather than a way of life? Would the college "academicize" culture to the point where it lost its communal roots? Would words replace praxis, and books replace behavior?

The experience of one tribal college illustrates the delicate balance between traditional modes of learning and curriculum and the role of tribal colleges in Indian country. The issue was the tribal college's efforts to establish a Native American Studies (NAS) curriculum. The issue was not just whether certain classes should be taught, but who should teach them, what qualifications the instructors should have, and who should make decisions regarding teacher competency in these areas of traditional culture. The resolution of this issue quickly became a major issue at the college, which had to be resolved before the institution could continue its development.

To resolve the NAS curriculum issue, meetings were arranged between college personnel and leaders of the Tribal Culture Committee representing the reservation's "elders" or "traditionalists." At the meeting, members of the culture committee expressed their individual and collective concerns about the college and its potential usurpation of their role as educators of "tribal ways." As the discussions developed, it became apparent that the college, through its NAS curriculum, might unintentionally destroy the Indian community as the living school for the transmission of tribal culture. A fear was expressed that the college classroom might deliberately, or even inadvertently, supplant tribal life.

After listening to these concerns, the college administrators and curriculum planners decided that the Tribal Culture Committee should have a major policy and instructional role in the development of the college. It was believed that to leave out this "cultural core" of the community would make the college an adversary of the tribe, and not its advocate. Consequently, it was decided that the culture committee would be given the responsibility to determine the scope, content, and faculty of the college's NAS/tribal studies curriculum, including the review and hiring of teaching faculty for these critical areas of "tribal interest." The intent behind this decision was to include the tribe's own invaluable cultural resource people. It was believed that if given a major role in the development of the college as policymakers, teachers, and administrators of programs within their areas of expertise, these cultural resource people would see the tribal college as an asset to tribal survival, and not as a threat.

However, the members of the Tribal Culture Committee expressed misgivings about their own academic credibility, as they, like most elders or traditionalists, did not have academic credentials—the majority having never finished high school. Soon, a discussion ensued about what might be done to allow members of the culture committee and their representatives an active role in the planning and teaching of Native American studies. Finally, it was decided that three steps should be taken. First, it was necessary for the curriculum developer to assure these repositories of tribal culture that their unique expertise was credible, often exceeding that of academic outsiders. Secondly, it was necessary to reaffirm the college's belief, and even insistence, that local cultural leaders have a substantive role to play in shaping and teaching the Native American studies curriculum, particularly those classes related to the tribe and its language. Finally, after further discussion, it was decided that the best way to approach the issue of academic credibility was to establish within the reservation community itself an official process for the certification of competence in the tribal culture and language. Consequently, information was collected from all the reservation's cultural leaders and a tentative agreement was reached that the Tribal Culture Committee would act as the tribe's "Tribal Teacher Certification Board." As such, it would create and issue teaching credentials to those members of the community deemed qualified to teach specific classes in the curriculum areas concerning the tribe and its culture.

Shortly after these steps were taken, an off-reservation community college challenged the teaching credentials of the "culture faculty" and insisted that a state university professor review the courses and test their competency. To their surprise, they discovered that the university "expert" was himself a student of the Tribal Culture Committee. Since then, no major external challenges have been made against the college or its faculty.

Similar external challenges to the academic credibility of the tribal colleges have been a constant issue during their development. In several instances these challenges have been no more than poorly disguised efforts to use white standards to control Indian education. These challenges have served to remind Indian leaders and educators that the most important aspect of the tribal college movement is that, as a tribally controlled and chartered institution, every tribal college is independent and need not yield to the regulatory powers of the state, nor any other educational jurisdiction.

In practice, however, this educational independence is partly illusory, since every tribal college must comply with external regional standards if it wants to be regionally accredited and see its graduates able to transfer to non-Indian colleges and universities. Consequently, every tribal college has had to adjust its curriculum and faculty qualifications to comply with regional standards, policies, and procedures related to accreditation. Such competing demands have meant that every tribal college has had to strike a balance between external educational expectations and those of the local community and culture.

Another major issue facing the tribal colleges is a product of their own success. Because of local availability, low costs, and unique cultural and language programs, increasing numbers of non-Indians are enrolling in tribal colleges. As long as these non-Indian students remain a minority, there is no problem. However, on reservations where the non-Indian population is significant, this has become a major financial and cultural issue. It is a financial issue because the Tribal College Act requires that all tribal colleges maintain an Indian majority in the student body or lose their federal funding. As the enrollment of non-Indian students increases, this restriction poses a sensitive issue that could eventually drive an even deeper wedge between the Indian and white populations living on some of the reservations. One solution has been to use a kind of "out-of-state tuition" format for non-Indians to offset federal funding losses and to get local non-Indians to pay their fair share in maintaining the college.[6] Presently, no non-Indian living on an Indian reservation pays taxes to maintain a tribal college, even in cases where non-Indians make extensive use of existing campus. The out-of-state tuition idea seems a reasonable solution but is one that some non-Indians may not accept.

A related issue is the colleges' potential domination by non-Indian student majorities. Leaders of those colleges with significant numbers of non-Indian students have to ask themselves whether, if unrestricted admission is allowed, the non-Indian students would eventually dominate campus social life, sports, and clubs, thereby changing the cultural and educational mission of the college.

In cases where these questions have arisen, careful negotiations initiated by Indian college leaders and tribal councils with the local non-Indian community have resolved some, but not all, of the issues involved. In some reservation communities it remains a major concern, which continues to threaten the special mission of the tribally controlled college movement (see Salish Kootenai College 1989, 14–15).

Some Economic Impacts of the Tribal Colleges

On most (if not all) Indian reservations, social and economic divisions exist between educated and noneducated Indians. Educational credentials on Indian reservations can be a major contributor to the factionalism that often exists between well-paid federal or tribal employees and the less-well-educated and more poorly paid, or unemployed, "traditional" Indians.

When faced with the prospect of a new tribal college on the reservation, some Indian people have expressed concern that perceived or real economic and social inequities might be exacerbated. Few people, including those Indian educators creating the tribal colleges, could predict with any degree of certainty what the short- or long-term effects of the college might be on the existing socio-economic patterns of reservation life. Certainly, the tribal college meant economic change: but what kind, and who would control it?

Tribal college curricula indicate that efforts are being made to address local economic issues through a variety of educational strategies that include efforts to enhance tribal self-determination by successfully challenging BIA and state control over reservation resources and development. For example, most tribal colleges have curricula to train tribal members in the protection and development of valuable tribal natural resources, including major research and teaching facilities in forestry, wildlife biology, range management, water quality research, aquaculture, and energy resource technology to mention only a few (see U.S. Senate Select Committee on Indian Affairs 1990). To enhance access to regional research and teaching opportunities in the sciences and technologies, a number of tribal colleges have joined with state research institutions and universities to create tribal faculty and student research opportunities that cannot be provided on the local tribal college campuses. At Montana State University, for example, a consortium arrangement called American Indian Research Opportunities (AIRO) has become a multiprogram structure involving all seven of the Indian tribal colleges in the state. One AIRO program, "Minority Bio-Medical Research," provides tribal college faculty and students with teaching, laboratory and field research opportunities, in conjunction with the university, in order to address the research needs of their reservation communities. Some of these programs include such exotic academic areas as molecular pharmacology, genetic engineering, and field research on diseases caused by water parasites common to the Montana region (Morris 1986, 12). Similarly, the four tribal colleges in North Dakota are currently developing a faculty exchange program in cooperation with state institutions of higher education in order to add to their academic programs (see U.S. Senate Select Committee on Indian Affairs 1990). Such multicampus consortium arrangements enhance cooperative scientific research which can make a major contribution to the development of young Indian educators and scientists.

In addition to these unique multicampus outreach efforts, tribal colleges provide the kind of educational and human services programs expected from local community colleges: basic math, human services, and voc-ed curricula such as electronics, mechanics, secretarial sciences, computer literacy and programming, and carpentry. These curricula are often developed in response to tribal or other local business developments. At the Blackfeet Community College in Montana, the college is assisting the tribe to assume greater control over tourism facilities near Glacier Park. At Fort Peck, in eastern Montana, the college is involved in the establishment of commercial mushroom production (see U.S. Senate Select Committee on Indian Affairs 1990). At Turtle Mountain Community College in North Dakota, the curriculum and faculty have contributed to efforts to revise and strengthen the tribe's constitution and bylaws as part of a long-term tribal development project. Such efforts are beginning to enhance tribal government and tribal college efforts to coordinate and strengthen the role of higher education in economic development on Indian reservations.

Tribal colleges also prepare students to compete academically with non-Indian students at off-reservation colleges and universities. In 1980, a study conducted in North Dakota found that 86 percent of the tribal college graduates who went on to four year colleges successfully completed college and received their B.A. degrees, as compared to a dismal 10 percent success rate for Indian students who went directly to one of the North Dakota state colleges or universities (see Pease Windy Boy 1986, 2). Equally dramatic is the fact that nearly 85 percent of those who graduated from a tribal college found employment, a stark contrast to an unemployment level of 50 to 85 percent, which is endemic on most Indian reservations (see U.S. Senate Select Committee on Indian Affairs 1990).

These unprecedented achievements in Indian higher education provide ample evidence that federal support for the tribally controlled college movement is not only good Indian policy, but good education policy as well. The argument can be made that as the tribal colleges continue to develop, they will, by necessity, undermine, overturn, and restructure federal, state, and local policies regarding the education of the American Indian. The Bush administration's refusal to use the more accurate tribal college FTE projections to set TCA annual budget appropriations provides a clear example of how the "politics of money" can be a determining force in Indian tribal affairs, despite policy announcements on subjects like "Indian self-determination." No one can really understand the full significance of the tribally controlled college movement without attending a graduation and observing the faces of new graduates and their families and friends. These struggling—and unique—Indian educational institutions have proven that with local Indian control, a learning environment can be created that enhances the desire and determination of Indian people to use education to ensure the culture's survival rather than its eventual destruction.

CONCLUSIONS

The American Indian tribal college movement is one model of Indian self-determination policy that works. It is a success earned by a dedicated coalition of Indian and non-Indian leaders, working on the reservations and in Congress, who recognize the value of community control of education, particularly for a cultural minority like the American Indian. Unfortunately, some real and now chronic fiscal issues continue to cloud the future of the tribal college movement, with the most obvious and substantial obstacles being the BIA and those in the federal government who continue to attack the Tribal College Act of 1978. The continuing threat and real loss of federal funds has battered some tribal colleges to the point of collapse, yet they continue to struggle to maintain an educational presence in Indian country. Management and program problems caused by federally inflicted financial uncertainties have stalled or slowed tribal college development, but they have not stopped it. Instead, the tribal college movement continues to grow, despite considerable opposition from unsympathetic congressional leaders and entrenched BIA bureaucrats who have put their personal careers above the needs of those whom they were elected to serve.

Because of the continuing uncertainty surrounding the annual fundings of the tribal colleges through PL 95–471, Senators Kent Conrad, Daniel Inouye, John McCain, Quentin Burdick, Dennis DeConcini, and Thomas Daschle introduced S. 2213 (see U.S. Senate Select Committee on Indian Affairs 1990). This bill amended Title III of the Tribally Controlled Community College Assistance Act of 1978 (25 U.S.C. 1831, *et seq.*) to double the original federal authorization of $5 million to $10 million "for each of the fiscal years 1990, 1991, 1992, 1993, and 1994." In addition the bill modified existing language to increase the federal match per college endowment authorized from $350,000 to $750,000 (see S. 2213: 4–5).

For the tribal colleges, their achievements involve more than simply formal education. The tribal college movement brings to the Indian reservation a growing sense of personal and community accomplishment, a renewed sense of confidence and pride in what Indians can do when they have the opportunity to lead. These struggling tribal institutions are changing how Indian people view education, but they also show how they see themselves intellectually and collectively. With the confidence earned at their local tribal college, a growing number of Indian people have a greater awareness of themselves as thinkers and problem solvers. This renewed confidence in Indian intellectual abilities is one of the key achievements of the tribal college movement, and one that gives real meaning to the policy of Indian self-determination.

With the emergence of the Indian-controlled college, Indian people have come to realize that higher education need no longer be something imposed from without, but rather can be something sought from within. "It is our college, our education, and we can learn with confidence and pride. No longer can education make us strangers in our own communities" (Morris 1981–82). Such comments by Indian students and reservation community members remind us that education is not just about buildings or books, but also about the more subtle issues of personal and community attitudes toward education, and the role of such attitudes in creating a motivating climate for formal and lifelong learning. In testimony before the U.S. Senate Select Committee on Indian Affairs on S. 2213, Joseph McDonald, president of Salish Kootenai College, was asked to identify the single most important contribution being made by the tribal colleges to Indian country. He answered "Hope. . . . Whether [the student is] coming right out of high school, a recovering alcoholic, a new single head of household, [or] a recent widower," the tribal college provides every enrollee with hope (U.S. Senate Select Committee on Indian Affairs 1990, 11).

For the tribal college movement to succeed, it needs immediate and sustained national public and private support, both financial and political. What is not needed are more externally directed research studies on how to develop Indian communities; instead, more policies must give active support and recognition to what can potentially be accomplished if the Indians are allowed even a frail opportunity to develop and control the institutional infrastructure of their own development, namely, their education, their natural and human resources, and capital.

Certainly, not everything that has been tried by the tribal colleges has succeeded, but Indian people now have the opportunity to learn from their own failures and errors, rather than having to endure those created by the policies and programs of others. Given the spectacular achievements of these remarkable Indian institutions of higher education, it would appear that the Indian is learning very fast.

NOTES

1. The tribally chartered tribal colleges are: Blackfeet Community College, Cheyenne River Community College, Dull Knife Memorial College, Fond Du Lac Community College, Fort Belknap Community College, Fort Berthold Community College, Fort Peck Community College, Little Big Horn College, Little Hoop Community College, Lac Coure Oreilles Ojibwa Community College, Navajo Community College, Nebraska Indian Community College, Northwest Community College, Oglala Lakota College, Salish Kootenai College, Sinte Gleska College, Sisseton Wahpeton College, Stonechild Community College, and Turtle Mountain Community College. Other Indian college members of the AIHEC that are not tribally chartered include Bay Mills Community College, Crownpoint Institute of Technology, D-Q University, Haskell Indian Junior College (federal), Southwest Indian Polytechnic, and United Tribes Technical College (federal).

2. There are a few articles and dissertations written by those who have participated in the tribal college movement, e.g., Stein, 1986.

3. The devastating effect of the Reagan budget cuts are still resonating in Indian country. Under the Reagan budget, JOM would have been totally cut, had not Congress restored these monies. Proposed cuts for the Office of Education totalled $20.7 million and for the BIA, $72.9 million (U.S. Senate Select Committee on Indian Affairs 1981, 1). Despite Indian opposition, dozens of Indian schools were closed and health services were reduced or closed. According to the Senate Select Committee on Indian Affairs, "It is possible that over the next 3 to 5 years, 13,000 to 20,000 housing units will be constructed without water and sewer facilities" (U.S. Senate Select Committee on Indian Affairs 1981, 14). All Housing and Urban Development (HUD) housing was to be cut by 1983. Similar cuts were requested for CETA (the Comprehensive Employment Training Act) and the Economic Development Administration (EDA) (U.S. Senate Select Committee on Indian Affairs 1981, 1, 14–15).

4. I was in Washington, D.C., at a meeting of Indian educators at the time of the announcement that Indian education was not a trust obligation. At the time, the then acting director of Indian education in the BIA apparently had not received word of this major policy announcement and continued to promise full recognition of the trust responsibility. When informed that the administration had rejected the "trust" concept, he immediately changed his speech to conform to this new reality. Obligations and truth have a short life in Washington, D.C.

A key to understanding the Reagan "budget wars" is an appreciation of his "New Federalism" philosophy which sought to transfer federal programs to the states. What the administration failed to appreciate is the legal nature of the tribes and their "trust" status under federal law. The New Federalism runs counter to federal-tribe relationships when it attempts to transfer federal obligations and responsibilities to the states.

5. Control of Indians through education has a long and mostly unhappy history.

Dartmouth was founded as an Indian school, and there were "Indian" rooms or dormitories at other colonial-period colleges, including Harvard and William and Mary. In the nineteenth century, Haskill College was founded as a boarding school and later as a college for the education of Indian youth. Bacone College in Oklahoma is another Indian college. However, until the founding of the Navajo Community College in 1968, no college was under the control of an Indian tribe.

6. A requirement of the Tribally Controlled College Act of 1978 is that the tribal college must be more than 50 percent Indian in enrollment to qualify for funding.

REFERENCES

American Indian Research Opportunities (AIRO). 1986. *AIRO Program Announcement*. Minority Biomedical Research Support Program. Director, Dr. David Young. Montana State University, Bozeman.

Astin, A. W. 1982. *Minorities in Higher Education*. San Francisco: Jossey-Bass.

Comtec (Washington, D.C.). 1986. *Newsletter of the Indian Education Information Service* (whole issue) 7 no. 2, (June 1986).

Dupris, Joseph. 1980. *American Indian Community Controlled Education: Determination for Today, Direction for Tomorrow*. ERIC Publication, HEW Contract 400–78–0023. Las Cruces, New Mexico: New Mexico State University.

Fries, Judith E. 1987. *The American Indian in Higher Education, 1975–76 to 1984–85*. U.S. Department of Education. Center for Education Statistics, Washington, D.C.: U.S. Government Printing Office.

Fuchs, Estelle, and Robert J. Havighurst. 1972. *To Live On This Earth: American Indian Education*. Garden City, N.Y.: Doubleday.

Morris, C. Patrick. 1981–82. Notes on Washington, D.C., meeting of AIHEC.

Morris, C. Patrick. 1982–83. Notes on Washington, D.C., meeting of AIHEC.

Morris, C. Patrick. 1985. " 'As Long As The Water Flows . . .' United States Indian Water Rights: A Growing National Conflict." In *Native Power: The Quest for Autonomy and Nationhood of Indigenous Peoples*, ed. Yens Brøsted et al. New York: Columbia University Press.

Morris, C. Patrick. 1986. "Native American Studies: A Personal Overview." *The Wicazo Sa Review* (Indian Studies Journal, Eastern Washington University, Cheney), 2, no. 2 (Fall).

Morris, C. Patrick. 1988. "Termination by Accountants: The Reagan Indian Policy." In *Special Symposium on Native Americans and Public Policy*, ed. Fremont J. Lyden and Lyman H. Legters. *Policy Studies Journal 16*, no. 4 (Summer): Special issue, 731–50.

Salish Kootenai College. 1989. *Self-Study*. Pablo, Montana: Salish Kootenai College.

Stein, Wayne. 1986. *A History of Tribally Controlled Community Colleges: 1968–1978*. Ph.D. diss., Washington State University, Pullman.

U.S. Department of the Interior. 1986. "Bureau of Indian Affairs 1987 Budget Request Is 923.7 Million." Release for February 5, 1986. Washington, D.C.: BIA.

U.S. Federal Register. 1987. "Administration of Educational Loans, Grants and Other Assistance for Higher Education to Administration." Part 40 of Chapter 1, Title 25, of the Code of Federal Regulations, 52, no. 41 (March 3): 6482–87.

U.S. Senate. 1969. *Indian Education: A National Tragedy—A National Challenge.* Special Subcommittee on Indian Education of the Committee on Labor and Public Welfare, U.S. Senate, 91st Congress, Senate Report No. 91–501. Washington, D.C.: U.S. Government Printing Office.

U.S. Senate Select Committee on Indian Affairs. 1981. *Analysis of the Budget Pertaining to Indian Affairs Fiscal Year 1982.* A Report of the Senate Select Committee on Indian Affairs of the U.S. Senate, 97th Congress, 1st sess. Washington, D.C.: U.S. Government Printing Office.

U.S. Senate Select Committee on Indian Affairs. 1990. *Senate Select Committee Hearing on S. 2213: To Increase the Federal Contribution to the Tribally Controlled Community College Endowment Program.* 101st Congress, 2d sess.; S. Hrg 1–1–692, *Hearing before the Select Committee on Indian Affairs, on S. 2167 Reauthorization Bill and S. 2213, April 9, 1990, Bismarck, North Dakota.* U.S. Senate, 101st Congress, 2d sess. Washington, D.C.: U.S. Government Printing Office.

Wright, Bobby. 1986. "An Assessment of Student Outcomes at Tribally Controlled Community Colleges." Paper presented at the 18th Annual National Indian Education Association Conference, 22 November 1986.

6

Indian Religion, the First Amendment, and the State

Lyman H. Legters

On November 21, 1987, in an unusual kind of Thanksgiving observance, representatives of the Church Council of Greater Seattle met with representatives of Northwest Indian tribes at a street corner in downtown Seattle. There, a proclamation was read and presented to the tribal representative by the ten ecclesiastical signatories. It was addressed to the twenty-six federally recognized tribes of Washington and Alaska and read as follows:

Dear Brothers and Sisters,

This is a formal apology on behalf of our churches for their long-standing participation in the destruction of traditional Native American spiritual practices. We call upon our people for recognition of and respect for your traditional ways of life and for protection of your sacred places and ceremonial objects. We have frequently been unconscious and insensitive and not come to your aid when you have been victimized by unjust Federal policies and practices. In many other circumstances we reflected the rampant racism and prejudice of the dominant culture with which we too willingly identified. During this 200th Anniversary year of the United States Constitution we, as leaders of our churches in the Pacific Northwest, extend our apology. We ask your forgiveness and blessing.

Pledging to uphold the American Indian Religious Freedom Act of 1978, the signatories added three affirmations:

1. The rights of the Native Peoples to practice and participate in traditional ceremonies and rituals with the same protection offered all religions under the Constitution;

2. Access to and protection of sacred sites and public lands for ceremonial purposes; and

3. The use of religious symbols (feathers, tobacco, sweet grass, bone, etc.) for use
   in traditional ceremonies and rituals.

The proclamation went on to offer assistance in the righting of previous
wrongs as well as advocacy and mediation in relation to government agencies
where religious freedom is at issue. It concluded:

May the promises of this day go on public record with all the congregations of our
communions and be communicated to the Native American Peoples of the Pacific
Northwest. May the God of Abraham and Sarah, and the Spirit who lives in both
the cedar and Salmon People, be honored and celebrated.[1]

It would be difficult to maintain, five years later, that this initiative, as
generous and stirring as it was belated, has had anything but symbolic
significance. The policies of the executive branch since 1980 and the rulings
of an increasingly conservative Supreme Court have seemed, if anything,
to move in an opposite direction.[2] Moreover, the congressional apology for
the Wounded Knee massacre hardly satisfies as atonement for centuries of
genocidal conduct.[3] So far as the narrower issue of religious freedom is
concerned, the promise of the American Indian Religious Freedom Act
(AIRFA) has been systematically thwarted by the executive and judicial
branches as they converted a substantive intent into a procedural charade.
Nonetheless, in a landscape as bleak as the one surrounding Indian religious
freedom in U.S. society and constitutional practice, symbols of the right
kind are not to be sneezed at, and the Church Council's apology shines like
a beacon, reminding us by what a wide margin our practices diverge from
principles that we claim to uphold.

The Pacific Northwest was also the setting for an episode that more nearly
typifies society's attitude toward and treatment of native religious tradition.
This is the infamous David Sohappy case, otherwise known as the Salmon-
scam, in which state and federal officials joined with a Washington state
senator to deny members of the Yakima Nation their treaty rights and the
constitutional guarantee of religious freedom.

In May 1991, David Sohappy, Sr., was buried on the Yakima reservation
at the age of sixty-six, with a twenty-one-gun salute by the Veterans of
Foreign Wars marking his military service in World War II. The ceremony
was conducted according to the Seven Drum ritual of the Feather Religion,
of which Sohappy had been a leader. This is a traditional religion claiming
a spiritual relationship with salmon and other wildlife. Central to that religious belief is the right, and indeed the obligation, to fish without regard
to regulations imposed by the surrounding white society or, for that matter,
tribal government. However, David Sohappy died, his health broken by
federal incarceration, without the satisfaction of any official acknowledgement that he was anything but a convicted poacher.

The Yakima Treaty of 1855 was one of several concluded in the same period that transferred enormous tracts of land out of Indian hands. The treaty provided, by way of minimal compensation, that Indians could continue to fish in their traditional manner along the Columbia River. In addition, when the Bonneville Dam was built in 1930, the federal government incurred an obligation, which it steadfastly ignored, to replace the housing and fishing sites lost to the flooding that resulted from the construction. David Sohappy, who had spent his life fishing from his Cooks Landing home along the Columbia, should have been the beneficiary of both federal obligations: to protect traditional Indian fishing rights and to replace the sites lost to the Bonneville Dam. Instead, in 1981 and 1982 he was singled out as a target of a sting, very like entrapment, which was supposedly designed to penalize the "poaching" of salmon.

In November 1981, the Lacey Act amendments were signed into law, making it illegal to possess, sell, or transport "illegally" caught fish or game across state lines. Sponsored by Senator Slade Gorton (R-Washington), the amendments were steered around the Senate Committee on Indian Affairs and passed almost unnoticed, except by the Washington State Department of Fisheries and the National Marine Fisheries Service (NMFS). The former, which was noteworthy for its long-standing racist approach to Indian matters, had already requested the sting operation in April of that year, anticipating passage of the amendments. NMFS, which at that time was the subject of litigation initiated by Columbia River tribes for its questionable management of resources, then sent undercover agents to purchase salmon from the nineteen individuals charged in the ensuing indictment. Thirteen subsistence fishermen were convicted in 1983; David Sohappy and his son were each sentenced to a five-year prison term. Whereas the Sohappys had sold 317 and 28 fish, respectively, two non-Indian fishermen, who were convicted of selling $20,000 worth of fish to Seattle restaurants, were sentenced to 30 days in jail in one case and only a fine in the other. Although the Lacey Act Amendments of 1981 state explicitly that "Nothing in this section . . . shall deprive any Indian or Indian tribe, band or community of any right, privilege, or immunity afforded under federal treaty, agreement, or statute with respect to hunting, trapping, or fishing or the control, licensing or regulation thereof," the trial court refused to entertain a defense based on treaty rights. Finally, to complete this chapter of persecution, Senator Gorton appealed to then Secretary of Interior James Watt to evict Sohappy's family from their home at Cooks Landing, alleging it to be "the last remaining focal point for illegal fishing activity on the Columbia River."[4]

Although Sohappy's position on treaty rights would presumably have been identical to that of the Yakima Nation to which he belonged, that was not necessarily true with respect to fishing. The tribe had its own rules about fish harvesting, and it was possible to hold that Sohappy's violation, however minor, had also offended against tribal law. It was, therefore, not at all clear

what the outcome might be when, in 1987, the Yakima, asserting their tribal
jurisdiction in the case, secured the temporary release of Sohappy from
federal prison in Minnesota in order to have him stand trial in the tribal
court. That trial ended on April 29, 1987, when the jury returned a verdict
of "not guilty" on all charges of illegal fishing. After eight hours of delib-
eration, the jury found that federal officers had acted improperly by en-
trapping Sohappy and others. Most significant of all for the present topic,
moreover, they ruled that tribal fishing regulations had infringed on the free
exercise of religion.

By way of contrast, the International Indian Treaty Council offered to the
Forty-Third Session of the UN Commission on Human Rights, meeting early
in 1987 at Geneva, Switzerland, the following characterization of Sohappy's
"selective persecution" at federal hands:

Mr. Sohappy has been in jail for seven months and we are now informed that he
will go to trial on April 13th. While in Federal custody David Sohappy has also been
denied his diet as a salmon culture person. That culture requires consumption of
Salmon [sic] for religious and health reasons. Mr. Sohappy has also been denied an
Eagle feather, a necessary article for his religion. Mr. Sohappy is a leader of the
Indian Seven Drum and Advanced Feather Religion. His health is now deteriorating. . . . Our delegation view [sic] Mr. Sohappy's treatment in the justice systems as
cruel and inhumane treatment by domestic and international standards.[5]

In June 1987, following Sohappy's acquittal in tribal court and after the
Yakima Tribal Council had urged President Ronald Reagan to pardon the
defendant, federal authorities reasserted their jurisdiction and the five Yakima fishermen were surrendered by the tribe. This outcome had been assured when Ross Swimmer, assistant secretary for Indian affairs, threatened
the tribe with a cutoff of federal funds.[6]

Among the many conclusions that might be drawn from this episode, the
one that seems inescapable within the present topic is that an Indian tribal
court displayed a keener appreciation of and sensitivity to the First Amendment to the U.S. Constitution, with respect to Indian religion, than did the
governments and courts of the state and federal systems of justice. Strangely
enough, the meanness of spirit exhibited by the petty denials during Sohappy's imprisonment is perhaps more eloquent than the larger constitutional issue in revealing an official determination to disparage Indian religion,
in flagrant contravention of constitutional requirements.

Although constitutional debate has, in general, been quite sharp in recent
years with the rightward tilt of the federal judiciary, and although the First
Amendment with its religion clauses has figured in the commemorations of
the Constitution and of Jefferson's Virginia Statute for Religious Liberty, it
is by no means clear that any of it bears significantly on the status of Native

American religion. Whether the Constitution is construed loosely or strictly, and whatever may be believed about the intent of the framers, American Indians appear almost never to count as beneficiaries of First Amendment guarantees concerning religion. For American society in general, and irrespective of the many disagreements among constitutional scholars, the twin clauses assuring free exercise and prohibiting establishment have been markedly efficacious: They have worked well, both for those mainly concerned to protect religion against state encroachment and for those anxious to keep the state free of religious entanglements. Especially since 1924, when all American Indians obtained citizenship, it is, therefore, difficult to justify the continuing failure of the U.S. constitutional system to treat Indian religion evenhandedly. Even allowing for occasional exceptions, it seems, on the whole, that they are being denied the guarantee of free exercise, while the establishment clause is being used against them.

This essential invisibility of Indian religion *as religion* is reflected symptomatically in the scholarly literature. Without going into an extensive review, but rather by taking only a few of the best contributions, it seems significant that Leonard Levy, Paul Kauper, and Milton Konvitz all mention Indian religion barely or not at all in their treatments of First Amendment clauses bearing on religious freedom. By the same token, in his study of American Indians and the law, Charles Wilkinson largely ignores the subject of religion.[7] These works are among the best in their respective fields, and I cite them here not by way of criticism, but rather to underscore the invisibility of the subject.

In a similar vein, in 1990 the Brookings Institution published the results of a symposium organized by the Williamsburg Charter Foundation and held in 1988 at the University of Virginia. Proclaimed as a "celebration and reaffirmation of the religious liberty clauses of the First Amendment," the symposium took as its point of departure the Williamsburg Charter. That document, which is printed as an appendix to the volume of proceedings, offers a kind of recipe for legitimate public discourse in a pluralist democratic order, suggesting also the desirability of an enlarged scope for religious viewpoints in such discourse. Its doctrinal basis is unexceptionable:

Religious liberty finally depends on neither the favors of the state and its officials nor the vagaries of tyrants or majorities. Religious liberty in a democracy is a right that may not be submitted to vote and depends on the outcome of no election. A society is only as just and free as it is respectful of this right, especially toward the beliefs of its smallest minorities and least popular communities.[8]

Now the charter itself, as an enunciation of principle, might not be expected to address particular affronts to the religious freedom it celebrates. However, the ensuing discussion disclosed no concern about this society's most glaring transgression of constitutional requirements with respect to religion: the denial of protection to American Indian religious practice. Despite the evident applicability of the concluding clause quoted above, the only kind of religions in the minds of the discussants (so far as the printed word allows us to conclude) were the mainstream faiths and denominations that have visibility in their buildings, their rituals, and their statements of belief.

A similar occasion occurred in Seattle in autumn 1986 under the auspices of the William O. Douglas Institute. In this instance it was a bicentennial commemoration of Jefferson's Virginia Statute that afforded opportunity for consideration of the current status of religious freedom in America. Up to a point, the greatest concern was lavished on the disabilities suffered by the so-called new religions: Scientology, the Unification Church, and the like.[9] However, there was a discernable shift in the attitudes of participants when one session was given over to Native Americans and the plight of their religious commitments and practices.

Hazel Umtuch (Yakima) began with a brief statement about "the land," its centrality in Indian ceremony, and the reasons why it is the subject of prayer and the object of protective concern in native tradition. Juanita Jefferson (Lummi) then told of her own passage from uneasy existence in white society to the healing effect of rejoining her people on the reservation and recovering the significance of native religious tradition. From the struggle against termination and the abridgement of treaty rights, she moved to a more positive participation in tribal life:

In the recovery of our Indian religious practices, we begin to experience a healing process, whether the ills are spiritual or mental or physical. We can know that healing, and celebrate it, and go on to a new stage. All of our rituals and ceremonies follow this basic pattern; whether it's an Indian naming ceremony, which is a way of strengthening a person, or being initiated into spiritual practices that begin with cleansing, the aim is always that one will become strong and well. And that, with this strength, one will go on to help others in this way of life.

Recounting an instance on the Lummi reservation when secular white authorities intervened to prevent the alleged bodily harm inflicted in an initiation ceremony, she understood the threat to Indian culture as a species of genocide, explaining "And so I also began to understand what it has meant for other cultures of the world to undergo the various forms of genocide." The particular case was lost, as has usually been the Indian experience when native ways come into conflict with those of the surrounding white society, but the Lummi and neighboring tribes were strengthened in their determination to protect their traditional religion.

The final statement, by Jewell Praying Wolf James (Lummi), was an extended chronicle of infringements of Indian religious freedom. I can do no better than to quote extensively from his presentation.

could conceivably have
t serves the needs and
its the organized tribes.
tuation has been pretty
rse, have been protected
evotion to constitutional
d, though certainly not
f self-governance. How-
ship has meant, for the
and culture, while self-
e putatively compelling

. The Native American
dvantage, no doubt, be-
stream culture) gradually
lgement that ceremonial
the California Supreme
te to justify prohibition.
in Scalia, writing for the
ure of toleration by em-
pper reading of the free
to say reactionary) com-
only the beginning of a
is reminded of a warning
law:

ociety that the Jews played
the shift from fresh air to
of Indians, even more than
l in our democratic faith.[15]

o clearly a constitutional
endment, it is tempting
st unrelieved assault on
tion, whereby the due
First Amendment guar-
here, to the degree that
e federal government in
endment rights.[16] How-
an also work to Indian
s is Philip Kurland's ar-
endment must be under-
t be a consistency of
ian religion between the

Having worked in different capacities with the Lummi Indian Tribe for the past decade, continuously active in natural resource management, I believe that we are both entitled and obligated to question national policies as they affect our people here in the Pacific Northwest. For what we are up against here in Indian Country is the question of survival itself.

In 1924, citizenship was conferred on American Indians, thus bringing us for the first time within the protection of the Fourteenth Amendment. In Indian Country we acknowledge that this was done to honor Indians who had fought in World War I, but we also suggest that it had something to do with grabbing more of our land and resources. In 1921 Charles Burke was made Commissioner of Indian Affairs. During his term in office, he had plans to defraud the American Indians of their land and natural resources. Such plans extended even to prevention of the traditional religious practices of the Indian people. He drafted and began to implement the Indian "religious crimes code." This code would imprison native Indians for thirty days for every "offense" an Indian is alleged to have committed. The first targets were the Hopi, Navajo, and Sioux. The Commissioner began to have traditional religious leaders in these communities imprisoned for practicing the ancient cere- monials. At that point three organizations from California came to the defense of the Indian people's right to practice their religions. These were the Indian Welfare League, the National Association to Help the Indians, and the Indian Defense As- sociation of Northern California. A member of the Indian Welfare League, a Los Angeles attorney named Ida May Adams, dreamed up the concept of making Amer- ican Indians citizens. She believed American Indians would be guaranteed First Amendment Rights if they were citizens. Thus, the 1924 Indian Citizenship Act was enacted by Congress.

In 1978, the U.S. Congress passed the American Indian Religious Freedom Act. Now, why is it we need such an act if we are truly "citizens"? Why do we need the 1978 Religious Freedom Act to guarantee first amendment protections? Well, once again, it is political. Our religious practices clash with corporate interests. To be allowed to practice our religious ceremonials would interfere with the ability of corporate interests to exploit natural resources. . . .

The Hoopas and Yuroks wanted to continue to practice their spiritual questing in the wilderness areas, undisturbed and in the tradition of their ancestors. However, the U.S. Forest Service had other plans for this area so important to Hoopa and Yurok ceremonials. The Forest Service planned on opening up the area with a federally funded road. This road would destroy the area's religious value to the natives. Because no president would order the federal agencies to abide by the 1978 Indian Religious Freedom Act, the Indian tribes have had to resort continuously to the courts to determine whether or not their religious ceremonies and practices will be respected and protected. The Hoopas and Yuroks only sought to be allowed to continue to practice their prayers in a clean, undisturbed environment.

The issue was the same with the Navajo Medicine Men and the Rainbow Bridge controversy. All the Medicine Men sought was the right to continue to practice their ancient ceremonials and prayers in the same areas as their ancestors. This "Rainbow Bridge" held great significance for the essence of their practices and the success of their prayers for their people's future and ability to survive. All they wanted was to go to the site and not be disturbed, to be allowed to pray and make spiritual contact. But, the United States decided to dam the area and flood the Rainbow Bridge with

water and tourists. You see, once the area was flooded th
could make money boating people to the Rainbow Bridg
destroy the site's value for the Navajos.

At first the U.S. took the position that the Navajo Medi
able to reach the site and practice undisturbed. The quest
deprived of the right to visit the site? And what were the to
cigarette butts, newspapers, wrappers, and other litter. Th
for the prayer ceremonials. The courts would then ask the N
was absolutely central to their practices, ceremonials, and

How about the Hopi? What is Hopi? Hopi means peace.
of peace. For centuries they have been sitting there with a
spirit, or even Jesus, would instill into their safekeeping a
kept alive by their daily prayers, their daily activities, and
to their survival, and maybe even that of all of us. They hav
relationship with everything in the world around them. Thi
was placed on their shoulders. A part of their vision was to
the land around them to stop the cancerous serpent that
ground waiting to surface. This serpent was let loose by the c
miners, and the politicians who helped force the removal
their lands and away from the site of their duties. Now th
Did they fail to pray hard enough? Did they not keep the
ceremonials properly? Where did they go wrong? Or was tl
hands and the contaminating destruction of the serpent's coa
unavoidable?

What about the Lummi Indians? Are they experiencing t
inatory activity from governmental officials and representat
enactment of the 1978 Indian Religious Freedom Act, the L
it means to have religious freedom. It meant that no pre
federal agencies to live up to and abide by the enactment, tl
be assured prosecution if we continued to advocate and e>
happened? Well, in the early morning hours, before the b
States made a move against the Lummi Indians. They sent t
sheriffs, the Bureau of Indian Affairs police, and Washingt(
homes of young and elderly Lummi tribal members. They er
and front and back doors. Some doors were kicked off the hin
with guns drawn upon wives and children. The people w(
and held at gun point.

The officers ransacked clothing, dressers, closets, and po
sugar and flour barrels. What were they after? They were a
owned by the Indian people for their ceremonial regalia. 1
people were in violation of the Eagle Protection enactme:
who have no place to go. These were people who would ha
allowed searches at reasonable hours, once the officers disj
rants. But this was not the way. No warrants were displa
people knew, this could have been some anti-Indian group (
of the Ku Klux Klan.

Lummi Elders, half-dressed, were handcuffed, with thei
feet, and their feet shackled together. They were all led to tl

ianship. The contradiction between these concep•
worked to Indian advantage: guardianship when
purposes of Indians, and self-governance when it s
However, as every Native American knows, the •
much the opposite. Religious freedom could, of co•
under the notion of guardianship, simply out of ¢
precept. Alternately, it could have been protect
infallibly, by Indians themselves in the pursuance
ever, neither option was allowed to rule. Guardi:
most part, denying the validity of Indian religior
governance has been consistently overridden by •
requirements of the laws of the majority.

The peyote cases are instructive in this regar
Church of North America (enjoying some modest •
cause it seems to resemble the churches of the mair
won from state courts and legislatures the acknowl(
use of the hallucinogen did not, in the words o•
Court, invoke any "compelling interest" of the st
However, in 1990, in the *Smith* case, Justice Anto
Supreme Court majority, retreated from the pos
phasizing the so-called war on drugs over any p
exercise clause.[14] The increasingly conservative (n•
position of the Court warrants concern that this i
course leading in precisely the wrong direction. On
issued by Felix Cohen, the great scholar of Indiar

The Indian plays much the same role in our American
in Germany. Like the miner's canary, the Indian mar•
poison gas in our political atmosphere; and our treatmen
our treatment of other minorities, reflects the rise and •

Because the issue of Indian religious freedom is
one, hinged directly to the meaning of the First A
to look for legal or juridical remedies for the alm
native religion. Clearly, the doctrine of incorpo
process clause of the Fourteenth Amendment mak(
antees binding on the states, has some importanc
the states may have been more egregious than t
trampling on religious freedom and other First A
ever, as the *Smith* case indicates, that doctrine
disadvantage. More promising for Indians perha
gument that the two religion clauses of the First A•
stood and applied conjointly. The result mi;
interpretation that would preclude whipsawing Ir

two clauses as separately applied. Unfortunately, Kurland's proposal has not won the minds of the courts.[17]

It is easy enough to assign blame for the uncomprehending approach of white society toward Indian religion. Undoubtedly, it is the U.S. Supreme Court, as the court of last resort in applying constitutional requirements, that bears ultimate responsibility, for it is the branch of government that supposedly functions without reference to the tides of sentiment and opinion that necessarily condition the behavior of elected officials. It is a standing reproach to the Court, and to government in general, that Indians despair of finding protection under the First Amendment for their traditional religion. They turn increasingly (as they did in the Sohappy case) to international bodies concerned with human rights. They devise strategies to gain protection under other constitutional provisions or by linking their religious concerns with environmental efforts which stand a better chance of a sympathetic hearing in the courts. Moreover, they are forced to propose amendments that would give efficacy to the very law—AIRFA—that was intended to restore their First Amendment rights. "Why the courts have chosen to apply more stringent tests to Indian religious cases is unclear. What is evident is the judicial system's inability to understand and properly assess Indian religious beliefs, especially regarding the importance of land."[18] Also evident, over and above the persistent ethnocentrism that denies Indians equal protection, is that government, even including the Supreme Court, becomes a scofflaw, and not just in Indian eyes. The continuing subversion of treaty and constitutional rights becomes a threat to the rule of law itself.

NOTES

1. Jon Magnuson, "Affirming Native Spirituality: A Call to Justice," *The Christian Century*, 9 December 1987, pp. 1114–17.

2. C. Patrick Morris, "Termination by Accountants: The Reagan Indian Policy," in *Native Americans and Public Policy* ed. Fremont J. Lyden and Lyman H. Legters (Pittsburgh, Penn.: University of Pittsburgh Press, 1992), pp. 63–84.

3. Nancy Butterfield, "Congress Apologizes for Massacre," *Northwest Ethnic News*, December 1990, p. 3.

4. *Treaty Council News*, June 1987, pp. 1–2, 11.

5. Ibid.

6. This account draws heavily on the full and often sympathetic coverage of the case in the Seattle press.

7. Leonard W. Levy, *The Establishment Clause* (New York: Macmillan, 1986); Paul G. Kauper, *Civil Liberties and the Constitution* (Ann Arbor: University of Michigan Press, 1962); Milton R. Konvitz, *Religious Liberty and Conscience* (New York: Viking Press, 1968); Charles F. Wilkinson, *American Indians, Time, and the Law* (New Haven, Conn.: Yale University Press, 1988).

8. James Davison Hunter and Os Guinness, eds., *Articles of Faith, Articles of Peace* (Washington, D.C.: Brookings Institution, 1990).

9. The apparent contrast between this emphasis and that of the Williamsburg discussion masks the unfortunate fact that the most fervent defenders of religious freedom pay little or no attention to the implications of their advocacy for American Indians.

10. The courts held that reserving the area for Indian ceremonials would amount to an establishment, while also measuring the Indian religious claims against the standard of indispensability. Vine Deloria, Jr., and Clifford M. Lytle, *American Indians, American Justice* (Austin: University of Texas Press, 1983), p. 239.

11. Lyman H. Legters, ed., *The Virginia Statute and Religious Freedom in America* (Unpublished conference proceedings, Seattle, 1986).

12. Robert S. Michaelson, "Law and Limits of Liberty," in *Handbook of American Indian Religious Freedom*, ed. Christopher Vecsey (New York: Crossroad, 1991), p. 119.

13. Ibid.

14. *Employment Division v. Smith*, 494 U.S., 108 L.Ed. 2d 876, 110 S. Ct. (1990), p. 5.

15. Quoted in Paul E. Lawson and C. Patrick Morris, "The Native American Church and the New Court: The *Smith* Case and Indian Religious Freedoms," *American Indian Culture and Research Journal 15*, no. 1 (1991): 85–86; this article is an appropriately scathing examination of the Supreme Court ruling.

16. On incorporation, see Levy, *The Establishment Clause*, ch. 7.

17. Philip B. Kurland, *Religion and the Law* (Chicago: Aldine, 1962).

18. Sharon O'Brien, "A Legal Analysis of the American Indian Religious Freedom Act," in Vecsey, *Handbook*, p. 42.

7

Indian Preference: Racial Discrimination or a Political Right?

Jerry D. Stubben

In an era when affirmative action is under legal and political scrutiny and the president of the United States vetoed the 1990 Civil Rights Bill because he feared it contained legislation that would require discriminatory employment quotas, employers on or near Indian tribal lands possess the legal right to discriminate in hiring against all other racial or ethnic groups. Although many may view such preference as nothing more than institutionalized racism and reverse discrimination, it is not. Indian preference is based on the political relationship between Indian tribes and the United States government. Thus, it is derived from the political status of American Indian tribes and their individual members, and not from racial or minority status, as is the case in affirmative action programs as derived from such aforementioned civil rights legislation. For those not familiar with Indian preference, this chapter will examine the cultural and legal basis for such preferential treatment of Indians.

THE CIVIL RIGHTS ACT OF 1964: TITLE VII

The main purpose of Title VII of the Civil Rights Act of 1964 (as amended in 1972) was to reverse past discrimination in both the public and private sectors by making it unlawful for employers to discriminate on the basis of race, color, religion, sex, or national origin.[1] Section 703 (a) states, "It shall be an unlawful employment practice for an employer to fail or refuse to hire or otherwise discriminate against an individual . . . or . . . to limit, segregate, or classify employees in any way which would deprive or tend to deprive any individual of employment opportunities . . . because of such individual's race, color, religion, sex, or national origin."

The act, however, exempted "employers who had twenty-four or less employees, federal, tribal, state and local governments and a bona fide private membership club (other than a labor organization) which is exempt from taxation under section 501 (c) of the Internal Revenue Code of 1954." The federal government was required to institute a policy, through executive orders, to ensure equal employment opportunities for federal employees.[2]

Section 702 allowed for two more exemptions to Title VII: "to an employer with respect to the employment of aliens outside any State" and to "a religious corporation, association, or society with respect to the employment of individuals of a particular religion to perform work connected with the carrying on by such corporation, association, or society." Exempting aliens and religious organizations from Title VII was based on "the fact that congressional statutes are not valid outside the boundaries of the United States as prescribed by international law" and on the concept of "separation of church and state as defined in Article I of the Bill of Rights in the United States Constitution."

A third exemption was allowed under Section 703 (i). Known as the Indian Preference section of Title VII, it states that "nothing contained in this title shall apply to any business or enterprise on or near an Indian reservation with respect to any publicly announced employment practice of such business or enterprise under which a preferential treatment is given to any individual because he is an Indian living on or near a reservation."

The basis for this third exemption is not as clearly defined in the context of international or constitutional law as the other two exemptions which relate to classifications of groups rather than government entities as defined under section 701(b). Indian preference is not guaranteed in the U.S. Constitution, as is the case with the religious freedoms that are enjoyed by religious organizations. Indian tribes are part of the constitutional structure of government.[3] However, tribal authority was not created nor protected directly by the Constitution, for tribal sovereignty predated the formation of the United States and continued after it, and tribes were acknowledged by the Constitution in the reaffirmation of previously negotiated treaties. Further relations between Indian tribes and the U.S. government were similar to those of other sovereign nations and were cemented through treaties and treaty substitutes.[4]

Without a constitutional basis, perhaps the basis for Indian preference lies in international law under the right of sovereign nations to be excluded from the laws of other sovereign nations, similar to the extraterritorial exemption given to U.S. employers outside the boundaries of the United States. However, unlike most other sovereign nations, Indian tribes must rely on the United States to protect their sovereignty from external infringement. The Supreme Court has been instrumental in defining Indian tribal sovereignty ever since the birth of the nation.

In the early 1800s, Chief Justice John Marshall made it clear that Indian tribes were sovereign before contact with the Europeans and that some, but not all, sovereign powers continued in existence after relations with Europeans and the United States had been established. In *Johnson v. McIntosh*, the Court ruled that the tribes' "rights to complete sovereignty, as independent nations, were necessarily diminished."[5] *Cherokee Nation v. Georgia* held that tribes are not foreign nations and that "they may, more correctly, perhaps, be denominated domestic dependent nations."[6,7]

The third case in the "Marshall trilogy" is *Worcester v. Georgia.*[8] Here, Marshall applied *Cherokee* but reached different conclusions. He emphasized that the Indians had their own political institutions and were engaged in self-government. The British, he noted, had never attempted to interfere with the domestic affairs of the Indians, and the colonies had followed a similar approach. In analyzing the Treaty of Hopewell, between the United States and the Cherokees, Marshall concluded that it explicitly recognized the national character of the Cherokees and their right to self-government. Nothing in the treaties indicated that the Cherokees had surrendered their national character, in spite of some phrases indicating that the Congress would henceforth assume some responsibility for their commercial relations with American citizens.[9]

In Marshall's view, tribes in aboriginal times possessed a sovereignty as complete as that of any European nation. After forming alliances with the United States, however, they surrendered their external sovereignty and thenceforth lacked sufficient sovereignty to claim political independence, rather remaining as sovereigns in their ability to shield themselves from any intrusion by the states. Therefore, it is the federal government's responsibility to ensure that this sovereignty is preserved.[10] This meaning of Indian sovereignty has generally been used since the early nineteenth century.[11]

The modern court has subscribed to this view of Indian tribes as quasi-sovereign tribal entities, moving slowly before employing the word *sovereignty* (so colloquial is it, with its implications from international law and policy) to describe the status of Indian tribal governments.[12] Senator Hubert Humphrey, the Senate sponsor of Indian preference in Title VII, while on the floor of the Senate, identified the special status of Indians as a basis for Indian preference: "This exemption is consistent with the Federal Government's policy of encouraging Indian employment and with the *special legal position* of Indians."[13]

Thus, unlike other minority groups in the United States, Indian tribes are something more than racial or ethnic entities. They also are political entities, and this makes them special. When members of other minority groups in the United States have dealings with the federal government, they are seen as individuals dealing with a political entity. When a tribe has dealings with the United States, however, two political entities stand face-to-face and must come to terms. Individual Indians have a special status that other minority groups may not have, including Indian preference, because they are members of a political entity, the tribe.[14]

Ebona identified differences that Indian tribes have in relationship to other minority groups, including a treaty relationship with the federal government as represented in the U.S. Constitution, congressional laws, Supreme Court decisions and executive orders; a reserved land base; a system of self-government; and the fact that most tribes are rurally isolated from the dominant society, in a self-imposed segregation.[15] These attributes of an Indian tribe are not applicable to any other ethnic or minority group in the United States.

The Supreme Court ruled in a similar vein in *United States v. Antelope*[16] by citing *Morton v. Mancari*,[17] in which it found that federal laws that apply to individual Indians and Indian tribes are not racially applicable but speak rather to the federal government's long-standing relationship with Indian tribes of a political nature.[18] Thus, it is the special status of Indians by virtue of a long-standing relationship between their tribal governments and the federal government, and not constitutional law or international sovereignty, that is the basis of Indian preference.

That the Supreme Court has continually characterized Indian tribes as foreign to the United States in their cultural and political traditions is difficult for most people to understand; therefore, they make little effort to do so and instead prefer to consider Indians as simply another racial minority.[19] The statutory recognition of the special status of Indian tribes will be dealt with in the following section.

INDIAN PREFERENCE: THE INDIAN REORGANIZATION ACT OF 1934

Indian preference in employment, although dating back to colonial times, was never fully implemented into law until Congress passed the Wheeler-Howard Act in 1934.[20] Commonly referred to as the Indian Reorganization Act (IRA), it stated:

The Secretary of the Interior is directed to establish standards of health, age, character, experience, knowledge, and ability for Indians who may be appointed, without regard to civil-service laws, to the various positions maintained, now or hereafter, by the Indian Office, in the administration of functions or services affecting any Indian tribe. Such qualified Indians shall hereafter have the preference to appointment to vacancies in any such positions.[21]

Congressional testimony by Representative Edgar Howard of Nebraska, co-sponsor of the IRA and chairman of the House Indian Committee, espoused the following reasoning for Indian preference in the Bureau of Indian Affairs:

The Indians have not only been thus deprived of civic rights and powers, but they have been largely deprived of the opportunity to enter the more important positions in the service of the very bureau which manages their affairs. Theoretically, the Indians have the right to qualify for the Federal civil service. In actual practice there has been no adequate program of training to qualify Indians to compete in these examinations . . . ; and even if there were such training, the Indians would have to compete under existing law, on equal terms with multitudes of white applicants.[22]

Further evidence presented by Howard and others identified that in 1934, less than 34 percent of the permanent civil service appointments in the Bureau of Indian Affairs were held by Indians and the vast majority of the positions held by Indians were in the lower salary grades. Few Indians held supervisory positions, and only 8 of the 103 Indian agencies had Indian superintendents. Due to this lack of Indian involvement in the Bureau of Indian Affairs, supporters of the act felt it was necessary for Indians with the requisite vocational and professional training "to enter the Indian service of their own people without the necessity of competing with white applicants for these positions."[23]

Representative William Hastings from Oklahoma espoused that "in his judgment, exempting Indians from the civil-service requirements would improve the Bureau of Indian Affairs by employing more Indians who speak the language and possess an understanding of their respective tribes, which presently was not found in the more qualified non-Indian college graduates that hold positions in the Bureau."[24]

In referring to testimony that the Indian preference policy was "set up against retention of the present civil service," Indian Commissioner John Collier testified before the House Committee on Indian Affairs that "we must not blind ourselves to the fact that the effect of this bill if worked out would unquestionably be to replace white employees with Indian employees."[25]

Representative Howard defended the replacement of white employees with Indian employees based on the following considerations:

The Indian character had suffered subtly and profoundly through the long exclusion of the Indians from normal human activity in managing their affairs, developing their powers, and giving scope to their ambitions. It should be possible for Indians to enter the service of their own people without running the gauntlet of competition with whites for these positions. Indian progress and ambition will be enormously strengthened as soon as we adopt the principle that the Indian Service shall gradually become, in fact as well as name, an Indian service predominantly in the hands of educated and competent Indians. Section 13 . . . gives to such Indians a preference right to appointment to any future vacancy. This provision in no way signifies a disregard of the true merit system, but it adapts the merit system to Indian temperament, training, and capacity.[26]

American Indians, through section 13 of the Indian Reorganization Act of 1934, were reaffirmed by the U.S. Congress to possess a "preference right" to employment within a federal agency. Although this preference right was only valid in employment in the Bureau of Indian Affairs, section 6 of the IRA expanded Indian preference in hiring to Indian and non-Indian logging companies by setting "a sliding scale for the reduction of contract prices for Indian timber where the purchaser employs Indian labor in the logging operations, the reduction being proportionate to the percentage of Indian labor employed."[27] Thus, the more Indian laborers a logging company employed, the lower the cost of timber purchased from federally managed Indian lands.

Discrimination against white employees of the Bureau of Indian Affairs did not appear to be the issue when it came to those who opposed Indian preference. Opponents of the IRA felt that sections of the legislation, such as Indian preference, sought "to set Indians apart as a separate race; meaning only continued segregations and the fostering of race prejudice."[28] They also argued that "increased Indian appointments would be at an increased cost to taxpayers and would only leave the power where it had always been, in the hands of the Commissioner of Indian Affairs and the Secretary of Interior."[29]

Commissioner of Indian Affairs John Collier, in an article entitled "Indians at Work" (in *Survey Graphic* for June 1934) expanded Indian preference as defined under section 13 of the IRA to include "a special Indian civil service in which [Indian] communities may appoint their qualified members for any position of local Indian service, and power of recall over local government employees is given to the communities."[30] Collier's interpretation of Indian preference under section 13 of the IRA set the stage for tribal governments to have a much greater impact on all hiring decisions upon their particular reservations.

INDIAN PREFERENCE AND CASE LAW

Even with the statutory enactment of Indian preference, "for reasons not entirely clear," the Interior Department did not enforce the provisions dealing with Indian preference in promotions. As time passed, these important Indian rights remained on the books virtually unnoticed.[31] All Indian commissioners since Collier at the inception of the IRA had made sure that Indians were favored at their initial hiring, but they had not given them preference in further promotions.[32] Consequently, although the percentage of Indians in the Bureau of Indian Affairs had risen from 34 percent in 1934 to 57 percent in 1972, few Indians had risen into positions of responsibility.[33]

Under pressure from Indian leaders who asserted these long-neglected rights of Indian preference in promotion as provided in the Wheeler-Howard Act, the commissioner of Indian Affairs, Louis Bruce, in 1972 convinced the secretary of Interior, Rogers Morton, to institute Indian preference to promotions within the BIA.[34]

Many of the most perplexing problems in Indian law involve the rights of non-Indians. Soon after Bruce's initiation of Indian preference at the BIA, the civil rights of non-Indians came under review of the Court when the Indian preference provision of section 12 of the Indian Reorganization Act of 1934 was challenged by non-Indian employees of the bureau, who claimed that the preference was contrary to the antidiscrimination provisions of the Equal Employment Opportunity Act of 1972 and violated the due process clause of the Fifth Amendment. The plaintiffs claimed that Indian preference was a racial preference which denied them due process and equal protection of the laws.[35]

A three-judge federal district court which was convened in the U.S. District Court for the District of New Mexico concluded "that the preference was implicitly repealed by section 11 of the Equal Employment Opportunity Act of 1972 proscribing discrimination in most federal employment on the basis of race."[36]

On appeal, the U.S. Supreme Court reversed and remanded.[37] In an opinion by Blackmun, expressing the unanimous view of the court, it was held that the Indian employment preference (1) "was not repealed by the Equal Employment Opportunities Act of 1972" and (2) "did not constitute an invidious racial discrimination in violation of the due process clause of the Fifth Amendment."

In *Morton v. Mancari*, the Court identified a long legislative relationship between Indians and the U.S. Congress and stated that the federal policy of according some hiring preference to Indians in the Indian service dates at least back to an 1834 Congressional Act mandating that "in all cases of the appointments of interpreters or other persons employed for the benefit of the Indians, a preference shall be given to persons of Indian descent, if such can be found, who are properly qualified for the execution of the duties."[38]

Since that time, Congress repeatedly has enacted various Indian preferences for the employment of clerical, mechanical, and other help on reservations and about agencies.[39] These have also involved the employment of herders, teamsters, and laborers, "and where practicable in all other employments" in the Indian service,[40] employment as matrons, farmers, and industrial teachers in Indian schools.[41] Moreover, Congress called for a general preference as to "Indian labor and products of Indian industry."[42]

The Court found "that the purpose of these preferences, as variously expressed in the legislative history, has been to give Indians a greater participation in their own self-government";[43] "to further the Government's trust obligation toward Indian tribes";[44] and "to reduce the negative effect of having non-Indians administer matters that affect Indian tribal life."[45]

It is against this background that the Court found that Indian preference had not been repealed by the Equal Employment Opportunity Act of 1972.

Referring to Title VII of the Civil Rights Act of 1964 as the first major piece of federal legislation prohibiting discrimination in private employment on the basis of "race, color, religion, sex, or national origin," the Court found that sections 701(b) and 703(i) of the act "explicitly exempted from its coverage the preferential employment of Indians by Indian tribes or by industries located on or near Indian reservations."[46]

The exemption under Title VII revealed to the Court "a clear congressional recognition within the framework of Title VII, of the unique legal status of tribal and reservation-based activities." The 1964 Civil Rights Act did not specifically outlaw employment discrimination by the federal government, yet the mechanism for enforcing long-standing executive orders forbidding government discrimination had proved ineffective. In order to remedy this, Congress, by the 1972 Equal Employment Opportunity Act, amended the 1964 Civil Rights Act and proscribed discrimination in most areas of the federal government.[47]

The Court concluded "that although the 1972 Act was designed to correct discriminatory hiring practices in the Federal government, including the BIA, nowhere in the legislative history of the Act is there any mention of Indian preference. . . . In fact, three months after the 1972 Act, Congress enacted two new Indian preference laws." These were part of the Education Amendments of 1972.[48] "The new laws explicitly required that Indians be given preference in Government programs for training teachers of Indian children. . . . It is improbable, to say the least, that the same Congress which affirmatively approved and enacted these additional and similar Indian preferences was, at the same time, condemning the BIA preference as racially discriminatory. . . . We therefore hold that the District Court erred in ruling that the Indian preference was repealed by the 1972 Act."[49]

In regard to the appellees' contention that Indian preference constitutes invidious racial discrimination, the Court, for the first time, "described the relationship of Indians to the federal government as political rather than racial."[50] Harry Blackmun's opinion for the unanimous court pointed out that:

Literally every piece of legislation dealing with Indian tribes and reservations, and certainly all legislation dealing with the BIA, single out for special treatment a constituency of tribal Indians living on or near reservations. If these laws, derived from historical relationships and explicitly designed to help only Indians, were deemed invidious racial discrimination, an entire Title of the United States Code (25 USC) [25 USCS] would be effectively erased and the solemn commitment of the Government towards the Indians would be jeopardized. It is in this historical and legal context that the constitutional validity of the Indian preference is to be determined.[51]

The opinion of the Court expressed the belief that "Indian preference does not constitute racial discrimination. . . . It is not even a racial preference. . . . Rather, it is an employment criterion reasonably designed to further the cause of Indian self-government and to make the BIA more responsive to the needs of its constituent groups to much the same degree as the constitutional requirement (Art I, § 3, cl 3) that a U.S. Senator, when elected, be an inhabitant of the state for which he or she shall be chosen. . . . The preference as applied is granted to Indians not as a discrete racial group, but rather, as members of quasi-sovereign tribal entities whose lives and activities are governed by the BIA in a unique fashion. . . . In this sense there is no other group of people favored in this manner and the preference applies only to employment of the Indian service and is not a blanket exemption for Indians from all civil service examinations."[52]

"On numerous previous occasions the Court specifically upheld legislation that singles out Indians for particular and special treatment. . . . As long as the special treatment can be tied rationally to the fulfillment of Congress' unique obligation toward the Indian, such legislative judgments will not be disturbed. . . . Where Indian preference is reasonable and rationally designed to further Indian self-government, the Court cannot say that Congress' classification violates due process."[53]

With the sanction of the Court, Indian preference became the norm among the Bureau of Indian Affairs, Indian Health Service, and other federal Indian agencies. Non-Indian employees in these federal agencies saw their chances of advancement nullified by Indian preference and began lobbying for legislation that would permit them to retire early with full benefits or transfer with preference to other federal agencies. Congress attempted to provide relief in 1976 when it enacted an early retirement bill for non-Indian employees. However, the legislation was vetoed in September by the president.[54]

Since the mid–1970s, Congress has included Indian preference in the enabling legislation of federal Indian agencies. Most recent was the Indian Education Amendments of 1988, which established an Office of Indian Education in the Department of Education and contains an Indian preference section that reads as follows: "All professional staff within the Office of Indian Education shall have experience with Indian education programs. The Secretary shall give preference to Indians in all personnel actions within the Office of Indian Education."[55]

In 1990 the General Accounting Office (GAO) indicated that federal agencies that have an Indian component, such as the Department of Education, often find that Indian preference may impact the affirmative employment and recruitment plans of other minorities. For example, in fiscal year 1989, Health and Human Services (HHS) found that the percentage of Hispanic employees in HHS in Region VIII, which encompasses the states of Colo-

rado, Montana, North and South Dakota, Utah, and Wyoming, was 6 percent. This was below the percentage of Hispanics in the region, which was
6.7 percent. This finding made it appear that HHS was not actively recruiting
Hispanic employees.[56]

HHS realized that as of September 30, 1989, 907 of the 1,266 Indian
Health Service (IHS) employees in the region were Indians. This large group
of Indian employees constituted nearly 33 percent of the total work force of
HHS in that region. HHS concluded that in order to "accurately" identify
their Hispanic work force percentage, IHS should be excluded because of
the Indian preference requirements of that single component of HHS. When
IHS was excluded, the percentage of Hispanic employees in HHS rose to
10.3 percent in the region. Therefore, in order to take into account both
the political rights of American Indians and the affirmative action status of
Hispanics, data concerning the IHS workforce was excluded.[57]

THE EXPANSION OF INDIAN PREFERENCE

Legally, Title VII and *Morton v. Mancari* sanction the political right of
the individual Indian to preference in hiring by federal Indian agencies and
employers on and near tribal lands. Practically, Indian preference has expanded beyond the federal government, the tribes, and nearby employers
to Indian organizations such as urban Indian Centers, Native American
Banks, Indian Art Councils, and Indian Law Firms, which may or may not
possess the legal or statutory status that would entitle such organizations to
implement Indian preference in hiring. In many such cases Indian applicants
receive preference based on tribal enrollment, which gives the applicant
additional points on employment tests, or positive consideration based on
knowledge of Indian culture and values.[58]

Such cultural preference is seen by Indian employers as a necessary qualification in order to work with Indian people or affairs. As Robin Bear of the
Winnebago Tribe of Nebraska pointed out, "The Non-Indian usually doesn't
understand the culture and beliefs of Indians . . . [or] understand the cultural
differences between Indians and Non-Indians."[59]

Because Indian groups are a "minority" within the larger non-Indian culture, Indian values are often misunderstood, stereotyped, or subjected to a
variety of prejudices by mainstream American culture. DuBray found that
unbiased and specific studies about American Indian cultural values are rare
in American colleges and universities. As a result, non-Indians who possess
academic degrees in such areas as social work, education, government, law,
medicine, business, and even engineering still do not possess the necessary
knowledge of Indian culture that is necessary to work with Indian clients.[60]

Whereas Section 703 (i) of Title VII of the Civil Rights Act of 1964 allows
for Indian preference on or near an Indian reservation, many tribes have
taken Indian preference one step further in implementing tribal preference

in hiring. Thus, an Indian who is an enrolled member of the hiring tribe will be given preference over Indians from other tribes.[61]

The following tribal job announcements are examples of direct and indirect tribal preference:

Yankton Sioux Tribe, Marty, South Dakota, Associate Social Worker, Indian preference policy will be in effect, preferably enrolled Yankton Social members.[62]

Cheyenne River Sioux Tribe, Eagle Butte, South Dakota, Associate Judge, Homebase Visitor, Community Youth Counselor, Jailer, Teaching Assistant, Teacher, Substance Abuse Counselor, Computer Clerk, Mental Health Technician and Health/Nutrition Counselor, CHEYENNE RIVER SIOUX TRIBAL MEMBERS ARE ENCOURAGED TO APPLY.[63]

Oglala Sioux Tribe, Pine Ridge, South Dakota, Police Officer. If Indian Preference is claimed, a certificate of Blood Degree or Tribal Affiliation must accompany the application.[64]

Since tribal enrollment records are kept by the tribal enrollment office, it is very easy for the tribal government or other tribal hiring entity to identify whether applicants for specific jobs are tribal members.[65]

There are positive reasons for tribal preference: Since many Indian reservations are fairly segregated communities with their own cultural identity, tribal preference promotes the hiring of tribal members who are viewed by the other tribal members as possessing a greater degree of tribally sensitive knowledge than Indians from other tribes.[66] Moreover, tribal preference promotes the maintenance of particular tribal practices and institutions by protecting them from the external effects of non-Indian or other tribal values and beliefs.[67] Interaction among tribes has occurred for thousands of years and continues today, so the impact that tribal preference may have on the cultural identity is very limited but still noteworthy, especially in tribes such as the Navajo or Pueblo, where being able to speak the tribal language is essential. Ability to speak a particular tribal language or possession of adequate cultural knowledge may limit the employment pool for a particular position to members of that tribe only.[68] Tribal preference may also allow the tribal government to have a direct impact on the unemployment rate of its particular reservation by hiring tribal members who are unemployed.[69]

There may also be some less positive reasons for tribal preference. Tribal preference may promote nepotism in allowing tribal officials to hire relatives, and it may allow tribal officials to hire members of the tribe who are more supportive of the political positions of the tribal government than other members of the tribe.[70]

CONCLUSION

Tribalism in the United States stems from ancient, nonfederal sources, but it has become entwined within our federal system of government. The Supreme Court articulated the responsibility for Indians with the federal government, with the former becoming the wards of the latter. The guardian, faced with few practical constraints, holds nearly full sway in its ability to either sap or energize Indian sovereignty.[71]

In the various constitutional articles that have been cited to justify the federal involvement with the Indians, we find the allocation by the framers of the Constitution of different functions to different branches of the national government. Only Congress, in the Commerce Clause (article I, section 8), has been specifically empowered to deal with Indians, and consequently, both the executive and judicial branches have become accustomed to allowing Congress to take the lead in determining Indian policy and to look to congressional intent in formulating their own ideas about the rights of Indians and the responsibilities of the federal government.[72]

Such is the case with Indian preference, where the Court, as the arbiter of Indian sovereignty, has interpreted such preference as a special treatment which can be rationally tied to the fulfillment of the unique political obligation of Congress toward Indians, and thus is a political right of the individual Indian rather than a special privilege of a racial group.[73]

In acknowledging the political right of Indians through preference in hiring, not only did the Court apply a constitutional test to Indian legislation, it also defined the relationship between the tribes and the federal government in a new way.[74] The Court defined the congressional intention, in Title VII (as amended in 1972) and previous legislation, as preserving the political relationship between the tribe and the federal government. At last, a constitutional yardstick had been fashioned that might be used to preserve tribal rights. The Court's reaffirmation of Indian preference energized Indian sovereignty, and it is no accident that following *Mancari*, the Interior Department began describing the relationship between tribes and the U.S. government as one of "government to government."[75]

Thus, Indian preference does not discriminate against other minority, ethnic, or racial groups. Instead, Indian preference is derived from the very heart of tribal sovereignty, that being the right of Indians to preserve their separate cultural and political identity from encroachment by both the majority population and other minority, ethnic, and racial groups in America. Moreover, it is a right that many American Indians see as necessary to their future existence as a tribal people.

NOTES

1. Act of July 2, 1964, P.L. 88–352, 78 Stat. 253.
2. P.L. 88–352, § 701 (b) 78 Stat. 253 (1964).

3. See Article VI, cl. 2, "all Treaties made . . . shall be the Supreme Law of the Land," and Article I, cl. 2, "and excluding Indians not taxed."

4. Charles F. Wilkinson, *American Indians, Time, and the Law* (New Haven, Conn.: Yale University Press, 1987), p. 103.

5. 21 U.S. (8 Wheat.) 543 (1823).

6. 30 U.S. (5 Pet.) 1 (1831).

7. Vine Deloria, Jr., and Clifford M. Lytle, *American Indians, American Justice* (Austin: University of Texas Press, 1983), p. 26; see also Wilkinson, *American Indians*, p. 55.

8. 31 U.S. (6 Pet.) 515 (1832).

9. Deloria and Lytle, *American Indians*, p. 32; see also Wilkinson, *American Indians*, pp. 55–56.

10. The Cherokees won the *Worcester* case, but Marshall's worst fears were realized. On hearing of the decision, President Andrew Jackson is reported to have remarked, "John Marshall has made his decision: now let him enforce it." Deprived of any real federal protection, the Cherokees reluctantly signed the Treaty of New Echota in 1835 and began their mournful march west on the Trail of Tears. See Deloria and Lytle, *American Indians*, p. 33.

11. Ibid., pp. 32–33; see also Wilkinson, *American Indians*, p. 56.

12. Wilkinson, *American Indians*, p. 53.

13. *Congressional Record* 12723, 1964.

14. U.S. Department of the Interior, Bureau of Indian Affairs, *American Indians, U.S. Indian Policy, Tribes and Reservations, BIA: Past and Present Economic Development* (Washington, D.C.: U.S. Government Printing Office, 1984), p. 24.

15. Andrew Ebona, "Federal Government Policies and Indian Goals of Self-Government," in *Pathways to Self-Determination*, ed. Leroy Little Bear, Menno Boldt, and J. Anthony Long (Toronto: University of Toronto Press, 1984), p. 90.

16. 430 U.S. 641 (1977).

17. 417 U.S. 535 (1974).

18. Deloria and Lytle, *American Indians*, p. 228.

19. Vine Deloria, Jr., "Higher Education and Self-Determination," *Winds of Change* 6, no. 1 (1991): 19.

20. Act of June 18, 1934, P.L. 73–383, 48 Stat. 984; also see *Congressional Record* 7139, 1979.

21. P.L. 73–383, § 13, 48 Stat 986, 25 USC § 472 (1934).

22. *Congressional Record* 11729, 1934.

23. Ibid.

24. Ibid., 11739.

25. Ibid., 11737.

26. Ibid., 11731.

27. Ibid., 11730.

28. Ibid., 11734.

29. Ibid., 11735.

30. Ibid., 10776.

31. *Congressional Record* 6841, 1975.

32. James E. Officer, "The Indian Service and Its Evolution," in *The Aggressions of Civilization*, ed. Sandra L. Cadwalader and Vine Deloria, Jr. (Philadelphia: Temple University Press, 1984), p. 94.

33. *Congressional Record* 6841, 1975.

34. See *Freeman v. Morton*, U.S. App. DC, 499 F2d (1974).

35. Alvin J. Ziontz, "Indian Litigation," in Cadwalader and Deloria, *Aggressions of Civilization*, p. 166.

36. 42 USCS § 2000e–16 (a) and 359 F Supp 585.

37. See *Morton v Mancari*, 417 US 535 (1974).

38. Act of June 30, 1834, § 9, 4 Stat 737, 25 USC 45 [25 USCS 45].

39. Act of May 17, 1882, § 6, 22 Stat 88; and Act of July 4, 1884, § 6, 23 Stat 97, [25 USCS § 46] 25 USC § 46 [25 USCS § 46].

40. Act of Aug. 15, 1894, § 10, 28 Stat 313, 25 USC § 44 [25 USCS § 44].

41. Act of June 7, 1897, § 1, 30 Stat 83, 25 USC § 274 [25 USCS § 274].

42. Act of June 25, 1910, § 23, 36 Stat 861, 25 USC § 47 [25 USCS § 47].

43. Hearings before Senate Committee on Indian Affairs, 73d Congress, 2d sess., pt. 2, p. 256 (1934).

44. HR Rep No. 1804, 73d Cong, 2d Sess, 8 (1934).

45. HR Rep No. 474, 23d Cong, 1st Sess, 98 (1834).

46. 417 US 546 (1974).

47. 417 US 547 (1974).

48. 20 USC §§ 887c (a) and (d), and § 1119a (1970 ed Supp II).

49. 417 US 544 & 549 (1974).

50. Deloria and Lytle, *American Indians*, p. 239.

51. 417 US 553 (1974).

52. 417 US 554 (1974).

53. 417 US 555 (1974).

54. Officer, "The Indian Service," p. 92.

55. 25 USC 2001, Sec 5341 (c) (1) (A).

56. U.S. General Accounting Office, Health and Human Services Department, *Hispanic Representation and Equal Employment Practices in Region VIII* (GAO/HRD–91–6, Washington, D.C.: U.S. Government Printing Office, November 1990).

57. Ibid.

58. John Echohawk, Executive Director, Native American Rights Fund, Boulder, Colorado, phone interview by author, January 1991.

59. Robin Bear, "Commentary," *Winnebago Indian News* (Winnebago, Nebraska), 10 January 1991, p. 2.

60. W. H. DuBray, "American Indian Values: Critical Factor in Casework," *Social Casework*, 66, no. 1 (1985): 30–37.

61. Cora Jones, Agency Superintendent, Bureau of Indian Affairs, Rosebud Agency, Rosebud, South Dakota, phone interview by author, November 1990.

62. "Jobs," *Lakota Times* (Rapid City, South Dakota), 15 January 1991, p. 10.

63. Ibid.

64. Ibid.

65. Fred LeRoy, Director, Northern Ponca Restoration Committee, Tribal Enrollment, Omaha, Nebraska, phone interview by author, December 1990.

66. Concerning the tribes' separate cultural identities, see Ebona, "Federal Government Policies," p. 90.

67. Saunie Wilson, Administrator, Loneman School, Oglala, South Dakota, interview by author, August 1991.

68. Jones interview.

69. LeRoy interview.

70. LeRoy interview; Echohawk interview.

71. Wilkinson, *American Indians*, p. 86.

72. Deloria and Lytle, *American Indians*, p. 34.

73. Vine Deloria, Jr., "Congress in Its Wisdom," in Cadwalader and Deloria, *The Aggressions of Civilization*, p. 117.

74. Ziontz, "Indian Litigation," p. 166.

75. Ibid.

PART II

Economic Development and Self-Governance

8

The Redefinition of Property Rights in American Indian Reservations: A Comparative Analysis of Native American Economic Development

Joseph P. Kalt and Stephen Cornell

American Indians are the most impoverished minority in the United States. At the same time, American Indian reservations are subject to unique legal and economic status, constituting what have been termed "nations within" a nation. After a century of dependence and subjugation, this status is undergoing dramatic change. American Indian reservations are achieving (or being subjected to, depending on one's point of view) sharply increased possibilities for self-determination. In the face of changing federal funding priorities, the economic well-being of many American Indians hinges increasingly on the tribes' own responses to these possibilities.

Beginning with a major policy statement in the Nixon administration and accelerating during the Carter and Reagan administrations, American Indians' assertions of their rights have been manifested in the specific policy of political and economic self-determination. Some reservations have responded by turning themselves into the equivalent of economic enterprise zones, offering (with widely varying success) tax and regulatory havens to outside investors. Some have become the equivalent of medium-to-large corporations, issuing financial instruments in the world capital markets and explicitly adopting corporate strategy and management practices. Indeed, tribes such as the Mescalero and White Mountain Apaches have become premier "private" managers of multiple-use forest resource economies. Still other reservations, however, have intentionally or unintentionally avoided raising the prominence of economic development strategies in tribal affairs, or else have chosen strategies with lower profiles and less ambitious goals.

Recent legal, political, and economic upheavals in Indian Country have meant renewed attention to economic affairs. The Reagan administration has produced two major reports on paths to Indian economic self-determination.

Tribes themselves have formed planning consortia and intertribal research organizations to develop and share accumulating knowledge on relevant economic and sociopolitical matters. Tribal councils, tribal members, and tribal newspapers are debating the dimensions of economic self-determination with increased urgency, as federal budget cuts and greater Indian responsibility place an unprecedented level of the economic and sociological opportunity costs of tribal decisions on the tribes themselves.

The central change in Indian economic affairs that self-determination has brought is that, for the first time, development programs are being designed and directed by Indian tribes instead of the federal government. Various tribes have launched projects ranging from ski resorts, mineral extraction, and forest and wildlife harvesting to industrial parks, on-reservation factories, and well-known gaming operations. There are signs that some versions of self-determination are meeting with sustainable economic success on at least some reservations. With varying degrees of solvency, a listing of substantial Indian enterprises includes the following:

—The Cherokees of Oklahoma own and operate an electronics manufacturing plant.

—The Passamoquoddy Tribe of Maine recently purchased the nation's largest cement plant and have now sold it at several times purchase price.

—The Mescalero Apaches of New Mexico and the White Mountain Apaches of Arizona each own and operate large lumber industries, ski resorts, and fee-hunting and -fishing industries. The Mescaleros also own and operate a golf course.

—The Quinault, Lummi, Swinomish, and several other tribes in the Northwest and Alaska own and operate fish canneries.

—The Blackfeet of Montana are a major player in the market for writing instruments.

—The Oneidas of Wisconsin, the Gilas of Arizona, and several other tribes own and operate office and industrial parks serving major metropolitan areas.

—The Warm Springs reservation in Oregon owns and operates a major sawmill and a large tourist resort.

—More than a hundred tribes operate bingo casinos, with seating capacities often in the thousands and revenues approaching the millions.

—The Choctaw of Mississippi own and operate a factory specializing in electrical wire harnesses for the auto industry, as well as a greeting card company.

Current circumstances have created a need and also an opportunity for research—and this chapter is a report on a research program in progress. The need arises from the demand by tribes and policymakers for answers to such questions as: Should the federal Bureau of Indian Affairs (BIA) be manager or consultant, or even a complete nonparty, to Indian businesses? Should tribal governments try to develop and own enterprises, or should they encourage tribal members or outside investors to bring business to the reservations? Should tribes rely on nonmembers to hold key managerial positions? How can tribes or tribal members gain access to capital markets?

The opportunity for research arises because the deciphering of the determinants of success and failure—and the definitions of *success* and *failure* as well—among American Indian tribes provides potentially profound insights into the sources of the wealth of nations, along with lessons that are applicable far beyond Native Americans. The move toward greater self-determination that is now taking place provides a unique context in which to observe a large number of poor, developing economies as they: (a) make selections over their governmental structures, (b) face cultural and political tensions brought on by economic change, (c) deal with the ancillary sociological and political effects of economic growth, and (d) implement investment and employment policies that are increasingly subject to marketplace tests of success. What is it, for example, that has allowed tribes such as the White Mountain Apaches and the Mescalero Apaches to arrive at governmental, managerial, political, and cultural structures that yield bursts of economic development, while other tribes show economic stagnation? How much does economic development depend on cultural, political, and governmental factors, and how endogenous are these factors in the face of economic forces? What lessons are there in the answers to these sorts of questions for the prospects of non-Indian developing economies, or even the prospects of the United States, the world's most developed economy, as it attempts to remain competitive in the world economy?

Phrased in these ways (i.e., as a topic in broadly conceived development economics), the issue of American Indian economic development obviously cannot be fully analyzed in a single study. Accordingly, this chapter has a much narrower goal: to tell some interesting stories that serve to generate a set of tentative hypotheses of relevance to the kinds of questions noted above. In fact, we would like to emphasize that any answers put forth are hardly definitive and are rather intended to provoke thought. Moreover, the "stories" to which we refer primarily concern the case experiences of tribes that we have been able to examine in some detail. Case studies provide the impetus for hypotheses; they do not result in convincing tests of theories. Anything said here that sounds like a generalized conclusion applicable to all tribes, at all times, and/or for all developing economies is primarily a reflection of our own inability to resist temptation. However, if the voyage of the *Beagle* taught us anything about method, it should be that starting in the field with cases can sometimes produce unusually useful hypotheses.

THE CHANGING PROPERTY RIGHTS OF AMERICAN INDIAN TRIBES

A revolution is taking place in the legal status of American Indian lands. The essential thrust of this revolution is the effective deregulation of broad classes of economic activity on Indian reservations. This has come about, in large part, as a result of the Indians' own aggressive assertions, over the last fifteen to twenty years, of their treaty and civil rights to self-determination and self-government. The resulting changes, which were won through many battles in the courts, administrative agencies, and legislatures, have significantly unraveled the historic (not to mention, demeaning) legal status of Indians as official wards of the federal government.[1]

The component of the Indian activist movement that probably has received the most attention from the news media has been the assertion of off-reservation claims to either compensation for the loss of traditional or treated tribal properties or the establishment of exclusive rights of use over such properties.[2] The legal and political wrangling that these developments have generated has indeed been newsworthy, and the resulting policy decisions undoubtedly have been economically significant to the parties involved. However, the changes in American Indian policy that are, or will be, most important and enduring are the alterations that are taking place in Indians' *on-reservation* rights.

The clear trend in public policy since the 1960s has consisted of de facto and de jure transfers of property rights in reservations away from federal and state governmental units and toward the tribes themselves.[3] The term *property rights* is used here in its economic, rather than legal, sense. That is, *property rights* here refers to the identity of the parties that, in fact, exercise decision making control over resources or actions (see next section, "Changing Rights and Changing Opportunities"). It is this control that is effectively being transferred, albeit in fits and starts and often with strings attached, to the various Indian tribes.

Many American Indian reservations are coming to resemble so-called enterprise zones. For many purposes, reservations now occupy the status of independent state governments. They are, for example, substantially free of state-level economic, environmental, and related regulation, as well as being exempt from state taxation of on-reservation tribal income and property.[4] The tribes themselves have powers of self-taxation, as well as the ability to levy fees and taxes (such as severance taxes) on the export of tribal resources. In addition, most tribes have broad powers of self-government, including the capacities to institute regulation of intratribal commerce and relations, adopt rules of property transfer and inheritance, and establish legislatures, courts, and police forces.[5]

With regard to economic development, Indian tribes have had the right since the 1930s to establish federally chartered corporations for the management of tribal enterprises. Historically, however, the Bureau of Indian Affairs has been the primary holder of property rights (i.e., the primary decision maker) in economic projects for most reservations. American Indian reservations are formally held in trust by the federal government, with the BIA serving as the primary administrator of the government's trust responsibility.

In order to affirm and direct a federal policy that was announced in 1970 to support Indian autonomy, the federal government adopted the Indian Self-Determination and Education Assistance Act of 1975. This has gradually altered the governmental role in Indian management. The role and the authority of the BIA are now in flux and vary considerably from tribe to tribe. Nevertheless, there has been a clear trend toward greater autonomy for the individual tribes. While the BIA maintains administrative authority over Indian reservations, on at least some reservations its de facto role appears to be evolving toward that of advisor, contract consultant, and funding source. As a recent Interior Department task force put it: "The Role of the Federal Government is . . . gradually changing from that of "guardian" to that of "mentor." The government can provide technical Assistance and advice on how to make reservation environments more supportive and attractive to business. But it cannot require—nor should it—that Indians accept this advice" (Department of the Interior, *Report of the Task Force on American Indian Economic Development* [Draft], p. v–5). Primary decision-making authority over investment, labor policy, marketing, pricing, and production increasingly resides with the individual tribes (or individual tribal members) *when demand for such authority is asserted.*

In the natural resource sector, which is of particular importance to many tribes, it is now the stated policy of the federal government that "tribal governments have the responsibility to determine the extent and the methods of developing the tribe's natural resources. The federal government's responsibility should not be used to hinder tribes from taking advantage of economic development opportunities."[6]

The implied solidification of tribes' property rights to the natural resources on their reservations is not illusory. Since they are formally under BIA jurisdiction, reservations' lumber, mining, and grazing activities generally are not subject to the planning of such agencies as the U.S. Forest Service, the National Park Service, or the Bureau of Land Management (BLM), the federal bodies with primary management responsibility for public lands of the type occupied by many Indian reservations. Similarly, with regard to wildlife-related matters, legal decisions reached in the 1970s and early 1980s have allowed tribes to throw off any vestiges of regulatory responsibility from state game and fish departments (which otherwise have authority for the regulation of fishing and hunting activities within a state).[7] The result is that the policy move to self-management of natural resources has taken American Indian reservations a long distance toward the status of private businesses— at least in their relations with the off-reservation world—and away from the status of publicly managed lands. As the American Indian National Bank observes: "Tribes today can be viewed as ethnic land-owning communities and as "quasi-corporations" responsible for the investment of tribal resources, [and] for managing those resources."[8]

Indeed, to the (hard-to-quantify) extent that Indian autonomy has had the effect of insulating some reservations from the oversight of federal and state regulatory authorities that regulate the private sector (e.g., the Environ-mental Protection Agency, the Occupational Health and Safety Administra-tion, the National Labor Relations Board, state gaming commissions, state and municipal zoning authorities, etc.), some American Indian tribes have enjoyed more extensive, complete, and secure property titles than private companies. That is, in a number of important respects, reservations are more "deregulated"—at least with respect to nontribal governments—than the vast bulk of the rest of the economy. This creates niches in the market that present American Indian tribes with classic opportunities for the exercise of comparative advantage. The question, of course, is how, and how well, tribes can respond to these opportunities.

CHANGING RIGHTS AND CHANGING OPPORTUNITIES

The Underlying Reality of Native American Economic Development

Before turning to a description of some of the current cases of Indian economic development, it is important to understand the setting of these stories. It is difficult to exaggerate the overall depressed state of Native American economic development, or the sorry history of associated public policies.[9] Unemployment rates on reservations commonly exceed 50 percent, and many reservations run at rates of 80–90 percent unemployment year after year. On some reservations, the only real employment is working in a government-funded office that delivers necessary social services to the un-employed. Along with the lack of economic opportunity for individuals comes accentuated socioeconomic problems of crime, familial instability, alcohol-ism, mental illness, and so forth.

On most reservations, the majority of investment dollars for enterprise development comes from the Bureau of Indian Affairs through grant and direct guaranteed loan programs. Default and/or forced refinancing rates on the latter are quite high; about one-third of the BIA's loans are overdue, nonperforming, or in default.[10] Federal attempts at business creation have a long and embarrassing history of "white elephant disease"; moreover, some analysts have asserted that, at least until very recently, there was not a single case of a successful reservation-based business of significant size that could withstand the market's profit-and-loss test in the absence of targeted governmental subsidy. Even now, it may be that the number of significant enterprises operating with stand-alone success may number in the single digits.

Despite tax advantages and niches in the market, many tribes and tribal members find it extremely difficult to attract capital. Perceived and, not uncommonly, real instability and opportunism on the part of tribal govern-ments and the BIA combine with the absence of track records to scare off investors. On the flip side, many tribes and tribal members have been burned so frequently and so severely by the proverbial fast-talking outsider that they are reluctant to pursue outside credit or equity capital, not to mention outside management and expertise.

Finally, the federal government and, particularly, the BIA are omnipresent, if not omnipotent. American Indian reservations remain, en masse, heavily dependent on public funding of social services—and none appears anxious to sever this pipeline. The amount of social service funding (e.g., per capita) does not appear to decline as one looks toward tribes with evidence of economic vitality. Many reservations' economic affairs are, for all intents and purposes, run by the BIA, which routinely takes upon itself the role of official trustee to negotiate contracts, determine resource utilization, manage financial records and accounts, veto or approve investment decisions, hire and fire labor, and otherwise direct and control reservation businesses.[11] As a result, any impression that the "new era" of Indian self-determination has transformed all reservations into bustling enclaves of *Indian-run* enterprises and tribal self-sufficiency is false.

Shifting the Opportunity Costs of Economic Development

While aggregate statistics do not paint a rosy picture, there is *something* new happening in reservation economic development. The essence appears to be this: the combination of more secure property rights, the access to (potentially) profitable market niches, and the de facto ability to wrest control of tribal resources from federal and state governments has meant that the tribes themselves are increasingly bearing the opportunity costs of their investment and management decisions.

Throughout most of their history, American Indian reservations have served as the mechanism by which non-Indian society has "kept" Indians. While original functions, such a incarceration, may have gone by the way, reservations have continued to receive bare minimum levels of subsistence support from the public sector but have held no secure *self*-controlled assets on which to build economies. Increasingly, however, tribes have accumulated assets—even if they are only the intangible assets of relative freedom from certain kinds of state and federal regulation. Thus, increasingly, a tribe's failure to take advantage of economic opportunities imposes a cost on that tribe in the form of the forgone returns from those opportunities. Some tribes (or tribal councils) may consciously choose not to act in the face of such opportunity costs.[12] As the present turmoil in the economic development strategies of tribe after tribe demonstrates, however, tribes do change and attempt to adapt.

This "opportunity cost" perspective is important because it suggests the testable prediction that the frequency of successful economic ventures should be on the rise—finally. The implication of the perspective is that the tribes

themselves are increasingly both central decision makers and residual claim-
ants. That is, they can both make decisions and, if they turn a profit, keep
the returns themselves; and it is the prospect of the latter that motivates
quality in the former. In previous times, this link was all but nonexistent,
as fundamental decision-making power lay with federal bureaucracies (especially the BIA) and bureaucrats:

Anecdote: The historic records of the White Mountain Apaches of Arizona, like those
         of so many tribes, recount as standard operating procedure that tribal
         council meetings were routinely conducted with the BIA superintendent
         seated next to the tribal chairman and that momentous decisions were
         turned over to the BIA because "it knows more than we do."

The public sector authorities may have been benevolently motivated, but
they were forbidden by law from keeping the returns to sound economic
decisions. Without the prospect of meaningful reward, and in the face of
some perverse incentives to "sell" poverty to the U.S. Congress (described
below), it is not terribly surprising that bureaucracy-based economic development has met with little success.
    The 1960s witnessed a surge of Great Society federal funds and programs
aimed at economic development on American Indian reservations. The con-
sequence was large numbers of BIA, Economic Development Administration, and related agency projects, ranging from hotel and motel construction
to small manufacturing facilities. Despite the appearance of overly simplistic
caricature, it seems that a fair assessment of these projects is that, by and
large, they were trendy and socially conscious, but economically hopeless,
publicly funded boondoggles ("Quite a few reservations have pretty scenery,
so let's promote tourism by building motels.") that end up as make-work
projects where employees far outnumber guests.[13] Then, too, the sorry, but
documented, history of neocolonial thefts of many reservations' natural resources took place within the context of BIA and other agency contract
negotiation, royalty systems, and management plans:[14]

Anecdote: The White Mountain Apaches recently received judgment against the
         BIA for mismanagement of the Fort Apache reservation.[15] Beginning in
         1916 and continuing well past World War II, extensive measures were
         taken by the BIA to increase water runoff from the reservation to the city
         of Phoenix. These included the grazing by non-Indians of over 100,000
         animals on range contemporaneously estimated to have a carrying capacity
         of 41,000, increasing the allowable timber cut far in excess of contem-
         poraneously assessed sustainable yield, and employing various "vegetation
         management" practices (cottonwood eradication, brush chaining, and
         burning) designed to maximize the yield of but one of the reservation's
         forest products: water.

However, times are changing. The gradual solidification of Indian economic rights now means that some tribes routinely ignore BIA-directed levels of resource harvest, some tribes aggressively reject or do "end runs" around BIA-negotiated business contracts, some tribes hide economic development and investment plans from the federal authorities for as long as possible, and some individually undertake investment projects that exceed BIA's entire capital grant budget.

Anecdote: The White Mountain Apaches now routinely exclude the BIA from important tribal council meetings.

It is in this kind of environment that Native American businesses and tribal reservations are now operating. The tenor of relations between tribes and the federal government may vary from pleasant to hostile, but the move toward autonomy is real.

Perspectives on the Policy Debate: Routes to Development

The move toward Indian economic self-determination is really a move away from the BIA (and the federal government). In reading through the mountains of publications, speeches, pronouncements, and reports being generated on the topic of Indian economic development, there is surprisingly little disagreement with the proposition that BIA-controlled economic development has been a marked failure in the past and provides no hope for the future. Tribes themselves rail continuously against the BIA, and even the federal government is unusually critical. The Reagan administration's Commission on Indian Reservation Economies described the Bureau of Indian Affairs with these words:

Bureau of Indian Affairs management of Indian trust resources creates numerous land, labor, and capital obstacles to Indian reservation economic development. In terms of land and resources, incompetent asset management undermines local initiative and raises costs to Indian tribes and businesses. . . . Bureau personnel are either under-qualified to manage their present responsibilities, or unable to provide expert technical assistance for business development. . . . A Byzantine system of over-regulation actually deters investment. . . . Exacerbating the development climate is the fact that BIA consumes more than two-thirds of its budget on itself. . . . The system is designed for paternalistic control and it thrives on the failure of Indian tribes.[16]

There are, in fact, three primary conceptions, or "models," of the BIA afoot in public discussion, and at least one of them is hinted at in the foregoing passages. Ranging from the benevolent to the accusatorial, the competing conceptions of the BIA in its role as development agency are as follows:

1. The BIA is staffed by well-meaning people who pursue the interests of American Indians—sovereignty, preservation of cultural values, and eco-

nomic well-being—within the broad mandate of trust responsibility provided by Congress. The BIA takes its trust responsibilities seriously and, in particular, cannot simply give up control of Indian assets and affairs in the absence of concrete evidence, so far largely lacking, that tribes possess the experience, expertise, management systems, governmental stability and planning capacities to manage their own economies successfully.

Anecdote: The BIA is now heavily staffed, in Washington and in the area offices, by Native Americans who are intended to be sensitive to Indian problems and perspectives.

2. The BIA is a typical Byzantine bureaucracy primarily interested in its own power and survival. It is not interested in working its way out of a job by turning reservations over to tribes or by bringing real economic development to Indian Country. The BIA budget depends, in a classic Niskanen way, on the congressional perception that American Indians are poor and have little prospect for progress. Accordingly, the BIA has become very adept at producing and marketing poverty to Congress.[17]

Anecdote: The BIA has shown considerably more willingness to contract social service delivery (still funded by the BIA budget) to tribes than to give up control over economic management and assets: As of 1985, 51 percent of social service appropriations were funding contracts for social service delivery, compared to 30 percent for economic development, 31 percent for natural resource management, and 14 percent for trust management.[18]

3. At least currently, the BIA and its policies are designed to implement a racist policy of terminating reservations and the special legal status of reservation peoples; at least, the BIA is intended to keep the land, water, and resource assets from really being owned and controlled by Indian tribes.[19]

Anecdote: The primary sources of this view are Indian leaders who view the Reagan/ Ross Swimmer administration's "privatization" movement (see more below) as a means of transferring tribal assets out of the hands of tribal governments and, ultimately, out of the hands of tribal members.

Anecdote: The BIA continues to set levels of allowable timber cuts (and, whether by design or circumstance, associated water runoffs to Phoenix) for the White Mountain Apaches which far exceed the levels the tribe will accept.

A full examination of the BIA is beyond the scope of this study (although our reading of the record of the BIA resonates with the Byzantine bureaucracy model). It does seem fair—in fact, an understatement—to say that the record of BIA-managed economic development is bad enough to warrant turning to radically different approaches. If nothing else, the BIA operates under an incentive scheme that leaves any link between sound performance by Indian enterprises and bureaucratic reward tenuous, if not perversely twisted (per the Byzantine bureaucracy model).

Alternatives to Federal Management and Control

In its barest essentials, the keys to Indian economic development have two crucial components: Reservations need capital, both human and financial; and reservations need an economic and legal environment that can attract and hold that capital. Human capital means expertise: in management, labor relations, business planning, law, manufacturing, technology, communications, and on and on. It is the case, and will be for a long time to come, that many Indian communities lack the experience and expertise needed to run successful businesses. Financial capital, meanwhile, is needed to pay the bills that building a viable enterprise entails. The BIA and other agencies historically have been ill-equipped (if not ill-intentioned) to supply either the expertise or the financial capital at the levels and under the terms that are needed to generate successful economic development.

In reality, there are only two generic alternatives to BIA/federal management of Indian economic affairs. First, there is the bringing of private (member and nonmember) capital and private employers to the reservation. Second, there is the creation of tribally owned capital and businesses on the reservation. Obviously, these two approaches are not mutually exclusive, but they are distinct enough as development strategies that they have polarized much of the current debate.

The Reagan/Swimmer administration has made the expansion of private business development on reservations the centerpiece of its development policy. This policy was enunciated in the 1984 *Report and Recommendations of the Presidential Commission on Indian Reservation Economies*, which recommended that tribal governments transfer existing enterprises to private ownership (initially) in the hands of tribal members and that the attraction of private enterprises to reservations constitutes the central objective of tribal development policies. In order to overcome risks that private businesses perceive when contemplating operating on a reservation under that reservation's laws and government, tribal governments are urged to divorce tribal judicial systems from their political interference, consider surrendering certain rights of sovereignty (such as the right to adjudicate some types of business disputes and the right to exemption from suit), and opening tribal court decisions to federal court review where this is constitutional or where statutory rights are involved.

At the core of the private enterprise–based policy on Indian development is the observation that many tribes are unable to attract capital and employers because of the perception that tribal governments are unreliable in business dealings. Essentially, the view is that some combination of "meddling" by tribal governments and unintentional political instability which translates into vacillating business policies increases the risk and hassle of doing business on reservations. This view is not without foundation (although the 1984 commission report noted that "there is a reluctance throughout the commercial banking industry to deal with Indian reservations because of the unresponsiveness of the BIA").

When one party to a bargain or contract is also the enforcer (sovereign adjudicator) of that bargain or contract, strong incentives exist for the enforcing party to engage in opportunistic behavior: changing implicit or explicit terms and conditions for the purpose of economic gain. If there are any sunk costs once a relationship is undertaken (as when a mine or factory is opened), an opportunistic enforcer has some ability to alter the terms of the bargain unilaterally without causing the sunk investment to pick up and walk away.[20] Such alteration may be explicit, as when the length of a contract is unilaterally changed or the level of a royalty is raised above what was initially agreed on, or opportunistic behavior may simply take the form of less-than-promised diligence in meeting contract terms (because "the pressure is off"), thereby raising the captured party's costs or worsening its efficiency.

The problem with opportunistic behavior is that it can give a party a bad reputation and raise the cost of attracting future investment dollars. Opportunistic expropriation through conscious action or unintended instability, if anticipated, can cause investors either to refuse to commit capital to reservations or to stiffen the conditions and charges under which capital is committed. Many large international corporations, for example, employ systematically higher hurdle rates of return (i.e., the rates that prospective ventures must promise before they are undertaken) when dealing with developing economies with opportunistic records or unstable property rights. This, of course, limits the flow of capital to the affected countries.

The discouragement of private investment, business formation, and business relationships on reservations through the perceived threat of opportunistic action by tribal governments is a severe handicap to economic development. This threat arises because sovereign tribal governments necessarily find it extremely difficult to bind themselves credibly to long-term, arm's-length agreements regarding on-reservation property rights of private businesses and investors.[21] To be sure, measures such as the adoption of appropriate reservation business codes and constitutional separations of political and economic authority can be helpful to a tribe. Ultimately, however, as the enforcer of such agreements, even a well-intentioned tribal government cannot readily bind its successors. Of course, moreover, a tribe may not want a form of government that binds it in long-term economic relationships, despite the price paid in the form of discouraged development.

How do well-functioning marketplaces handle the problems of binding parties to nonopportunistic behavior when the threat of such behavior is present? There are really two ways that are of relevance here. First, parties submit their long-term agreements to third-party enforcement, either through courts or arbitration. For American Indian tribes, this submission to outside enforcement and authority is often seen as a relinquishing of sovereignty. Second, parties integrate themselves into a single firm in order to give each the same objective: overall firm profitability.[22] For American Indian tribes, this integration into a single economic unit means tribal ownership and control of enterprises.

Tribal government ownership is frequently characterized as noncapitalist, incompatible with private enterprise, or a form of central planning, or even socialism. This is silly. To the extent that a tribe has property rights in its reservation—rights to use, control, and disposal—and can engage in economic transactions over those rights with the rest of the economy, a tribe is most reasonably thought of as, itself, a firm with respect to its dealings with others. Moreover, a tribe's internal organization (e.g., its government) is the analogue to the forms of corporate governance that typical private sector firms or, perhaps even more appropriately, municipal corporations employ. Indeed, contained in the economic definition of a firm is the observation that firms are institutions that, internally, are fundamentally nonmarket allocators of resources that use some form of nonprice, central planning to achieve their objectives.[23]

The dichotomy that pits privatization as free enterprise against tribal ownership as a noncapitalist function obscures the reality that the transfer of property rights toward tribes that is now taking place is transforming tribes into firms insofar as their economic relationships with outside parties are concerned. The subjugation of the authority of the BIA and other governments is the same thing as the creation of private property rights for the quasi-corporations that are tribes. To own its own resources and have the right to make its own decisions on their use is to confront a tribe with categorically the same choices that a firm faces (e.g., to allow bingo, to allow nonmember wildlife harvesting, or to either buy a good or service from another firm or make it in-house). The appropriate questions to ask are not residing in misdirected and ideologically laden inquiries into free enterprise versus central planning. Rather, the appropriate questions to be asking concern the optimal boundaries between within-firm (i.e., tribally controlled) and outside-firm transactions.

What are the strengths and weaknesses of managing a tribe's economy predominantly as a tribally owned corporation versus a collection of separate markets? To return to the discussion above, perhaps the natural thing to think is that tribal ownership by unreliable tribal governments provides no solution to the capital market's concern over opportunism. This misses the point that when a business enterprise is tribe-as-corporation property, rather than outside-party property, the tribal government has no incentive to engage in opportunistic expropriation of that business any more than a private sector corporate manager has an incentive to run one of his or her divisions into the ground. This is not to say that a tribal government would not lack the expertise or would not constitute the wrong form of corporate governance for effective management of a particular enterprise. Such problems might make it very hard for a tribe to attract capital to fund the enterprise, but such inefficiency is the inefficiency of a particular corporate structure rather than a symptom of opportunistic governments. By integrating the interests of tribal businesses with the interests of tribal management, the tribe-as-corporation finds it easier (all else equal) to raise capital because it can more credibly (albeit still imperfectly) bind itself with commitments to the sound performance of on-reservation enterprises.[24]

Anecdote: The Mescalero and White Mountain Apaches are arguably the most aggressively anti-BIA-control, pro-tribal-control tribes in the country. They also appear to be relatively good at raising capital.

The boundaries of the well-functioning firm and, by implication, the economically appropriate tribe-as-corporation are determined by the strength of within-firm economies of scale and scope relative to the costs of allocating resources through arm's-length, market transactions.[25] Under certain circumstances, it is easy to identify the kinds of factors that determine a firm's economies of scale and scope. One of the limits of the effectiveness of markets arises when there are significant spillover effects among economic activities, such that one firm's actions impose uncompensated costs (or benefits) on other firms. Without some mechanism for making spillover costs internal to the offending firm, that firm is effectively subsidized by others and has incentives to engage in too much of the spillover-generating production. The textbook example of this situation is, of course, environmental pollution. It is not that markets cannot solve these kinds of spillover problems if tradable property rights are present (i.e., allowing damaged parties to charge culprits for spillovers). Rather, markets can often encounter very high transactions costs and simply be too expensive to use in such contexts. Under such circumstances, bringing all affected activities under the control of a unitized firm offers a viable nongovernmental solution to the control of spillovers; if division A imposes costs on division B, unitized management can directly balance the tradeoffs between A's productivity and B's productivity.[26]

For American Indian reservations, the most obvious settings in which significant environmental spillover problems are likely to arise are in agricultural-, forest-, and natural resource–based economies. A forest-based economy, for example, confronts the reality that the timber cut affects harvestable wildlife resources and hydrology, which in turn affects grazing, which affects hydrology, which affects wildlife, and so on. Unitized economic management provides a mechanism by which the implied tradeoffs between the various outputs that a forest economy can yield can be optimally balanced.

The direct implication is that an approach to development based on the tribe-as-unitized-firm is likely to be particularly well-suited to agriculture-, forest-, and natural resource–based reservations. By the same token, a reservation economy of independent private enterprises organized through formal and informal market transactions is likely to be best suited to reservations without spillover-linked production processes, for example, reservations whose comparative advantage lie in the provision of labor and/or regulatory havens.

An obvious drawback to tribes-as-firms is that sovereign tribes are also governments. As such, they are susceptible to all of the commonplace problems of governments acting as economic enterprises. These range from political factionalism and patronage to nontransferability of ownership and rationally ignorant voters-shareholders. We recognize these impediments to tribes-as-firms, but tribal governments are de facto owners of firms located within their jurisdictions, by reason of their sovereignty. The tribe-as-firm goes to the heart of the problem by moving the tribe closer to the role of residual claimant and raising the opportunity costs of poor performance. Whether this positive influence is strong enough to counteract the negative aspects of governmental ownership in any particular case turns on the political, cultural, and economic factors discussed below.

At an operational level, the most obvious drawback to tribes-as-firms is the implied need for top-quality management talent and expertise. While private sector corporate leaders "rule" through effective politicking with boards of directors, other managers, stockholders, and employees, the kind of politicking that is required to become a tribal leader may not frequently come packaged with the managerial, financial, and strategic skills that the control of tribal enterprises requires.

Anecdote: The most frequently cited impediment to reservation economic development in testimony before the presidential commission was "weak business management by tribal governments."

Moreover, when a tribe lacks the necessary expertise and skills in its member population, the tribal members' mistrust or distaste for outsiders may prevent the tribal government from going off-reservation in search of needed human capital. In short, tribal ownership may improve access to capital markets, all else being equal; however, all else may not be equal, because tribal ownership may translate into a shortage of managerial skill by placing greater demands for such skill on tribal members themselves.

From many tribes' perspectives, the central advantage of the tribes-as-corporations approach to development over the privatization approach is the strengthening of tribal sovereignty that is implied by the former orientation. Any talk of reducing or surrendering any amount or dimension of tribal sovereignty is a red flag to tribal governments and the bulk of their constituents. Within six weeks of the appearance of the presidential commission's report in November 1984, the National Tribal Chairman's Association voted eighty-four to eighteen to reject the commission's recommendations, based primarily on the perceived diminution of sovereignty that the commission's recommendations envisioned. As one tribal leader explained: "The thing is that the Federal Government wants to gain control of tribal resources, and the way they're going to do it is to bring in these outside investors the Commission's talking about, which is a pretty clandestine way of going about it."[27]

Why is the privatization of reservations so objectionable to so many? Like other bureaucrats and top corporate managers who fight budget cuts and takeovers, some tribal leaders are undoubtedly threatened by the prospect of losing control over reservation resources. Less cynically, however, there is legitimate concern among leaders and rank-and-file tribal members that privatization of the reservations could lead to losses of sovereignty more profound than a mere surrender of certain judicial powers. The prospect of tribal assets being spirited away by sophisticated but unscrupulous outsiders preying on desperately poor and ill-informed tribal members may be thought to belong to a bygone era of allotments and assimilation. The recent experience of many Indians under the Alaska Native Claims Settlement Act, as well as experiences of the Navajos and many other tribes that are rich in energy resources, indicates that times are not so different.[28]

Even if it is financially enriching, the appearance of significant nonmember capital on the reservation introduces new, non-Indian players into tribal politics and tribal social structures, and severe social strife frequently undermines tribal cohesion under such circumstances.[29] Economists, in particular, are just coming to recognize the roles that cultural mores and institutions play as social organizers and implicit contract enforcers.[30] Culture is a public good subject to free riding (by individual tribal members responding to expanded private sector options, in this context); however, if tribal members themselves choose to forgo their free riding in favor of tribal autonomy and a tribe-as-corporation approach to economic development, imposing a policy of privatization from Washington is unjustified paternalism. The bottom-line benefit of tribal control of tribal resources lies, to a substantial degree, in allowing American Indian reservations the chance to achieve success on their own terms. These terms, *as with all societies and all individuals*, involve both narrowly defined economic goods and services and broader cultural values.

TRIBES AS CORPORATIONS: TAKING PROPERTY RIGHTS FROM THE BIA

The vast majority of American Indians on reservations and the vast majority of tribes continue to be largely controlled in their economic affairs by the

BIA. The opportunity to observe the relative performances of privatization and tribe-as-corporation strategies of economic development are quite limited. The listing of significant, capitalized reservation enterprises is discouragingly short, and almost every time an apparent success story is uncovered, another information source confounds the picture by pointing out ongoing subsidization, stark operating problems, deep managerial difficulties, or resulting intratribal strife.[31] Still, as best as can be determined, there are some notable examples of sustainable economic development. The most successful tribes that can be found appear to be stridently independent of the BIA and emphatically designed on the tribe-as-corporation model of development rather than the privatization-of-reservation-markets model. Tellingly, they occur on forest-based reservations, which are well suited to unitized, tribe-as-firm management. Moreover, tribal government has a decidedly corporate structure and management expertise has been imported from off the reservation.

Some (Relative) Success Stories: The Arrow-Coase Theorem as a Management Philosophy

It has been a common theme in much recent thinking about American Indian economic development that to be truly sovereign and independent, a tribe has to develop a strong business base. The 1984 presidential commission, for example, wrote: "Without sound reservation economies, the concept of self-government has little meaning." This view may put things backwards. The experience of successful tribes suggests that to have strong reservation economies, tribes have to first have sovereignty. That is, a precondition of economic development must be assertions of a tribe's property rights in its own reservation. Without this, and with continued BIA/federal de facto ownership of reservations, the indefiniteness of property rights and the absence of a compelling designation of the residual claimant to the use and misuse of tribal resources means that the carrot-and-stick effect of opportunity costs on the tribe's behavior will be lost.

Although existing case law and a fairly good record of success would suggest that almost any tribe so inclined could establish "clear title" for itself, the number of tribes that have actively taken a consistent and uncompromising go-it-alone approach is fairly small. The tribes who have taken this approach have done so through repeated court battles designed to secure tribal rights to charge for (i.e., tax) the sale of tribal resources, tribal rights to self-management, and tribal rights to engage as a party to contracts and the issuance of financial instruments.[32] It has also been achieved by the subjugation of the power (i.e., property rights) of the BIA and other public agencies (such as state game and fish departments) through adept political maneuvering and the waving of the "self-determination" flag when pressed to relinquish autonomy to the BIA. In some cases, such as on the Mescalero

Apache and the White Mountain Apache reservations, the result has been the creation of a bundle of property rights that is not duplicated, even in the non-Indian world. Specifically, these two tribes have established themselves as for-profit owners and operators of what amount to national forests. What are the results of this unique arrangement? Has the transfer of property rights to the tribes altered their economic performance and made them more efficient?

The Apache Cases. The Mescalero Apache reservation consists of approximately a half million acres of forest and rangeland situated in south-central New Mexico and virtually surrounded by the Lincoln National Forest. It is home to approximately 3,000 Apaches. Under the longtime leadership of Chairman Wendell Chino, the Mescaleros have embarked on a broad-based strategy of tribally controlled and tribally owned economic development. The tribe engages in a major logging operation and operates a year-round golf and ski resort (Inn of the Mountain Gods and Sierra Blanca). It also aggressively markets fishing, hunting, and camping opportunities to southern New Mexico and west Texas.

Although hard data are difficult to come by, anecdotal evidence and direct observation suggest that at least the skiing and outdoor recreation enterprises of the Mescaleros are profitable. The reservation's housing stock is notable for its size and modernity, and the employment rate of tribal members is high. BIA data indicate unemployment rates in the range of 30 percent, but these data (which play a role in BIA and other agencies' funding levels for social services) may be inaccurate; other sources indicate that there is little or no involuntary unemployment on the reservation.[33] Obviously, if this is true, the Mescaleros truly are an outlier and represent a remarkable success story of self-managed and sovereign economic development.

The White Mountain Apaches are a tribe of approximately 9,000 people occupying 1.6 million acres of forest and rangeland in east-central Arizona. Like the Mescalero reservation, Fort Apache sits in the midst of national forest land. Approximately 750,000 acres of the reservation are covered by commercial timber, making it the largest contiguously managed ponderosa pine forest in the world. Approximately 400,000 acres of the Fort Apache reservation are prime grazing land. The reservation now has abundant wildlife and possesses approximately 3,000 surface acres of reservoirs and 500 miles of rivers and streams. Slightly more than 60 percent of the waters of the Salt River, which is a primary source of water for the Phoenix metropolitan area, originate on the reservation.

First under Chairman Ronnie Lupe, and now under Chairman Reno Johnson, the White Mountain Apaches have an aggressive program of tribally directed economic development founded on a natural resource base. The White Mountain Apaches operate nine enterprises and generate approximately $80 million per year in revenues. The largest enterprise is the Fort Apache Timber Company (FATCO), with annual sales on the order of $30 million per year. The FATCO sawmill is fully modernized and shows labor productivity (output per man-hour) that is considerably higher than most other mills in the western United States. A recent study of productivity indicates that average productivity in the Western Wood Products Association has been on the order of 7.4 labor hours per thousand board feet of lumber produced, while FATCO operates at 5.7 labor hours per thousand board feet. FATCO lumber is also apparently of high quality, sustaining prices which are 15 to 20 percent higher than average for the Rocky Mountain region.[34]

Over 95 percent of the FATCO work force consists of tribal members, and the annual payroll is approximately $9 million. The long-time general manager is not a tribal member. FATCO annually delivers timber royalties to the tribe equal to approximately 25 percent of sales. Significantly, FATCO has been consistently profitable (at a time when the lumber industry nationwide has been suffering) and is reported by some observers to be the most profitable tribal business in the country.

The White Mountain Apache ski resort (Sunrise) was begun in 1972 over opposition from some environmental interests. The resort is the largest and most heavily utilized in Arizona, servicing the rapidly growing populations of Phoenix and Tucson with seven chair lifts, fifty runs, two lodges, and a planned airport facility. Annual revenues are on the order of $7 million per year. In seasons of good snow, Sunrise appears to now be profitable. The facility employs approximately 650 full-time-equivalent workers, approximately 60 percent of whom are tribal members. The current general manager of Sunrise is not a tribal member.

In addition to the lumber and skiing operations, the White Mountain Apaches operate a system of retail enterprises, a construction company, a tribal cattle herd, and irrigation projects. Like the Mescaleros, the White Mountain Apaches have aggressively developed an outdoor recreation business based on hunting, fishing, and camping or hiking.

Significantly, when compared to many other tribes, the vast bulk of the tribe's total employment (over 85 percent) is in tribal enterprises rather than tribal government. Unemployment is officially in the range of 25 to 30 percent, although this reflects a rapid growth in the number of entrants to the work force. Housing in absolute terms remains well below non-Indian norms but is relatively better than on the majority of reservations.

Optimal Management of a Forest; or, Was Ronald Coase an Apache? In the foregoing descriptions there is a somewhat hidden set of facts that, taken together, constitute a remarkable picture. Both the Mescalero and White Mountain Apaches are operating forest-based, multiple-use economies that are subject to marketplace tests of performance and intended for the purpose of making money. Interestingly, U.S. national forests are also supposed to be managed as multiple-use units that provide forest products, grazing, recreation, and other amenities and commodities in a mixture that reflects sound environmental policy and, at least in part, economic benefits and costs. The Mescalero and White Mountain Apaches are dramatically out-performing the U.S. Forest Service and other public land agencies. For economists interested in an example of unitized, multiple-use, privately owned forests, the Apaches are the premier example.

The most striking attribute of the Apaches' management is the emphasis on recreation. Following their skiing operations as flagships for both the Mescalero and White Mountain Apaches are their big game hunting oper-ations. These provide an important window on the impact of the transfer of ownership of tribal resources to the tribes. At the present time, male ("bull") elk can be hunted in great numbers in the national forests adjoining the Mescalero and White Mountain reservations. In Arizona, for example, elk hunting permits (firearms and archery) are allocated by lotteries to approx-imately 1,700 hunters at a fee of approximately $60 each. The White Moun-tain Apaches, meanwhile, sell approximately forty trophy-only (i.e., mature male) elk permits to a two-year waiting list at a price averaging $10,000 per hunter. The tribe recently tested the market price with an auction and obtained a price of $15,000. The Mescaleros face similar competition from the state of New Mexico, in addition to private marketing by large ranches, and charge approximately $6,000 per elk hunt.

How can the Apaches charge so much for their elk hunting? Without going into the psyches of the people who pay $10,000 for an elk hunt, the answer is that the Apaches provide a level of quality that public land officials are unable to duplicate. This quality takes many dimensions:

—Wilderness experience: While the nearby public lands are relatively crowded with hunters and their vehicles and paraphernalia traversing heavily roaded forests, the Apaches emphasize the experience of wildness in a setting more reminiscent of tra-ditional frontier hunting grounds. Apache hunts are rugged with no guarantee of success. Given population levels, however, the Apaches provide dramatically higher success rates than public sector suppliers, as well as rates of success that exceed those offered by large for-profit ranch suppliers (such as the famous Vermejo Ranch, a New Mexico subsidiary of Pennzoil).

—Trophy quality: The White Mountain Apache, in particular, are in the business of providing trophy hunting recreation. Elk antler size is the measure of trophy quality, and the White Mountain Apaches' average antler size is off the map relative to the public sector competition. The average White Mountain elk scores over 340 on the "Boone and Crockett" scale, compared to something in the range of 50–70 points for the state of Colorado and approximately 275 points for the Vermejo Ranch.[35] The average White Mountain elk is 7.5 years old at the age of harvest, compared to 1.5–2.5 years in Colorado. Most other states appear to have elk with average ages at harvest not exceeding 4 years.[36]

—Professionalism: The Mescalero and White Mountain Apaches have reputations among their customers for being the upper crust of the market in terms of the professionalism of the tribe's staff and organization. (Dealing with state game and fish departments can often be like dealing with state motor vehicle bureaus.)

The Apaches' elk hunting and related fee-fishing and other fee-hunting operations were originally challenged by state officials, who asserted (among other things) that the Apaches were ill-suited to wildlife management and threatened the conservation of game and associated recreational opportunities. However, the results that have actually obtained have been precisely the opposite, just as the theory of property rights would have predicted. By turning fish and game into *economic* resources for the Apaches, incentives were created to preserve, protect, and invest in those resources. The results are remarkable by any standard and leave the Apaches teaching the rest of the world how to manage multiple-use forests.

From available biologic information, the Mescalero and White Mountain Apache elk herds appear to be among (there is no single measure available) the healthiest major elk populations in the world. Not only do the reservations produce more and larger males in their populations than can be found among publicly owned herds, but the Apache populations show steady population growth under tribal management. The Mescalero herd shows a ratio of males to females far higher than major competitors. Pregnancy rates among Apache elk also tend to exceed those of publicly managed populations. Finally, Apache elk herd populations are managed to prevent overgrazing of range and forage, while unhunted elk populations in areas such as Yellowstone National Park appear to be causing significant, if not catastrophic, ecological damage.[37]

Interestingly, the incentives for sound wildlife management that the Apaches confront show up in concrete differences between their unitized forest management practices and the practices seen on public lands. National forest managers operate under an incentive system in which the funding agent—Congress—is able to monitor relatively gross measures of value: board feet of timber cut and visitor days. State game and fish bureaus, meanwhile, face incentives to provide maximum numbers of recreational days, with little or no ability to provide discriminating measures of high- and low-quality recreation to their funding agents. In the case of the national forests, there appears to be a fortuitous synergy: As logging roads are built (often as part of timber sales that have costs far in excess of revenues), measured visitor days rise along with board feet of lumber cut as sight-seeing driving increases. It turns out that roads, however, are a major disturbance to elk populations. At $10,000 to $15,000 per trophy elk, the White Mountain Apaches' road-building policy is dramatically different from that in the national forests. Apache roads are generally required to be single-track and ungraveled; upon the termination of logging, they are reseeded and blocked to subsequent travel; wildlife-disturbing straight stretches of road are minimized; and roads are not allowed to be built within specified distances of meadows where elk congregate. In addition, the tribe has designated its own wilderness areas, requires unlogged buffer areas around meadows and streams, and forbids all travel of any kind in spring calving areas, a policy that has been fought for repeatedly by environmental groups, but not instituted in national forests. Finally, as perhaps the epitome of Coasian management, both the Mescalero and White Mountain Apaches require members who wish to hunt trophy animals to purchase that right on the same terms as the sales made to nonmembers.

In fact, there is an important lesson in the Apache experience for the management of U.S. public lands. The Apaches provide an answer to the perennial question that polarizes debates over U.S. public land policy: Are the public lands tilted too much in favor of industrial, nonrecreational utilization or too much in favor of recreational and environmental interests? Taking the American public's willingness to pay as the measure of the value that the public attaches to alternative uses of the public lands, the Apache experience indicates that the American public wants a bundle of multiple uses tilted more in favor of particular kinds of high-quality recreation (skiing, fishing, and trophy hunting) and less toward the industrial products derived from the nation's forests. That is, the most striking change in the management of Apache lands upon subjecting those lands to private market incentives has been the rapid move of the Apaches into the high-quality recreation niche that the public lands have failed to fill.

Ruminations on the Sources of Development and the Limits of Economics

While gratifying to economists (for whom all people are Adam Smith's rationally self-interested version of Pavlov's dogs), the relative economic success and the absolute ecological success of the Apaches are in some sense too easy to analyze: Incentives (i.e., property rights) were changed and, pari passu, behavior changed in rational fashion. The more interesting stories are the "failures." After all, the legal and political base for the property rights regime that the Apaches have forged for themselves is fundamentally the same for the vast majority of American Indian tribes. Why haven't they all taken the Apache route?

Consider, for example, the area of recreational development. The Hualapai Tribe of northern Arizona possesses antelope and desert bighorn sheep and markets these to nonmembers at premium prices. However, the tribe was forced to suspend its antelope hunting at a time when populations elsewhere in the region were on a steady rise, and desert sheep harvesting has had to be severely curtailed. The Wind River reservation (Shoshone and Arapaho) of Wyoming took over control of its fish and game from the state but very quickly found itself being preempted by federal authorities when common pool (i.e., unrestricted tribal hunting) management resulted in exceedingly rapid depredation of wildlife populations.[38] Similar stories apply in whole or in part to tribes in Utah, Colorado, Alaska, and Montana. Many other tribes, moreover, possess more than adequate wildlife resources to tap the niche in the market that the Apaches have identified, but they fail to do so by default or choice.

What is really going on with the Mescalero and White Mountain Apaches? Several facets of these cases stand out and begin to suggest hypotheses about the path to economic development by American Indians and, perhaps, other societies as well. At least in relative terms, the Apaches have acquired the two fundamental ingredients (addressed above) on which economic development is based: human and financial capital, and the legal and economic environment needed to attract and hold it. In particular, the following attributes of the Apache context seem to be at the core of their relative success as self-determined tribes.

Leadership and the Rent-Seeking Process. A core component of any society's legal and economic environment is its ability or inability to shut down wasteful rent-seeking processes (i.e., processes of using social resources to fight over the allocation of existing wealth, rather than directing resources and incentives toward the creation of new wealth). From Latin America to an excessively litigious U.S. society, rent seeking can destroy or divert resources from productive use. The key to shutting down rent seeking lies in the creation of definitive rules of law: definitive property rights to action and resources. Without definite rights, whether private, bureaucratic, or public, parties have incentives to invest in changing their rights.[39] Rules of law are fundamentally a problem of enforcement, and enforcement is a relationship between leaders and their constituents.

The Apaches have a long history of strong civic (as opposed to solely military) leadership by charismatic individuals, from Cochise through present administrations. These leaders appear to embody a self-defined standard of public service in the interest of the tribe, and the tribe itself exhibits very low tolerance for self-aggrandizement or corruption. The Mescalero Apaches have had the same, strong leader for thirty years, and the White Mountain Apaches have only had two chairmen in the last seventeen years. Many American Indian tribes have faced significant problems of "banana republic" corruption or lack traditions of hierarchical leadership. The Navajo, for example, had little early history of comprehensive governance and seem to continue to exhibit more strongly communalistic or flatly democratic, consensus-building approaches to tribal decision making.[40] Such decision making turns leadership itself into a common pool asset that is subject to exhaustion through factionalism and instability.

Leadership and Hierarchical Business Management. The hierarchical structure of most business management is not a quirk of capitalism but rather reflects the underlying efficiencies of specialization in ownership, management, and labor. The White Mountain Apaches have a decidedly corporate management structure, with the equivalent of senior vice presidents in charge of each division of the tribe's enterprises. Each of these division heads, whether a tribal member or not, is a remarkably strong personality. The tribal chairman appears to serve the role of keeping consensus among these managers concerning the overall goals and plans of the tribal economy.

Resource Endowments. Both the Mescalero and White Mountain Apaches have rich resource endowments in their timber, range, snow, and wildlife. This alone, however, seems to account for very little, and does not account at all for why the burst of development waited until the era of aggressive self-management to appear. Numerous tribes have rich natural resource endowments, ranging from oil, gas, and coal (e.g., the Navajos, the Crows, and the Northern Cheyenne) to nonenergy minerals (e.g., the Laguna Pueblo reservation). Even prior to the collapse of market prices for their assets, evidence of sustainable economic development for the average tribal member was hard to uncover.

On-Reservation Property Rights and the Common Pool. The Mescalero and White Mountain Apaches' regulation of member access to reservation wildlife is indicative of the tribes' abilities to shut down the common pool and avoid the tragedies of the commons, namely, resource races leading to rapid exhaustion. This may be founded in the Apaches' very long history of tribal ownership of capital assets, originating in the early 1600s with the raiding and reselling of the Spaniards' livestock. Traditions of significant capital asset ownership among, for example, Great Plains tribes were historically weak.[41] Recent examples of the tragedy of the commons are found on the Wind River reservation (described above) and, perhaps most notably, among the Navajo.[42]

Labor-Management Relations. A significant problem in many Indian businesses arises from conflict in efficient hierarchical and hire-and-fire labor-management relationships. Many tribes encounter great difficulty in establishing manager-follower command systems and in instituting layoffs when economic conditions warrant. These problems impede the specialization of labor and can emaciate businesses financially. Moreover, reputations of tribes for political "meddling" in enterprises by tribal governments are frequently earned when the problem of layoffs arises. The Apache tribal councils have fairly consistently been able to back management when layoffs are needed by conveying their necessity to the tribe. In fact, the White Mountain Apaches exhibit and stick to quite high standards of performance at many levels of employment. We have little clue as to the origins of these practices among the Apaches, other than to note that they are consistent with a sense conveyed by the tribe that "we will do whatever is necessary to succeed."

Nationalism. The White Mountain Apaches are particularly notable for their willingness and ability to attract human capital and expertise from off-reservation, and often non-Indian, sources, as well as a willingness to engage in service-oriented commerce with non-Apaches. Very few, if any, Native

American tribes are racist in the *Webster's* sense of adopting "a program or practice of racial discrimination, segregation, persecution, and domination." Mirroring the situation in many developing countries with histories of colonialism, however, many Native Americans are strongly nationalistic, as the debate over sovereignty demonstrates. In business dealings, this is frequently reflected in an unwillingness to hire outside experts and managers, as well as preferences for self-sufficiency and internally generated capital. However, the Apaches are fiercely nationalistic and proud of their Apache identity, but they do not appear to regard the infusion of outside human and financial capital, nor day-to-day commerce with non-Apaches, as the kinds of things that affect their self-identity in excessively adverse ways. Part of their identity, in fact, appears to arise from a self-image as a people who thrive on and adapt to cross-cultural confrontations. Tribal leadership, moreover, generally does not see even very-high-level non-Apache managers as weakening their position at the top of the tribal power structure.

Definitions of Success. A central debate among Native Americans is whether economic success will alter or even destroy the autonomy of tribal cultures. For some, this prospective effect of economic development is regarded as a negative. While economics-qua-economics is practiced (and preached) as acultural, it seems obvious that cultural institutions provide criteria by which elements of individuals' utilities, including self-esteem and self-identity, are measured and acquired; moreover, cultural institutions reduce the transactions and enforcement costs of running a society.[43] It is hardly irrational for individuals to trade off material goods and services in favor of a broader cultural definition of success.

The Apache notion of cultural success does not appear to be in much conflict with either the form or results of a tribe-as-corporation strategy of economic development. The operative definition of success appears to derive from a strong sense that being Apache means being able to take charge of changing situations for purposes of economic gain. To quote the Tribal Chairman of the Mescaleros: "[We are balancing] the best of both worlds—the white man's and the Indian's. From the white man, we have picked up the work ethic, while we have retained the Apache's independence. . . . What we're aiming for eventually is an Apache takeover—a takeover of management of all of our projects."[44]

Many other tribes explicitly, and often with great intratribal tension, see development as involving a trade-off between goods and services and their culture. The much-publicized 1986 Navajo election, for example, centered precisely on the individual tribal members' perceptions of this issue. For tribes with this kind of internal conflict, the definition of success may be incompatible with either a tribe-as-corporation or a privatization approach to development. If being a Navajo means refusing to shut down common pool grazing or accept hierarchical labor-management relationships, then narrowly defined economic development and the concept of being a Navajo may be noncomplementary. Indian *self-determination* means the right to choose either path, but self-determination will also subject tribes to the opportunity costs of their choices and definitions of success.

The foregoing discussion does *not* imply that certain Indian peoples necessarily must become "westernized," "modernized," "capitalistic," or otherwise culturally altered in order to be successful societies. First, as we have already stressed, the definition of success is not unidimensionally economic. When individuals have preferences over such matters as the modes of social interaction that organize their societies, the pace and direction of economic development, and the political and economic institutions through which collective action is taken, the Apache route to success will not be likely to resemble the Navajo route, the Sioux route, the Japanese route, or the German route. Second, there may be more than one path to even narrowly defined material success. Apache quasi-corporate management styles might be effectively replaced by cooperative or partnership organizational forms by the Navajo or by individual entrepreneurs among the Sioux. The range of societal adaptations to the twin problems of resource scarcity and social cohesion is not so broad as to preclude pressure on cultures to adapt their institutions and definitions of success. However, as the modern world demonstrates, neither is the feasible range of social forms so narrow as to force convergence of societies to an equilibrium of stark homogeneity.[45]

CONCLUSIONS

The most remarkable thing about federal policy with respect to American Indian economic development is its failure. It is not only too easy to cite the indicators of ongoing poverty; it is particularly striking how difficult it is to cite bona fide cases in which individual reservation enterprises are economically successful (i.e., are making *net* contributions to the economy). Moreover, it is even more difficult to uncover an entire reservation economy that absorbs fewer of society's resources than it produces.

In some ways the sorry state of the reservations' economies and their standards of living is surprising. Like many ethnic minorities, American Indians have a history of subjection to discrimination in both economic and legal spheres; they have ample tales of being swindled out of assets and opportunities; and they have sweet-and-sour relationships with state and federal governments, which serve as sources of income and services while also regulating the Indians' civil and economic rights. Unlike many ethnic minorities, however, American Indians have had, at least nominally, some tangible and legal assets—their reservations and certain kinds of unique legal status. Nonetheless, American Indians remain the country's poorest minority.

The explanation for the economic status of American Indian reservations is, of course, extremely complicated. At least a major part of the problem, however, has been that American Indians, either as tribes or as individual residents, have not really owned their reservations. Reservations have been the de facto property of the federal government, especially the BIA. Public sector property rights of this type are attenuated: The BIA (or, ultimately, Congress) is unable to claim the benefits of sound, successful economic development and may even face incentives to avoid such development; moreover, BIA decision makers bear little penalty for poor performance. This attenuation consequently translates into a dilution of incentives for good performance. We should not be surprised at the results.

The gradual transfer and solidification of the tribes' rights in their own reservations over the last decade or so is correlated with inklings of real economic development. This is probably not an accident and attests to the importance of de facto ownership in the explanation of the economic status of Indian reservations. As tribes come to really own their own resources, and as they really come to plan, manage, and bear the consequences of the use of reservation resources, they become more directly subjected to the incentives for developing wise economic policies and management. The advantage of *self-determination* is that the response to such incentives can be made in ways that are more likely to be compatible with each tribe's cultural, political, and economic situations.

The transfer of property rights in Indian reservations from the public sector to the tribes has arisen from the federal policy of Indian self-determination and the tribes' demands for sovereignty. It is conventional wisdom that in order to be truly sovereign polities and economies, Indian reservations need strong economies and good business environments. From this has followed recommendations for one version of the privatization of reservation economies: To build strong economies, reservations need to attract independent, grass-roots, entrepreneurial capital and employers. While this source of economic development should not be totally rejected for all tribes, there is evidence that to develop strong economies, tribes first need true sovereignty; moreover, another version of the privatization of reservation economies may be that to build strong reservation economies, tribes should act—and should be allowed to act—as the owners of their own resources. The evidence and anecdotes discussed here suggest that this approach to development can provide some tribes with an effective route to success, as defined in the tribes' own terms.

NOTES

We have benefited greatly from the insightful comments of a number of individuals, including Robert Brauchli, Philip S. DeLoria, Thomas Hall, Henry Lee, Patrick Murphy, Robert Nelson, and Ronald Trosper. Invaluable research assistance and field work have been provided by Harry Nelson, Leland Leachman, and John Gamman. The financial support of the Ford Foundation, the Energy and Environmental

Policy Center, and the Institute of Politics at Harvard is also gratefully acknowledged. Perhaps most important, this work could not have been undertaken without the cooperation of numerous American Indian tribes, including the White Mountain Apaches (Arizona), the Mescalero Apaches (New Mexico), the Navajo (Four Corners), the Hualapai (Arizona), the San Carlos Apaches (Arizona), the Crow (Montana), and the Northern Cheyenne (Montana).

1. See U.S. Commission on Civil Rights, "Staff Memorandum: Constitutional Status of American Indians," New York, March 1973, p. 3. On the deeper roots of Indian political activism, see S. Cornell, *Return of the Native* (New York: Oxford University Press, 1988).

2. See, for example, F. G. Hutchins, "Writing Old Wrongs," *New Republic*, August 30, 1980, pp. 14–17; and T. Williams, *Don't Blame the Indians* (Atlanta: GSJ Press, 1986).

3. The most comprehensive review of the Indians' current legal status is probably C. Wilkinson, *American Indians, Time, and the Law* (New Haven: Yale University Press, 1987).

4. U.S. Commission on Civil Rights, "Staff Memorandum."

5. Ibid.

6. U.S. President [Ronald Reagan], *American Indian Policy* (Washington, D.C.: Bureau of Indian Affairs, January 24, 1983).

7. *Puyallup Tribe v. Wash. Department of Fish and Game*, 391 U.S. 392 (1970); *U.S. v. Jackson* 600 F2d 1283 (9th Cir. 1979); and *Mescalero Apache Tribe v. New Mexico* 677 F2d 55, *cert granted*, 103 SCt 371, 459 US 1014, 74 LEd2d 506, *aff'd*, 103 SCt 2378.

8. American Indian National Bank, "Indian Owned Businesses: An Entrepreneurial Explosion," *Indian Finance Digest*, pilot edition (1984): 4.

9. The most recent comprehensive examination of the matters discussed in this section is the U.S. Department of the Interior *Report of the Task Force on American Indian Economic Development* (Washington, D.C.: U.S. Government Printing Office, 1986).

10. H. Nelson, "Analysis of Loan Performance in the Bureau of Indian Affairs' Credit Program," *Project Report*, John F. Kennedy School of Government, Harvard Project on American Indian Economic Development (draft, Harvard University, April 1987).

11. To be sure, many tribes lack the experience and manpower to handle such affairs, but there is also evidence that the BIA itself lacks such traits. Some tribes have successfully taken the BIA to court for the mismanagement of tribal assets. See *White Mountain Apache v. U.S.*, 11 Claims Court 614 (1987).

12. See, for example, D. Champagne, *Strategies and Conditions of Political and Cultural Survival in American Indian Societies* (Cambridge, MA: Cultural Survival, 1985), and "Socio-Cultural Responses to Coal Development: A Comparison of the Crow and Northern Cheyenne" (draft, University of Wisconsin-Milwaukee, 1986).

13. For a brief review, see U.S. Department of the Interior, *Report of the Task Force on American Indian Economic Development* (Washington, D.C.: U.S. Government Printing Office, 1986), ch. 2.

14. The litany of these problems has now attained the status of folk wisdom. A very readable and representative overview is found in "The New Indian Wars," *Denver Post*, October-November 1983.

15. *White Mountain Apache v. BIA* (1987).

16. *Report and Recommendations of the Presidential Commission on Indian Reservation Economies* (Washington, D.C.: U.S. Government Printing Office, November 1984).

17. For a representative statement of this view, see the 1984 *Report and Recommendations of the Presidential Commission on Indian Reservation Economies*; quoted from Indian Finance Act section, p. 46. On the theory of bureaucracy, see W. Niskanen, *Bureaucracy and Representative Government* (Chicago: Aldine-Atherton Press, 1971).

18. From U.S. Department of the Interior, *Report of the Task Force on American Indian Economic Development*, Table 2, ch. 9.

19. For a representative statement, see "Indians Resist Shift in Economic Goals Urged by U.S. panel," *New York Times*, 14 January 1987, as well as the repeated positions taken by the National Congress of American Indians in *NCAI News* since 1985.

20. See B. Klein, R. Crawford, and A. Alchian, "Vertical Integration, Appropriable Rents, and the Competitive Contracting Process," *Journal of Law and Economics* 20(2) (October 1978): 297–326.

21. As suggested above, a well-intentioned tribal government cannot bind the BIA, which is also a de jure and de facto party to tribal agreements; moreover, capricious postagreement behavior by the BIA appears to be every bit as much a problem as opportunistic behavior by tribal governments.

22. See note 20 above.

23. See R. Coase, "The Nature of the Firm," *Economica* 4(16) (November 1937): 386–405; and R. Eccles and H. White, "Price and Authority in Inter-Profit Center Transactions," *American Journal of Sociology*, supple. (1988).

24. Tribes-as-corporations can still exercise opportunistic tendencies in joint ventures. Consequently, the capital markets are primarily interested in supplying financial capital in the form of debt, rather than equity, just as with most developing countries around the world.

25. See Coase, "The Nature of the Firm."

26. *Unitization* is borrowed from the language used by the oil and gas industry to describe how firms solve the problems of the common pool when multiple parties try to draw on the same reservoir. For a discussion of unitization (or merger) as a solution to problems of externalities, see R. Coase, "The Problem of Social Cost," *Journal of Law and Economics* 3 (October 1960): 1–44; and J. Hirshleifer, *Price Theory and Applications*, 2d ed. (Englewood, N.J.: Prentice-Hall, 1980), pp. 535–37. The possibilities of the unitization of spillover activities within a merged firm have led some economists to go so far as to recommend the privatization of national forests and parks as a mechanism for more efficiently producing the multiple, and often competing, outputs that they can yield. (See, for example, J. Baden and D. Lueck, "A Property Rights Approach to Wilderness Management" in *Public Lands and the U.S. Economy*, ed. Johnston and Emerson ([Boulder, CO: Westview Press, 1984, pp. 29–67]).

27. See note 19 above.

28. See note 14 above.

29. See notes 14 and 12.

30. See, for example, G. Becker, "Altruism, Egoism, and Genetic Fitness," *Jour-

nal of Political Economy 14(3) (September 1976): 817–26; G. Becker, "A Theory of Social Interactions," Journal of Political Economy 82(6) (November–December 1974): 1063–93; J. Hirshleifer, "Competition, Cooperation and Conflict in Economics and Biology," American Economic Review Proceedings 68(2) (May 1978): 238–43; and J. Coleman, "Social Capital in the Creation of Human Capital," American Journal of Sociology 94, supple. (1988): S95–S120.

31. Compare, for example, the treatment of the Blackfeet Tribe's writing instrument industry in Public Broadcasting Service, "The New Capitalists: Economics in Indian Country" (1985); and J. Cook, "Help Wanted—Work, Not Handouts," Forbes, 4 May 1987, pp. 68–71.

32. Wilkinson, American Indians.

33. See "Sierra Blanca," Boston Globe, 5 January 1986; and Public Broadcasting Service, "The New Capitalists."

34. Data provided by Robert Brauchli, tribal attorney, White Mountain Apache Tribe. March 1987.

35. G. Wolfe, Population Dynamics of the Vermejo Park Elk Herd (Doctoral thesis, Fort Collins, Colorado State University, 1985).

36. Joe Jojola, Wildlife Biologist, White Mountain Apache Game and Fish Department has supplied the bulk of the data (March 1987) reported here and below.

37. See A. Chase, Playing God in Yellowstone (Boston: Little Brown, 1986).

38. "Big Indian Elk Kill Leads to Call for Game Law," New York Times, 18 December 1983.

39. For an interesting perspective on property rights as a common pool resource, see T. Anderson and P. Hill, "Property Rights as a Common Pool Resource," in Bureaucracy v. Environment ed. J. Baden and R. Stroup (Ann Arbor: University of Michigan Press, 1981).

40. See, for example, "Navajo Election Offers Choice between Two Cultures," Boston Globe, 2 November 1986.

41. For an excellent account of the development of property rights among eastern tribes, see W. Cronon, Changes in the Land (New York: Hill and Wang, 1983). Other discussions of the problem of common property are found in Chase, Playing God in Yellowstone, and C. Martin, Keepers of the Game (Berkeley: University of California Press, 1978).

42. See G. Libecap and R. Johnson, "The Navajo and Too Many Sheep: Overgrazing on the Reservation," in J. Baden and R. Stroup, Bureaucracy v. Environment, pp. 87–107.

43. See note 28 above.

44. Wendell Chino, quoted in U.S. News and World Report, 5 April 1982, p. 65.

45. For a very cogent discussion of the "twin problems," see D. North, Structure and Change in Economic History (New York: Norton, 1981).

9

Economic Development as the Foundation for Self-Determination

Theresa Julnes

THE NATIONAL NATIVE ECONOMIC DEVELOPMENT STUDY

The purpose of this study was to report how economic development decisions in native nations have been made and managed in the past and to examine what obstacles may be hindering future economic development. This survey of Indian nations and corporations in the United States will provide an assessment of some of the trends of current economic development. The major goals of the survey were to make an assessment of the characteristics associated with successful economic development and to propose what assistance may be desired by tribes to promote economic development in the future.

The goals of the study are expressed through three research questions (with subquestions identifying the components of each major question):

How are economic development decisions made and managed?

1. Decisions made by the government or by the people?
2. Businesses managed exclusively by tribal members or with some or all outside management?

What perceived obstacles are there to economic development?

1. Lack of capital?
2. Lack of control?
3. Lack of trained management?
4. Lack of trained personnel?

5. Lack of natural resources?
6. Lack of financial resources?
7. Intrusion of BIA requirements?

What perceived *assistance is needed for economic development?*

1. Outside consultant planning?
2. Outside help to implement economic development?
3. Outside help to develop resources?
4. Outside help to market resources?
5. Outside management skills?
6. Outside technical skills?
7. Outside agency help (such as BIA)?
8. Input from family groups?

A major concern of this study is to determine the amount of economic development that each tribe is engaged in. For those tribes that are undertaking economic development, we examine what profits have been generated and for what length of time (a new enterprise will typically take time to show a profit). Other independent variables represent demographics relating to economic development, such as the size of the tribe and the number or percent of tribal members employed. These results will help to identify characteristics among tribes operating successful economic development ventures. These variables can be summarized as follows:

What is the current amount of economic development?

1. Any economic development?
2. Profit from economic development?
3. Amount of time for which economic development has existed?

What are the current demographics?

1. Size of tribe?
2. Number of tribal members employed?
3. Percent of tribal members employed?

Policy initiatives will be strongly influenced by the responses given by each tribal leader in regard to the adequacy of funds available for economic development and the amount of employment generated. Given the diversity of governmental structures existing among tribes, not to mention the variability of resources, it is no wonder that few quantitative studies in the literature evaluate tribal economic development. The few studies that have

been reported provide only a glance at the interworkings of tribal governments and their economic development strategies and do little to explain
why economic development has been successful in some places and not in
others. This study progresses beyond these earlier studies and quantifies
some of the components of economic development outlined in the three
research questions. It is hoped that empirically quantifiable data, along with
interpretive observations, will demonstrate the need and evidence for sound
public policy supporting the suggested strategies for tribal economic development.

STRUCTURE OF NATIVE GOVERNMENTS AND
DECISION MAKING

When considering strategies for development, it is important to consider
the organizational characteristics of Indian governments. Native governments are less complicated in structure than local or state governments and
tend to be less "bureaucratic" in nature. Two typical characteristics are an
aversion to putting anything down in writing and an aversion to the use of
hierarchical structures. This is also reflected in the community volunteer
involvement in the operation of native governments.

From the perspective of economic development, enterprises undertaken
by tribes tend to be those that require fewer bureaucratic structures; frequently, they tend to be small businesses (see aggregate responses to questions no. 5 and no. 12 in the Appendix). Given the fact that there are
differences in language and culture that will influence acceptable economic
endeavors, the businesses of native peoples are a reflection of the traditional
activities and values (as they relate to natural resources) of native cultures
in general.

It is also important to note that businesses operated on reservations are
a reflection of the tax incentives available to native governments. Much of
the negative media about tribal operations have centered on businesses that
sell tobacco and liquor, which, of course, are exempt from state taxes. Legal
battles continue over whether native governments have the right to sell tax-
exempt products to the general public.

METHODOLOGY

A questionnaire (see Appendix) was mailed to the leadership of each Indian
nation and corporation in the United States. The addresses for the tribal
offices (and the leader) of each tribe were provided by the regional offices
of the Bureau of Indian Affairs (BIA). Interestingly, although it is the parental
arm of the government over Indian affairs, the BIA did not have accurate
records concerning many tribes. Further, addresses were incorrect for 1.5
percent of the tribal offices. Since the U.S. Postal Service forwards mail for

eighteen months after addresses have been changed, some of the addresses provided by the BIA were more than eighteen months out of date.

After an original and a follow-up mailing of the questionnaire, one-third of the questionnaires were returned completed. In the responses from the completed questionnaires, the decision paths to economic development, as well as the perceived obstacles associated with achieving economic development, are explored and examined. This study tabulates the responses received in order to quantify the types of successes (and failures) reported and to indicate the most significant obstacles to economic development. In essence, the data used in this work will assess what economic development activities exist and what can be done to promote further development.

FINDINGS

First, we will look at how respondents answered specific questions. The strength of the mean responses to some of the research subquestions will demonstrate the overall need for financial policy initiatives. This will be emphasized later in the discussions of interrelationships of multiple variables.

DEMOGRAPHICS

The size of tribes was categorized as small (499 or fewer), medium (500–1,800), or large (1,801 or more). A third of the responses to the questionnaire came from each group (question no. 1). This distribution of responses does not reflect the population distribution as reported in the *Report and Recommendations of the President of the United States* by the Presidential Commission on Indian Reservation Economies (1984). Two influences account for the difference: first, the BIA merges some smaller tribes together for agency contact (as separately, the tribes could not maintain a tribal office); and second, it is assumed that more of the larger than the smaller tribes would respond due to their better staff capabilities. Consequently, as one would expect, the average populations of responding tribes are higher than the average of all tribes.

The proportion of tribal members employed by the tribe's economic development efforts is also of note (question no. 12). The questionnaire results reveal that the average tribe employed eighty-seven persons in economic development work, with fifty-nine tribal members, six native nontribal members, and thirty nonnatives. Thus, approximately 68 percent of the persons employed on economic development ventures are tribal members. Consequently, one can conclude that tribes are using economic development to reduce unemployment on the reservations.

HOW ARE ECONOMIC DEVELOPMENT DECISIONS MADE AND MANAGED?

As already mentioned, native governments are less bureaucratic than other government structures. The majority of tribal governments use the representative method (voting) for making economic decisions (see question no. 14). In 50 percent of the responding tribal governments, the tribal council (elected by the people) makes economic decisions. Thirty percent of tribal governments create a separate branch of government to make these decisions. In the remaining 20 percent, economic decisions are considered by the general council (all tribal members present at a scheduled meeting).

One-third of all tribes have their own business enterprises managed exclusively by tribal members, while 9 percent of tribal businesses are managed by outside managers. The other 58 percent are managed by tribal members with the help of outsiders (question no. 13). Thus, only a minority of tribes fully manage their own enterprises.

WHAT PERCEIVED OBSTACLES ARE THERE TO ECONOMIC DEVELOPMENT?

The perception that obstacles to economic development exist is an important consideration in determining a nation's ability to create economic opportunities. If government leadership is limited by the amount of resources available, its ability to plan for the development of such resources will also be limited by the tribe's vision of the development opportunities possible. The questionnaire listed seven possible obstacles: (1) lack of capital, (2) lack of control, (3) lack of trained management, (4) lack of trained personnel, (5) lack of natural resources, (6) lack of financial resources, and (7) intrusion of BIA requirements (see question no. 16). The five largest *perceived* obstacles of those respondents who believed obstacles existed were: (1) lack of capital (mean, 3.650); (2) lack of economic resources (the ability to obtain capital, mean, 3.377); (3) lack of natural resources (mean, 3.278); (4) lack of trained management (mean, 3.171); and (5) lack of trained personnel (mean, 3.153).[1]

Almost all tribes said that they lacked capital (96%), 83 percent said they lacked financial resources, 76 percent said they lacked trained personnel, and 57 percent perceived a lack of natural resources that could be developed. A high percent of responding tribes indicated that the seven obstacles listed were major deterrents. Perhaps such tribes will have to rely more on ventures whose success is based on proximity to population areas, such as gambling casinos, than on the development of natural resources.

WHAT PERCEIVED ASSISTANCE IS NECESSARY FOR ECONOMIC DEVELOPMENT?

In addition to perceived obstacles, a tribal nation's leadership vision is bound by its *perceived* need for assistance. A tribe's conceptual development, of course, is contingent on its ability to acquire this assistance. The questionnaire listed eight areas in which tribes might perceive that assistance would be necessary. These involved needs for (1) outside consultant planning, (2) outside help to implement economic development plans, (3) outside help to develop resources, (4) outside help to develop markets, (5) outside help with marketing skills, (6) outside help with technical skills, (7) outside help from other governments, and (8) input from family kin groups (see question no. 17).

Of the eight suggested assistance areas, the three strongest *perceived* needs were (1) the need to develop management skills (mean, 3.398); (2) the need to develop technical skills (mean, 3.336); and (3) the need for assistance in planning (mean, 3.214).[2]

Over 94 percent of the respondents felt that their tribe needed programs to help develop technical skills if they were to undertake development plans. Nearly 92 percent expressed a need or desire for programs to help develop management skills to assist in economic development plans. Nearly 87 percent felt that help was needed from both outside agencies and internal kinship groups. Approximately 82 percent indicated that they needed help from outside consultants for both planning and implementing economic development. Fewer than 51 percent of the tribes felt that they had the information necessary to develop or market products.

These perceptions suggest a strong need to develop skills internally, but also a willingness to accept external help. It could be inferred that educational assistance programs should be developed by each tribal government to meet its needs for internal skills. The specifics of educational assistance programs would, of course, have to be tailored to reflect both the current and the potential resources of each individual tribe.

WHAT IS THE CURRENT AMOUNT OF ECONOMIC DEVELOPMENT?

Over two-thirds of the responding tribal governments reported some economic development (see question no. 4). However, nearly 60 percent reported that economic development provides 10 percent or less of the funds needed to finance their governments (see question no. 2). Additionally, over 60 percent of these tribes have netted less than $250,000 from these efforts. Fewer than 10 percent made over $1,000,000 on such ventures (see question no. 6). Thus, while many tribes have profited from economic development, few have made enough money to support the tribe's self-governance.

The average length of time for which tribes have engaged in economic development is 10.9 years (see question no. 8). Most tribes engage in multiple ventures (86%, see question no. 5). Very few have developed their natural resources (3.5%) or engaged in agriculture (2.4%) as primary ventures. Most tribes without economic development were considering the possibility of engaging in such ventures. Moreover, many of these tribes were considering the development of their natural resources, but the possibility of acting on such ideas depends on the use of tax-incentive businesses like gambling casinos and the sale of tax-exempt products like alcohol and tobacco to finance such efforts.

MULTIVARIATE ANALYSIS

Analysis of variance was performed with the independent variables—current amount of economic development and demographics—on each of the components of the three research questions: (1) how economic development decisions are made and managed, (2) what obstacles there are to economic development, and (3) what assistance is needed for economic development. Most of the results could have been anticipated from an analysis of what makes any business successful. That is, nations with more resources will have fewer perceived obstacles, and success breeds success.

Multivariate analysis reveals, as one would expect, that strong relationships exist between "the lack of financial resources" and "the need for assistance to develop economic enterprises."[3]

HOW ARE ECONOMIC DEVELOPMENT DECISIONS MADE AND MANAGED?

It was found that neither of the independent variables had a significant effect on how economic decisions were made. However, if none of the tested variables (representing the amount of economic development or the demographic variables of size and number and the percent of tribal members employed) provided answers, then obstacles, rather than government decision making, would appear to be of greater importance in explaining success in development. Appreciably, it is far easier to formulate strategies to overcome obstacles than it is to effect a strategy to change the decision-making structure of a nation's government.

It was also found that the management of economic development is not effected by the tested variables representing the amount of economic development (that is, whether or not development exists) nor by the amount of revenue generated by economic development. Although the demographic variable of size has no relation to how economic development is managed in Indian nations, the demographic variables—tribe size, number of tribal members employed, and percent of tribal members employed—bear a significant relationship to the business operations of tribal nations. The number of tribal members employed was significantly higher for those tribes employing some or all outside management than for those relying solely on internal management ($p < .0283$). Similarly, a significant relationship ($p < .0234$) was found to exist between those nations with at least some outside management and the percent of tribal members employed. Figures 9.1 and 9.2 illustrate these differences.

Figure 9.1
Number of Tribal Members Employed by Economic Development, by
Exclusively Internal Management and at Least Some, if Not All, External
Management (P < 0.0283)

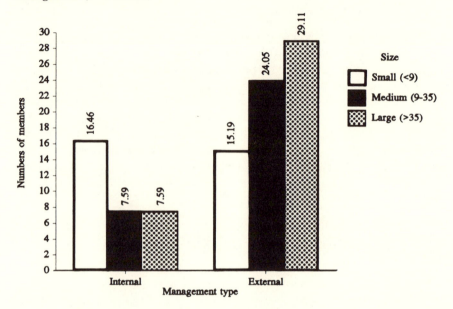

WHAT PERCEIVED OBSTACLES ARE THERE TO
ECONOMIC DEVELOPMENT?

Lack of financial resources was one of the strongest perceived obstacles.
When compared with tribes experiencing successful economic development,
it becomes evident that those tribes that earned less with their economic
ventures perceived a lack of financial resources as a primary hindrance
($p < .0020$). Figure 9.3 demonstrates this difference.

Another important area of influence on *perceived* obstacles was the cor-
relation with the population size of the nations involved. It was found that
those tribes with smaller populations stated that lack of resources, both
natural and financial, were the most significant obstacles to economic development. The most significant obstacle was lack of natural resources
($p < .0002$), but lack of financial resources (as a source of capital; $p < .0313$)
was also significant for smaller nations. Figures 9.4 and 9.5 illustrate these
significant differences.

WHAT PERCEIVED ASSISTANCE IS NECESSARY FOR
ECONOMIC DEVELOPMENT?

The perceived need for assistance was significantly related to many of the
tested variables. It was reported by the tribes without economic develop-

Figure 9.2
Percent of Tribal Members Employed by Economic Development, by
Exclusively Internal Management and at Least Some, if Not All, External
Management (P < 0.0234)

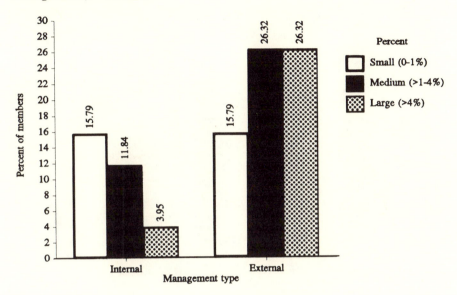

ment that lack of assistance in planning for economic development was felt significantly more by them than by tribes with development ($p < .0211$). More tribes without economic development also felt that assistance is necessary to help implement economic development ($p < .0135$) than tribes that were successfully developing their resources. Additionally, assistance in the form of input from kin groups was felt to be significantly more needed ($p < .0393$) for those tribes that have not launched economic ventures. Figures 9.6, 9.7, and 9.8 represent these differences between tribes with and without economic development.

Those tribes with economic development felt significantly stronger ($p < .0229$) about the need for assistance to help market products. Moreover, those tribes with higher sources of revenue from their economic development felt that more information was needed for economic development ($p < .0054$) than the tribes without high sources of revenue. Figures 9.9 and 9.10 illustrate these differences between tribes with and without high sources of revenue.

Those tribes that earned less with their economic development ventures than others also felt that outside help was needed, but this finding was not statistically significant ($p < .0876$). However, this finding helps to demonstrate the significance of tribes recognizing the importance of the need for outside help. If assistance is welcomed, rather than being forced upon them

Figure 9.3
Perceived Obstacle of Economic Resources, by Amount of Revenue Generated by Economic Development (P < 0.0020)

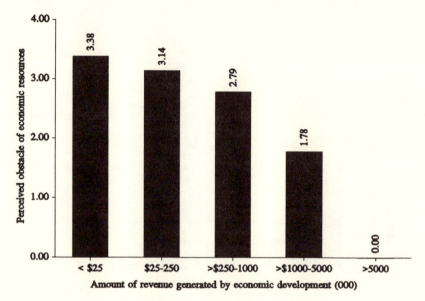

as some previous federal government interventions have been, such efforts will have the best chance for success.

CONCLUSION

The problem found by this study is not so much the inability of the Indian nations to use resources but rather their inability to get their resources to generate income. In essence, as is the case in the private business world, *it takes money to make money.*

Unraveling the determinants of successful economic development among Indian nations should provide a framework to assist other tribes with their economic endeavors. As noted by Joseph Kalt and Stephen Cornell in chapter 8, the real measure of self-determination is the performance and control of economic development. As increasing numbers of tribes are defining their political and governmental strategies, the impact and need for economic strength is causing them to focus on their economic resources.

This study has examined three major determinants. The first was how economic development decisions are made and managed; that is, the native governmental decision-making process. The second was the *perceived* obstacles to economic development. Finally, the third determinant was the *perceived* assistance needed for economic development.

These questions, as well as others, were asked of tribal leaders across the

Figure 9.4
Perceived Obstacle of Natural Resources by Small, Medium, and Large
Enrollments of Tribal Membership (P < 0.0002)

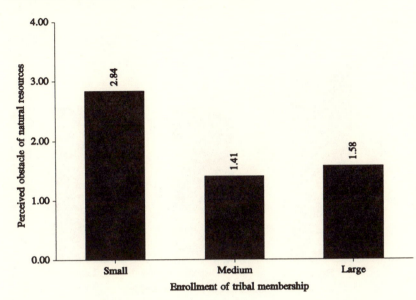

United States. The results provide an assessment of the current extent of
the tribes' economic development. Although few nations reported self-sufficiency through the use of governmental economic resources, their responses should target assistance toward economic self-sufficiency, and,
therefore, self-determination.

POLICY INITIATIVES

As control of Native American lands and government is slowly moving
toward self-government, economic independence is necessary. In Kalt's examination of the experiences of a number of tribes, they outline strategies
and signs of economic success. Kalt and Cornell's work (see chapter 8) also
traces the political and sociocultural roots of decision making as well as
depicting alternate paths to economic development.

Kalt and Cornell point out that the economic well-being of many American
Indians hinges increasingly on their tribe's own responses to the possibilities
for self-determination. The authors concentrate on the policy alternatives
on-reservation, while mentioning the off-reservation claims for compensation. (That is, the efforts to gain off-reservation claims that are concerned
with the lawsuits against the federal government and private individuals for
land treatied but taken away from Indian nations.) Indeed, settlements for

Figure 9.5
**Perceived Obstacle of Economic Resources by Small, Medium, and Large
Enrollments of Tribal Membership (P < 0.0313)**

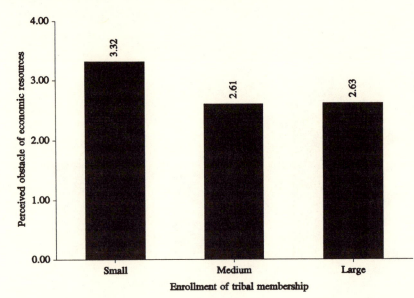

off-reservations claims have become the basis of future economic development for some tribes.

Initiatives for native enterprises should be twofold: first, the need for
access to financial resources, and second, the need for assistance toward
improved management of existing and future enterprises. The traditional
bank loan structure has not worked well with tribes. Moreover, to assume
self-determination, increased tribal employment must be a goal of both policy
initiatives and the resulting programs that they generate.

Currently, many resources exist for assisting tribes with economic development. One such useful directory is the *Economic and Community Development Resource Guide for Native Americans* published by the
Association on American Indian Affairs. Knowing how to use resources and
how to develop strategies are difficult tasks. A need for assistance in getting
started is evident in the questionnaire responses. External assistance can
indeed nurture internal skills.

One policy strategy that has worked extremely well in the state of Michigan
is a planning and development organization, the American Indian Business
Development Consortium, Inc., which is intended to serve as an information
and technical assistance resource within a geographic region.[4]

Another successful coalition (here, start-up finances were provided by the
federal government) is the Council of Energy Resource Tribes (CERT). To
build strength in negotiations with energy companies, twenty-five tribes

Figure 9.6
Perceived Need for Planning Assistance by Tribes with and without Economic
Development (P < 0.0211)

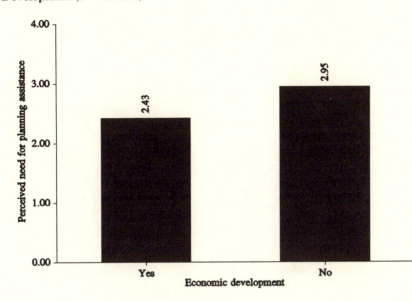

have joined together in CERT to pool technical assistance for energy development.

It is hoped that by sharing resources, tribes may find better opportunities
to develop their own economic plans. The survey results indicate that the
tribes have a strong perception of where their strengths and opportunities
lie. Policy support could further develop these perceptions into economic
reality with the help of Strength, Weakness, Opportunities and Threats
(SWOT) analyses for economic development.[5] Benefits would be realized
from federal funds directed toward jointly determined development and
training needs.

This survey shows that most Indian tribes have a long way to go before
they can utilize the income generated from the development of their resources to support total self-government. Tribes, at this time, are dependent
on external resources to build a foundation of strength and opportunity.
Many reservations do not contain the natural resources that can be developed. With a blending of resources with those of the outside world, which
will, in turn, link the white and Indian communities more intricately, many
tribes will have to depend more on access to white customers (e.g., gambling
casinos) than on the existence of natural resources. Policy will have to utilize
whatever opportunities are available to each tribe and its community.

Figure 9.7
Perceived Need for Implementing Assistance by Tribes with and without
Economic Development (P < 0.0135)

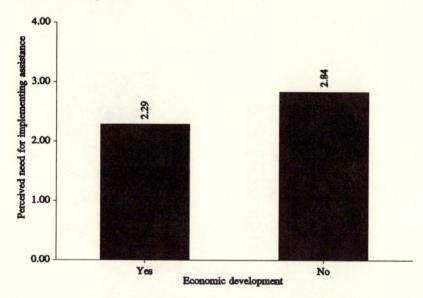

Figure 9.8
Perceived Need for Input Assistance by Kin or Family Groups, by Tribes with
and without Economic Development (P < 0.0393)

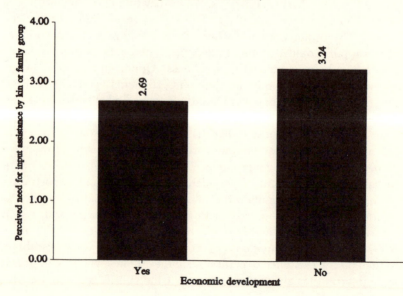

Figure 9.9
Perceived Need for Marketing Assistance by Tribes with and without Economic Development (P < 0.0229)

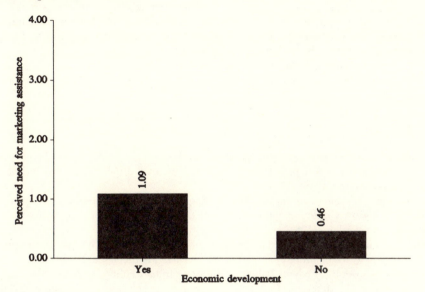

Figure 9.10
Perceived Need for Information Assistance, by Amount of Revenue Generated by Economic Assistance (P < 0.0054)

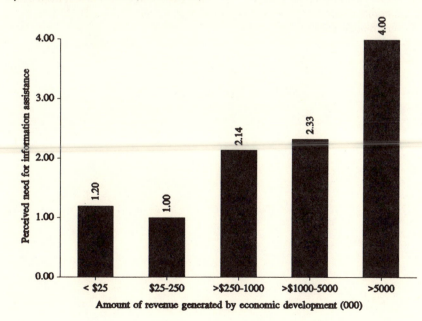

NOTES

1. Using a rating scale of 1 to 4, where 1 is "least strongly" and 4 is "most strongly."
2. Using a rating scale of 1 to 4, where 1 is "least strongly" and 4 is "most strongly."
3. Statistical relationships are reported: $p < .01$ = most significant; $p < .05$ = significant; and $p < .10$ = nearing significance.
4. A consortium with the support and cooperation of the state.
5. An analytical approach taught in most business schools and utilized by business analysts.

REFERENCES

Anders, Gary C. "Revenues from Tribal Natural Resources Should Alter Indian Social Institutions, Not Just Benefit the Few." *Journal of Contemporary Business* (1st quarter 1980): 57–74.

Association on American Indian Affairs. *Economic and Community Development Resource Guide for Native Americans*. New York: Association on American Indian Affairs, 1987.

Deloria, Vine, Jr., and Lytle, Clifford M. *The Nations Within: The Past and Future of American Indian Sovereignty*. New York: Pantheon Books, 1984.

Jorgensen, Joseph. "Federal Policies, American Indian Politics and the 'New Federalism.'" *American Indian Culture and Research Journal, 10,* no. 2 (1986): 1–13.

Jorgensen, Joseph. "Sovereignty and the Structure of Dependence at Northern Ute." *American Indian Culture and Research Journal, 10,* no. 2 (1986): 75–94.

Presidential Commission on Indian Reservation Economies. *Report and Recommendations of the President of the United States*. Washington, D.C.: U.S. Government Printing Office, 1984.

APPENDIX

1.   How many enrolled members are there in your tribe?

Population Range	Percent	N
1 - 499	33.3%	4 1
500 - 1,800	33.3%	4 1
1,801 - 53,151	33.3%	4 1

2.   How much of your tribal government is funded from economic
development? (The original question asked of other sources as well
as from economic development).

Range	Percent Response
zero to ten percent	59.5%
eleven to twenty percent	9.5%
twenty-one to thirty percent	6.0%
thirty-one to forty percent	2.6%
forty-one to fifty percent	6.0%
fifty-one to sixty percent	1.7%
sixty-one to seventy percent	0.9%
seventy-one to eighty percent	1.7%
eighty-one to ninety percent	3.5%
ninety-one percent to one hundred percent	8.6%
TOTAL	100.0%

3.   How much total money is necessary each year to finance your
       tribal government? (If you wish to be specific, exact or more
       approximate, figures are welcome).

6.0%	Under $25,000
13.7%	$25,000 to $75,000
13.7%	$75,001 to 175,000
7.7%	$175,001 to $250,000
27.4%	$250,001 to $1,000,000
31.6%	Over $1,000,000

4.   Does your tribal nation or corporation have any economic
       development? (If development has only reached the planning
       stages, please answer No and see question #9).

67.7%	Yes
32.3%	No

If No, skip to question #9.
If Yes, please continue.
5.   If Yes, which area(s) is this economic development in? (Check as many as apply).

      2.4%   Agriculture
      3.5%   Natural Resources
      0%   Production
      8.2%   Gaming (Bingo, etc.)
      85.9%   Other, please specify <u>with multiple businesses</u>

6.   If Yes, how much yearly net revenue (profit) is there from economic development? (If you wish to be specific, exact or more approximate, figures are welcome).

      30.9%   Under $25,000
      37.0% $25,000 to $250,000
      17.3% $250,001 to $1,000,000
      11.1% $1,000,001 to $5,000,000
      3.7%   Over $5,000,000

7.   Are these revenues (from economic development and other resources) sufficient to run your tribal government?

      15.7%   Yes
      84.3%   No

8.   How long has this economic enterprise existed? (If more than one type of enterprise, the number of years each has existed).

      10.92 mean years

9.   If your tribe does not currently have economic development, is your tribe considering economic development?

      47.3%   Yes
      2.3%   No
      50.4%   Yes, but considering additional

10.   If No, why not?

Various responses, see qualitative analysis.

If no economic development or consideration of economic development, skip to question #14.
Otherwise, please continue.

11. If your tribe is considering economic development, which area(s) is this economic development in? (Check as many as apply).

0 %	Agriculture
1.9 %	Natural Resources
6.7 %	Production
4.8 %	Gaming (Bingo, etc.)
86.7 %	Other, please specify <u>with multiple businesses</u>

12. If your tribe has economic development, how many people does the economic development employ?

  6969/80   Mean   87.11

Of these,
how many are tribal members?

  4759/81   Mean   58.75

how many are natives, but not tribal members?

  450/76   Mean   5.92

how many are non-natives?

  2360/77   Mean   30.65

If not 100% tribal employed, would members be interested in employment if training was made available?

81.4 %	Yes
10.0 %	No
9.6 %	100% tribal

13. If your tribe has economic development, is the development managed by tribal members or by outside managers?

33.3 %	Tribal members
9.2 %	Outside managers
57.5 %	A combination of Tribal members and Outside managers

14.   How are economic development decisions made by your tribal
      nation or corporation?

      44.4%   by tribal **council** only (skip to #16)
      12.1%   by tribal **members** at council meetings (no other
                       review process) (skip to #16)
      21.0%   by **separate branch** of tribal government (such
                       as an economic development board) (see #15)
      1.6%   other, please specify _____
                       _____
      21.0%   no economic development considered (skip to #16)

If decision is made by a **separate branch** of tribal government,
please continue.
Otherwise, please skip to question #16.

15.   What is this **separate branch of government** called?
      Various Responses.

Some questions about the problems with economic development.

16.   A major <u>obstacle</u> to economic development is:

a.   The **lack of capital** for economic development?
            95.9%   Yes
             4.1%   No
If Yes, how strongly do you feel this is an obstacle?
      Very Strongly   **67.8%**   Strongly   **30.4%**
      Somewhat   **1.8%**   Hardly at all 0 %
            Mean without Nos **3.650**   Mean with Nos **3.508**

b.   The **lack of control** over the projects by your tribal nation or
      corporation?
            28.4%   Yes
            71.6%   No
If Yes, how strongly do you feel this is an obstacle?
      Very Strongly   **42.4%**   Strongly   **45.5%**
      Somewhat   **9.1%**   Hardly at all 0 %
            Mean without Nos **2.765**   Mean with Nos **0.931**

c.   The lack of **trained management** for administering
      development?
          83.1%   Yes
          16.9%   No
If Yes, how strongly do you feel this is an obstacle?
      Very Strongly   38.2%   Strongly   41.2%
      Somewhat   16.6%   Hardly at all 0%
          Mean without Nos 3.171   Mean with Nos 2.667

d.   The lack of **trained personnel** for working on economic
      development?
          76.6%   Yes
          23.4%   No
If Yes, how strongly do you feel this is an obstacle?
      Very Strongly   37.9%   Strongly   44.2%
      Somewhat   17.9%   Hardly at all 0%
          Mean without Nos 3.153   Mean with Nos 2.452

e.   Insufficient tribal **natural** resources for economic
      development?
          57.3%   Yes
          42.7%   No
If Yes, how strongly do you feel this is an obstacle?
      Very Strongly   60%   Strongly   28.6%
      Somewhat 10%   Hardly at all 1.4%
          Mean without Nos 3.278   Mean with Nos 1.976

f.   Insufficient tribal **economic** resources for economic
      development?
          82.9%   Yes
          17.1%   No
If Yes, how strongly do you feel this is an obstacle?
      Very Strongly   52.5%   Strongly   41.6%
      Somewhat   5.9%   Hardly at all 0%
          Mean without Nos 3.377   Mean with Nos 2.869

g. The **requirements** of the Bureau of Indian Affairs?
          60.3%   Yes
          39.7%   No

If Yes, how strongly do you feel this is an obstacle?
    Very Strongly   **40.3%**   Strongly **38.9%**
    Somewhat   **20.8%**   Hardly at all 0 %
        Mean without Nos **2.976**   Mean with Nos **1.917**

Next, some questions about economic assistance.

17.   For your tribe's economic development, **as chair of the tribe** do you feel that:

a.   Help from outside consultants is necessary for **planning** economic development?
        81.8%   Yes
        18.2%   No
If Yes, how strongly do you feel this is necessary?
    Very Strongly   **39.4%**   Strongly **38.4%**
    Somewhat   **22.2%**   Hardly at all 0 %
        Mean without Nos **3.214**   Mean with Nos **2.648**

b.   Help from outside Tribe is necessary in **implementing** economic development?
        82.8%   Yes
        17.2%   No
If Yes, how strongly do you feel this is necessary?
    Very Strongly   **30.7%**   Strongly **37.6%**
    Somewhat   **29.7%**   Hardly at all 2 %
        Mean without Nos **3.000**   Mean with Nos **2.512**

c.   Your tribe has the necessary information to **develop** its resources?
        49.6%   Yes
        50.4%   No
If Yes, how strongly do you feel this is so?
    Very Strongly   **25.9%**   Strongly **51.7%**
    Somewhat   **17.4%**   Hardly at all 0 %
        Mean without Nos **3.070**   Mean with Nos **1.467**

d.   Your tribe has the necessary information to **market** its resources?
        31.1%   Yes
        68.9%   No

If Yes, how strongly do you feel this is so?
        Very Strongly   26.3%   Strongly   39.5%
        Somewhat   31.6%   Hardly at all 2.6%
            Mean without Nos 3.064   Mean with Nos 0.902

e.   Your tribe needs or desires programs to help develop
      management skills to assist in development plans?
              91.8%   Yes
              8.2%   No
If Yes, how strongly do you feel this is needed?
        Very Strongly   48.6%   Strongly   46%
        Somewhat   5.4%   Hardly at all 0%
            Mean without Nos 3.398   Mean with Nos 3.149

f.   Your tribe needs or desires programs to help develop
      technical skills to undertake development plans?
              94.2%   Yes
              5.8%   No
If Yes, how strongly do you feel this is needed?
        Very Strongly   46.4%   Strongly   42.9%
        Somewhat   10.7%   Hardly at all 0 %
            Mean without Nos 3.336   Mean with Nos 3.160

g.   Your Tribe needs help from outside agencies (help is necessary
      from agencies such as the BIA) for economic development?
              87.7%   Yes
              12.3%   No
If Yes, how strongly do you feel this is needed?
        Very Strongly   47.2%   Strongly   37.7%
        Somewhat   14.2%   Hardly at all .9%
            Mean without Nos 3.279   Mean with Nos 2.901

h.   To have successful economic development, organization and
      input from tribal kin groups is necessary?
              86.2%   Yes
              13.8%   No
If Yes, how strongly do you feel this is necessary?
        Very Strongly   49.5%   Strongly   34.3%
        Somewhat   15.2%   Hardly at all .9%

Mean without Nos **3.296**   Mean with Nos **2.861**

18. In the decision-making process for economic development, how
     strongly do you, **as tribal chair**, regard these influences?
                    (On a scale of 1 to 4)

     a.   The Bureau of Indian Affairs.   (**Mean   2.383**)
     Very Strongly   **11.7%**   Strongly   **29.2%**
     Somewhat   **45.0%**   Hardly at all   **14.2%**

     b.   Outside financial resources.   (**Mean   3.116**)
     Very Strongly   **37.2%**   Strongly   **41.3%**
     Somewhat   **17.4%**   Hardly at all   **4.1%**

     c.   Family groups.   (**Mean   2.725**)
     Very Strongly   **25.8%**   Strongly   **32.5%**
     Somewhat   **30.0%**   Hardly at all   **11.7%**

     d.   Other, please specify.   (**Mean   3.750**)
     Very Strongly   **63.9%**   Strongly   **27.8%**
     Somewhat   **5.6%**   Hardly at all   **0%**

19. Could your tribal government exist **exclusively** on your
     economic development revenues?
              17.8% Yes
              82.2% No
     If no, please explain.   **Various   responses.**

20. If you have or are considering economic development, what
criteria do you use to chose which area to pursue (e.g., income
differences in gaming over production, providing jobs, etc.)?
     Various   responses.

If you have any additional information or other comments that you
wish to share with me about your tribe's economic development,
please feel free to do so in the space provided below.
     Various   responses.

10

Who Is Subsidizing Whom?

Ronald L. Trosper

Indians are stigmatized by the idea that they receive subsidies from the federal government. Many economists and other social scientists believe that societies that receive permanent subsidies are in a position that is unhealthy and cannot last forever. Federal policymakers want to promote economic development in order to decrease budget expenditures for the benefit of Indians. These opinions suffer from issues of *truth in labeling*: Who is subsidizing whom, when all subsidies are examined? We need a complete picture of subsidies in order to determine who is truly being harmed by them.

On the Flathead Indian Reservation, Indians who are members of the Confederated Salish and Kootenai Tribes (the "tribe" or "tribes") are providing a subsidy to non-Indians greater than the ones received by Indians. This chapter explains the nature of the subsidy situation, which results from a hydroelectric dam located on Indian land. Although the particular subsidy on the Flathead Indian Reservation is of one type, the truth is that other Indians are also subsidizing non-Indians in many ways. The unusual part of this example is that Indians have some hope of ending their subsidy of non-Indians. In the year 2015, the tribe will be able to purchase the dam at book value and operate it. If the tribe can then sell power at opportunity cost to the highest bidder, the subsidy will end. Since other Indians are also subsidizing non-Indians, what should happen eventually on the Flathead Indian Reservation suggests a policy that could be carried out to benefit other Indians.

THE KERR DAM SITE

Kerr Dam sits six miles downstream from the mouth of Flathead Lake, on land owned by the Confederated Salish and Kootenai Tribes of the Flathead Indian Reservation. Montana Power Company (MPC), the owner of the dam, paid the tribes approximately $10 million in 1989 to rent the site. This rental is charged to MPC's customers. Valued at its opportunity cost of 5 cents per kilowatt hour, the total of 1,100 gigawatt hours produced each year is worth about $50 million per year, after expenses and capital costs. Because of the regulation policies for electric power, customers pay actual cost, not economic value. As a result, Montana Power's ratepayers pay $40 million per year less for their power than it is worth.[1]

The Salish and Kootenai Tribes receive approximately $16 million per year in federal government contributions to their livelihood. This figure includes all the costs of BIA operations on the reservation, welfare payments, education payments, Indian Health Service expenditures, and so on. These are programs seen by many as special programs for Indians, due to their history. Social Security, Medicare, and other programs available to Americans in general are omitted from this figure.[2]

Because the dam is used for peaking and for load-frequency control, game trout living in the seventy-two miles below the dam number only thirty per mile. Most Montana rivers of similar water quality have trout numbering in the hundreds per mile, ten times that observed. The diminished trout population indicates the general state of the river, which used to be an important source of subsistence and is now potentially an excellent source of recreation as well. The loss of these environmental benefits is a cost not currently borne by MPC or its customers and is not included in the above figures.

From these facts, I conclude that Indians still are subsidizing the settlers by at least $24 million per year. The subsidies of the nineteenth century and earlier have been replaced by modern ones. Americans currently believe that the subsidies have ended, but this subsidy will continue until the tribe begins its period of operating the dam in 2015.

This chapter reflects on the social and historical meanings of this and similar contemporary facts. I suggest some policies that would improve the general social productivity of both Kerr Dam and the Flathead River, while improving Indian lives. These policies, implemented on a national basis, would set things straight at last. Basically, we should let the rightful owners manage their assets, allow them to charge prices determined by opportunity costs, and stop the subsidies.

On the Flathead Reservation, in addition to returning the dam site, I would return operation of the National Bison Range and its two wildlife refuges to the tribes. I would not attempt to dislodge non-Indians from land where they live, including resort property on Flathead Lake.

Generalizing these policies to the nation, I would return hydroelectric facilities and national parks (and similar facilities such as monuments and wilderness areas) to the Indians. Neither action disrupts the homes of non-Indians. Dams are particularly easy to transfer, since so many are federal and others are governed under cost-of-service regulation. Parks and other similar lands are also easy to transfer. These policies make sense on grounds of equity and efficiency.

KERR DAM HISTORY

The Salish and Kootenai Tribes still have a claim to Kerr Dam because of their own efforts and their good luck with allies. Between 1927 and 1930, pro-Indian lobbyists led by John Collier and supported by a powerful Montana Senator, Burton Wheeler, assured that the tribe retained the land and would receive an annual rental. They thus went against the will of the secretary of the interior. In 1935, Congress amended the Federal Power Act to require that annual charges (the rentals) be adjusted after twenty years had passed from the start of operations, with an adjustment every ten years thereafter.

The dam began operating on May 20, 1939. Rental was $238,375 per year. Twenty years later, the tribe filed for an increase in rental. When they needed to have the license clause enforced in the early 1960s, liberals sat on the relevant hearing panels. In each case, before the Federal Power Commission and the Court of Appeals, the margin was one vote.[3] In 1967, the Federal Power Commission ruled that the rental should increase to $950,000, effective May 20, 1959. Using the ten-year provision, the tribe again filed suit to have this rental increased, and the Federal Energy Regulatory Commission increased it to $2,600,000, effective May 20, 1975. The annual charge remained at that level until the expiration of the license in 1980 and for each of the annual licenses issued during the consideration of a new license.

The Montana Power Company applied for a new license on June 1, 1976. The tribes applied on July 2, 1976. The Federal Energy Regulatory Commission assigned the case to an administrative law judge on July 20, 1983, saying "A hearing shall be held to determine whether the plans of one applicant are better adapted to conserve and utilize in the public interest the water resources of the region."[4]

The original goal of the tribe's application was to provide leverage for an increase in the annual rental. As the case proceeded, however, the tribe became increasingly interested in obtaining the license and operating the dam. Public comment by members of the tribe at open hearings strongly supported the tribe's acquiring the license.

The case addressed two main issues. First, if the company obtained the license, what should be the annual charge? Second, should the tribe obtain the license? Regarding the annual charge, the tribe's expert recommended a value of $47 million. The company maintained that the rental should either remain at $2.6 million or be lower. The experts for the secretary of the interior gave a figure of between $24 and $25 million, halfway between requests of the company and the tribe.[5] The reason for the experts' opinion was that they attributed half the rental to MPC, based on an earlier court ruling. All experts except those of the company valued power at opportunity cost.

With regard to the second question, the administrative judge stated that he "looked forward to the Tribes establishing precisely their plans as the potential licensee of the project and specific and concrete arrangements for this purpose so that the Commission could understand what was sought to be licensed."[6] He wanted to have proof of a purchaser. Although one large utility in California showed interest, no definite contract could be achieved in 1984. The tribe did not, in fact, have anything to sell.

The judge also wanted to know how the tribes would transport the electricity to market. This required wheeling. The dam is twenty-two miles from a major Bonneville Power Administration (BPA) substation at Hot Springs. The tribe presented estimates that the construction of a power line would cost $16 million. The judge pointed out that compliance with the National Environmental Policy Act required an environmental impact statement. Since one had not been completed, transmission was not proved possible. The tribes also argued that the Federal Energy Regulatory Commission (FERC) should force MPC to wheel on its lines. FERC denied the issuance of such an order "because the Tribes are not an electric utility entitled to seek a compulsory wheeling order."[7]

On August 30, 1984, the administrative law judge ordered the tribe to "show cause why the Tribe's application should not be summarily denied."[8] At the same time, he seems to have given the company the impression that if he awarded them the license, the annual charge would be in the range of $25,000,000. He also again urged the parties to settle the case. A staff person from the settlement staff of FERC was asked to assist. The parties began to negotiate in September, 1984.

While the litigation proceeded, a former member of the tribal council announced that he had offered and the company had agreed to settle with the company for a $30 million lump sum as rental for twenty years (*not* per year, but one payment for the twenty years), with the sum to be distributed on a per capita basis to all members of the tribe. They would amount to a one-time payment of $5,000 per tribal member. Council elections were scheduled for December 1984. A number of councilmen believed that this up-front offer of $5,000 would be popular.

The tribal council entered the bargaining in a difficult position. Their leverage on a license had been removed because they had been unable to find a clear purchaser and had been unable to wheel power. The ability to sell on an open market had been disallowed by FERC. Internal politics indicated a low rental might be acceptable should an election occur.

The parties bargained. The outcome of the bargain was a joint license. The company would operate the dam for thirty years. The tribes would be able to operate it for the last twenty years of the license and any subsequent annual licenses. The tribe would need to purchase the dam; the conveyance price will be the book value of the dam at takeover, original cost less accumulated depreciation. The earliest date for takeover is September 1, 2015. The annual charge would be $9 million per year, indexed to the Consumer Price Index, with June 1985 as the base month.[9] With inflation, this rose to approximately $10 million in 1989.

The outcome of the bargaining was not fair. Federal regulation worked to deny the tribe any chance to sell power from Kerr at opportunity cost. Tribal plans had to be specific, and transmission was a problem. Because the administrative judge included the impact on consumers as one of his important issues, he needed to know exactly which consumers would be affected. He seemed unable to assume that the tribe could sell the power during a fifty-year license period. The tribe knew the appropriate rental, approximately $50 million. The issue was not the true value of the site; it was the competence of the tribe to manage the dam.

FEDERAL GOALS

Both Republicans and Democrats place economic development as a major priority on Indian reservations. The desire is to reduce the cost of Indian programs. The usual proposals are modest, involving seed money for tribal or individual enterprise. Others propose special terms for outside interests on the reservation, such as would occur in enterprise zones. The Indian Development Finance Institution was originally proposed as a method of recapitalizing Indian economies. As legislation, however, it became a much smaller program. In addition, Indians were asked to help finance it.[10]

Current proposals are much too limited to accomplish the goal, given the extent of Indian poverty. In addition, they usually undercut the powers of tribal governments, thus presenting Indians with a choice between strong governments and economic development. Indians usually chose strong governments, for their own efforts have had the most effect in protecting what assets they still own.

My proposed policy resembles "privatization," which has been proposed for federal dams in the Northwest. Rather than sell the assets to corporations, I would give them to tribal governments. Each dam would have one owner, since the Bonneville Power Administration would no longer control many dams. Owners would be able to sell to the highest bidders. If the wholesale market for electricity is allowed to become competitive, electricity prices that are currently subsidizing hydroelectric consumers would increase to the proper market prices. This would improve the general efficiency of the nation's economy.

How many other tribes have lost much more? Because the tribe is a joint licensee, I can plausibly argue that it is a net subsidizer because it has a valuable piece of land. Other tribes are also net subsidizers, even if they do not "own" land under current law. The Salish and Kootenai Tribes were lucky; because the Montana Power Company is a private company, the conflict of interest is less than between the interests of the tribe and the federal government. Other tribes should also be in advantageous positions but are not, because federal dams sit on their land.

I can be specific. One half of Grand Coulee Dam is on the Colville Reservation. Chief Joseph and all the other federal dams below Grand Coulee benefit from its storage. Other Indian tribes of the Columbia River, through lost fishing sites, have rights to other dams. Dworshak is near both the Nez Perce and Coeur d'Alene Reservations.

On the Missouri River, Garrison Dam inundated the best parts of the Fort Berthold Reservation, and payment was inadequate.[11] Oahe Dam impacted the Standing Rock and Cheyenne River Reservations. Big Bend Dam is on the Crow Creek and Lower Brule Reservations. Fort Randall is on the Yankton Reservation.[12]

On the Colorado River, both Hoover Dam and Glen Canyon Dam are important. Hoover Dam is upstream from the five tribes that participated in *Arizona v. California*.[13] Glen Canyon Dam is on the Navajo Reservation. In the arid southwest, consumptive use rights have received great attention.[14] The taking of power values should also be examined, since both dams are important power generators. Standards for consumptive use rights take into account the intent of reservation establishment, not limited by technology known at the time. The principle should be extended to instream flows as well.[15]

Where there are no dams, there are parks. The Blackfeet Reservation abuts Glacier National Park. Yellowstone is near Wind River. Olympic National Park is near many tribes in Western Washington. The idea of returning federal land to Indians has been implemented on a small basis.[16]

WHY RETURN DAMS AND PARKS?

Each tribe's current land ownership is a result of a century of takings. Some takings are easier than others to reverse. In the case of the allotment policy, non-Indians now own the land. Current owners may be little connected to the original owners. In the case of the residential sites along Flathead Lake, for instance, many owners will have paid full price for the land. Even if owners receive payment for their land, returning that land would be unfair to current owners, who are forced to change plans. Finding the true beneficiaries would be difficult.

Hydroelectric dams and national parks are still owned by the entity which took the resources in the first place. Beneficiaries are the general public. A group of people such as the ratepayers of Montana Power are related to those who have benefited over the years from subsidized electricity. Current ratepayers are not benefiting from the ongoing subsidy.

Indians are owed something by those ratepayers. The bill for poorly compensated land taking should be paid for in a generalized way, without singling out particular people to have their lives disrupted. The return of land to the Hopi, for instance, hurt individual Navajo, who were themselves impoverished, subjugated people. A policy to return land now owned by others would simply repeat the mistakes of the allotment policy.

Simply transferring money to Indians has a number of drawbacks. The Indian Claims Commission effort, which was studied in a recent book, illustrates the difficulties.[17] The amount to be transferred should be the present value of a significant amount of income; upon seeing the amount, courts reduced it. The receiving generation is in an advantageous position. In 1972, the Salish and Kootenai Tribes received two cash settlements. One was a claim based on application of the allotment policy. The other was payment of Kerr Dam's increased rental from 1959–1972. The tribal council decided to divide up the money among the membership. This was approximately $6,000 each. (Congress required that $400,000 be invested.) I used the money as a down payment on my first house. Many other tribal members invested the money, while others spent it. People on welfare had their welfare payments suspended until they had used up the money. A disproportionate amount of these monies may have been spent on consumption. When invested, the benefits belonged to the individuals such as myself. People born after 1972 received nothing directly, except for benefits from the invested funds.

Transferring productive assets which cannot be consumed easily is better than transferring cash. Land and cash are different. Land, for Indians, is not at all like cash. Good evidence of this is the very low rates of sale of land by Alaska Native corporations. They have been able to sell land since the Alaska Native Claims Settlement Act, and have not done so.[18] One can be confident that large, productive assets such as dams and parks would not be subdivided or alienated. Just to be sure, one could, with the consent of the new owners, impose limitations on long-term sale of them. I think few tribal governments would object to having limitations placed on sale of the assets. Sales of electricity could have limits such as thirty or forty years, the useful life of competing fossil fuel plants.

A second objection to transfer of cash is that the real value of assets changes with time in unpredictable ways. A final objection to cash transfers is that excessive discounting is usually applied. Economists apply discount rates in order to analyze correctly the amount of today's consumption to give up for future consumption. This is a question of transfer between generations, or between periods of time in a person's life.

Such discounting is not appropriate as a criterion for the distribution of assets among a current generation of people in different groups. Alternately, if one is going to insist upon the relevance of current market prices, then such prices should be used in a consistent way, by including inflation in the valuation of land when discount rates are applied.[19]

IS THIS CASE UNIQUE?

Kerr Dam is not unique. The Navajo Nation is paid far less for its coal, oil, and gas than opportunity cost.[20] The same is true of other tribes selling fossil fuels. Until the Council of Energy Resource Tribes began a program to help tribes charge rights-of-way at opportunity cost, the BIA was charging a low percentage of the value of land in other uses. The general pattern is that the federal government, which has assumed a "trust responsibility" for managing Indian assets, has a poor record in obtaining the best price for Indian resources.

HOW MUCH SHOULD BE RETURNED?

I do not want to return the entire United States to Indians; neither do I think the current situation is tenable. Should one become caught up in detailed ex post analysis of particular assets, as I have done with Kerr Dam? Perhaps there is no alternative. A specific policy measure would need to define how much to return. By how much, I mean enough to allow Indians to live decent lives with economic independence, but not so much wealth that other people in society would feel themselves unfairly treated.

The difficulty is that most of the land in the United States would be under a cloud if all poorly or uncompensated transfers were to be reversed. I would propose that areas held in approximately the first centennial of the Declaration of Independence or the Constitution would be a good date. One hundred years ago, the federal government had not yet set forth to use its overwhelming military and economic power to break up reservations and Indian society. Usually, reservations at the late nineteenth century were contiguous holdings a part of which was described in each tribe's treaty. Even Indians removed from each of the Mississippi had land in Indian Territory. For tribes not subject to the allotment policy, some other event that is like the allotment policy could be used.

INDIAN ABILITY

The FERC judge threatened to dismiss the tribe's application because it could not prove that it was a bona fide applicant; FERC itself required that the tribe be a utility in order to wheel power. Unable to prove itself able to operate the dam, it was not able to obtain the license. This result is unfair. It is a practical example of how an erroneous idea has been allowed to determine the fate of people. Discriminatory attitudes should not determine ownership rights.

On first inspection, the test appears to be self-fulfilling prophecy designed to give a negative answer. The tribe was unable to sell electricity because it had no way to transport the power. In order to wheel electricity it needed to show it was an electric utility. I suspect the actual test was stronger. If there had been a sales contract, another reason to say no would have been presented. The judge could have ruled that a larger subsidy for Montana ratepayers compared to Californians or Indians was in the public interest. I suspect an underlying idea was an assumption that Indians do not have the ability to run Kerr Dam.

One counterargument to this is that the tribe could hire expertise, as other owners of assets do. An example is Montana Power Company's investors, who are not themselves electrical engineers but rather have a staff of such experts. Although this is a good point, it is rarely accepted. One reason might be the assumption that one needs expertise to supervise expertise. Another reason is prejudice. To persuade readers of the reasonableness of these proposals, I need to show that Indians can, in fact, manage complicated resources. There is plenty of evidence that when tribes do control large resources, they manage them well. Indians are particularly good at managing natural environments with multiple resources.

Take forests, for instance: Joseph Kalt argued that the White Mountain Apache are managing their forest better than public agencies do.[21] The annual conferences of the Intertribal Timber Council show tribes leading the BIA in forest management.[22] The School of Forestry at Northern Arizona University has discovered that Indian Tribes are more receptive to advanced ecological approaches to forest management than are other major managers of forests in the southwest.[23]

Indians are taking leadership roles in managing the salmon fisheries in the state of Washington.[24] Throughout the implementation of the Boldt Decision, Indians have had to prove competence in order to manage their half of the fishery.[25] They have consistently been able to do so. Surely, this is based on centuries of fishing in the coastal waters as well as on an ability to learn about fish from the same centers of learning that non-Indians use. The settlers usually manage fisheries and other game species with an open-access approach, which tends to wipe out the resource. In centuries of living from salmon, with adequate technology to wipe out the resource, Pacific Coast tribes did not do so.

The untold story of Philadelphia, Mississippi, is that the Mississippi Band of Choctaws are the leaders in developing the local economy. They attract and keep large, relatively labor-intensive assembly plants which are competitive with foreign manufacture of components for American goods. Coverage of the recent release of a movie about Philadelphia has totally missed the presence of an Indian tribe there, a tribe that is leading a stagnant rural society into economic development.

Historians have shown that the Five Civilized Tribes were managing quite well in Indian Territory prior to application of the allotment policy to them. The Cherokees pioneered public education. Their government was so strong that the United States had to abolish it and assume the right to appoint their Principal Chief in order to carry out allotment of their lands. Even earlier, the Cherokee had established a strong agricultural economy in the valley of the Little Tennessee River.[26]

On my reservation, the Confederated Tribes are clearly more sophisticated than other local governments in matters of environmental policy, tribal jurisdiction, public relations, and governmental management.

I showed in my article about ranching on the Northern Cheyenne Reservation that Indians and non-Indians were equally proficient in managing ranches.[27]

Jack Weatherford's recent book, *Indian Givers*, gives example after example of technical and social innovations which originated with Indians of the Americas (both North and South). He relies on recent scholarship to argue that Native Americans "transformed the world." An amazing number of the plants developed by Indian scientists before contact became central to the Industrial Revolution. We know that the Agricultural Revolution preceded the Industrial Revolution; cold-weather plants such as the potato were the foundation of increased agricultural productivity in cold northern Europe.[28]

Agricultural surpluses from the Agricultural Revolution financed the Industrial Revolution. England's Industrial Revolution started with factories manufacturing cotton. The long-strain type of cotton used in those factories originated in America. Fully 60 percent of the harvest of staple crops around the world are plants developed in the Americas.[29]

Indian expertise in medicine was equal to that of non-Indians in the nineteenth century; who does not recall that the special curing potions sold by vendors were said to be taken from Indians? The stereotype is based on reality: Aspirin, quinine and anesthetics are examples. England's naval might was aided by the cure for scurvy discovered in northern Canada by Jacques Cartier when Indians cured his party.[30]

Even the great cornerstone of American identity and political power, the Constitution, contains major features taken from Indian governments. The federal structure has no European model; the League of the Iroquois is the source. Separation of civil from military leadership was common in the Americas but rare in Europe. Impeachment of a president follows the model of impeachment of a *sachem* (tribal chief), with the exception that among the Iroquois, the women had the power of impeachment. The polite decorum of our Senate contrasts with the rudeness of the British House of Commons because our senators learned their manners from Indian traditions of public speaking. For these and more examples, see Weatherford's chapter 8, "The Founding Indian Fathers."

In chapter 7, "Liberty, Anarchism and the Nobel Savage," Weatherford traces the profound influence that Indian respect for individual liberty had on sixteenth-century European philosophers. Because Native American democracy was wider and deeper than any in Europe, politically, the Enlightenment was rooted in the Americas. Weatherford concluded:

Although today the notion of the noble savage usually reaps only scorn and historical footnotes as a quaint idea of a less-informed era, the idea had ramifications of great width and magnitude. The noble savage represented a new ideal of human political relations that mutated into hundreds of political theories that have swept the world in the past five hundred years. The discovery of new forms of political life in America freed the imaginations of Old World thinkers to envision utopias, socialism, communism, anarchism and dozens of other social forms. Scarcely any political theory or movement of the last three centuries has not shown the impact of the great political awakening that the Indians provoked among the Europeans.[31]

In 1935, the Indian Reorganization Act gave the secretary of the interior the task of bringing government back to the Indians. The Iroquois, whose women had voted for centuries, not decades, declined to accept IRA constitutions. Surely Canassatego was amused.[32]

I do not want to fall into the trap of claiming that the Industrial Revolution or the development of modern democratic government was entirely due to ideas, techniques, and products developed by Indians. My point is that historically, Indians have been *equal to* non-Indians as contributors of fundamentals that are commonplace in America today. In imposing standards of competence as prerequisites for the ownership of resources, the dominant society is imposing conditions it did not have to meet in obtaining those resources. Its sense of superiority in these matters is misplaced, being based on an incomplete understanding of its own history.

It may be true that specific tribes at present are far behind in matters of management and technical expertise. A century of subjugation has to have had effects. A practical policy needs to address the fact that Indians will need to engage in a period of study in order to attain their lost equality. I remind people that such education can and does happen quickly. The dominant society trains its youth over a span of between fifteen and twenty-five years. We know that investments in education can take place relatively quickly. Their proper instructors should be other tribes, who have regained a degree of self-government, self-determination, and so forth. I do not believe that current managers of dams or parks should have anything to say about the capabilities of the potential new owners. Disinterested third parties, such as other tribes with proved records of success, should be the judges of competence.

TOO SIMPLE A PROCESS?

Academics studying Indians often tend to overlook simple explanations or simple issues, turning instead to complicated ones. The simplest fact about Indians is that their land was taken unfairly. The interesting questions accompanying the simple story should not obscure it.

If the process was simple, then reversing it may also be simple. I have proposed two types of reversal that meet this test. Both dams and national parks are examples of lands that were taken but not physically divided up among the settlers. Since they are still federal property, changing ownership to Indian tribes would be relatively easy. Access to the lands would change. The rules of pricing electricity, for instance, could move toward competitive rather than regulated methods. The services of national parks would change in unexpected ways. Anticipations about such changes would generate objections to these proposals. Unlike those on the federal agenda, however, these changes would work. Both equity and efficiency would advance, a combination economists could support. Equity would improve because Indians would receive a fair share. Efficiency would improve because electricity would be priced at opportunity cost.

WHAT IS A SUBSIDY?

This chapter began by identifying a hidden subsidy, that of the owners of Kerr Dam to Montana Power Company's ratepayers. It ends with a review of intellectual subsidies from the sixteenth century. The failure to recognize these subsidies permits non-Indians to feel smug and causes Indians to suffer from low self-esteem. Identification of both subsidies is required. Perhaps the majority of Americans will never in fact let Indians receive their fair share of the material rewards of America. However, perhaps enough people can recognize the injustice and thereby provide some psychological relief for the continent's first inhabitants. The Indian side of history is gradually coming out. This chapter suggests ways in which the material results of that history could be reversed.

NOTES

1. Annual rental of the Kerr site is $9 million in dollars dated June 1985 and indexed to the Consumer Price Index. Federal Energy Regulatory Commission (FERC), Docket No. EL84–12–001, *Confederated Salish and Kootenai Tribes of the Flathead Reservation v. Montana Power Company*, Order Approving Settlement and Issuing License, July 17, 1985. The next best technology for Kerr is baseload

coal. Cost estimates are from Electric Power Research Institute, *TAG—Technical Assessment Guide*, vol. 1, *Electricity Supply* (Palo Alto, Calif.: Electric Power Research Institute, December 1986), Exhibit B.5–3A. The levelized real cost is 50 mills. In its 1989 rate request, Docket 8.6.15 before the Montana Public Service Commission, Montana Power proposed to purchase power from Colstrip 4 at a rate of 47 mills, stating that this rate is the long-run avoided cost of their power supply. Testimony of R. John Leland. Actual generation plus payments from downstream dams, less the earned rate of return on capital and operating costs, totals slightly more than $50 million per year. The amount will vary if peaking or lead frequency control are undertaken.

2. U.S. General Accounting Office, *Montana Indian Reservations: Funding of Selected Services, Taxation of Real Property*, GAO/HRD–89–1BR, October 1988; Confederated Salish and Kootenai Tribes, "Self-Governance Demonstration Project Report to Congress," submitted to the U.S. Senate Select Committee on Indian Affairs, 101 Cong., 1st sess., February 9, 1989; Confederated Salish and Kootenai Tribes, "Economic Impact Study" January 1984. The total is preliminary, pending reconciliation of expenditure estimates from different years.

3. *Montana Power Company v. Federal Power Commission, The Confederated Salish and Kootenai Tribes, and the Secretary of the Interior*, 445 F. 2d 739 (1970), *cert. denied*, 400 U.S. 1013 (January 18, 1971).

4. 24 FERC 61,088 (July 20, 1983).

5. Gordon Taylor, "Direct and Answering Testimony on Behalf of the Confederated Salish and Kootenai Tribes" January and April 1984.

6. 28 FERC 63,065 (August 30, 1985).

7. 28 FERC 61,252 (July 25, 1984).

8. 28 FERC 63,065 (August 30, 1985).

9. 31 FERC 63,015 (April 16, 1985).

10. U.S. Senate, Select Committee on Indian Affairs, *Indian Development Finance Corporation Act*, Hearing on S. 721, 100th Congress, 1st sess., April 30, 1987. Total federal appropriations for the corporation were proposed to be $102 million. This contrasts to the range of $3.6 to $8.0 billion estimated as the shortfall in "Estimation of Capitals Needs for an American Indian Development Finance Institution," located in *An American Indian Development Finance Institution*, Committee Print of the Select Committee on Indian Affairs, U.S. Senate, 99th Congress, 2d sess., S. Prt. 99–102, April 1986, pp. 73–82. The smaller figure results from an estimated number of jobs needed and a capital/labor ratio. The larger results from multiplying a per-capita income gap by a capital/income ratio. The base year is 1979.

11. Ronald Cummings, "Just Compensation for Lands Taken from the Three Affiliated Tribes of the Fort Berthold Reservation for the Garrison Dam" (Manuscript prepared for the Legal Department, Three Affiliated Tribes, North Dakota, November 1984).

12. Michael L. Lawson, *Damned Indians: The Pick-Sloan Plan and the Missouri River Sioux, 1944–1980* (Norman: University of Oklahoma Press, 1982), p. 28.

13. 460 U.S. 605 (1983).

14. Gary D. Weatherford and F. Lee Brown, *New Courses for the Colorado River: Major Issues for the Next Century* (Albuquerque: University of New Mexico Press, 1986).

15. That instream flows have received insufficient attention is evident in American

Indian Resources Institute, *Tribal Water Management Handbook* (Oakland, Calif.: American Indian Lawyer Training Program, 1988), pp. 31–32.

16. Since 1973, beginning with the Menominee Restoration Act, some lands have been returned to Indians. For a list of specific cases with reasons, see Kirke Kickingbird and Karen Ducheneaux, *One Hundred Million Acres* (New York: Macmillan, 1973).

17. Imre Sutton, ed., *Irredeemable America: The Indians' Estate and Land Claims* (Albuquerque: University of New Mexico Press, 1985).

18. Byron Mallott, "Effective Communication: Reporting to the Folks Back Home," *Indian Forests—The Land—The People—The Future* (Twelfth Annual National Indian Timber Symposium, Final Proceedings, Fairbanks, Alaska, June 5–9, 1988), pp. 47–52.

19. See, generally, Sutton, *Irredeemable America*. Leonard Carlson noted the failure to account for inflation or interest in most claims (see "What Was It Worth? Economic and Historical Aspects of Determining Awards in Indian Land Claims Cases," pp. 97–102). In addition, Charles F. Wilkinson reviewed the ways in which Indian rights are not subject to certain otherwise usual effects of time. See "Insulation against Time," chapter in *American Indians, Time, and the Law* (New Haven, Conn.: Yale University Press, 1987), pp. 32–52.

20. Phillip Reno, *Mother Earth, Father Sky, and Economic Development: Navajo Resources and Their Use* (Albuquerque: University of New Mexico Press, 1981), pp. 106–32.

21. Joseph P. Kalt, "The Redefinition of Property Rights in American Indian Reservations: A Comparative Analysis of Native American Economic Development" (Harvard Project on American Indian Economic Development, May 1987).

22. For example, see *Indian Forests—The Land—The People—The Future*.

23. W. W. Covington and D. B. Wood, "Advancing Total Resource Management through Cooperative Native American Research, Development, and Application" in *Indian Forests—The Land—The People—The Future*.

24. Larry Kinley, "The Northwest Salmon Fishery," pp. 207–221; and Alvin Ziontz, "The Case of the Pacific Northwest Indian Fishing Tribes: Benefits and Costs of Overcoming Dependency," pp. 188–199, in *Overcoming Economic Dependency* (Chicago: D'Arcy McNickle Center for the History of the American Indian, The Newberry Library, Occasional Papers in Curriculum, No. 9, 1988). See also Fay C. Cohen, *Treaties on Trial: The Continuing Controversy over Northwest Indian Fishing Rights* (Seattle: University of Washington Press, 1986), pp. 154–78.

25. *U.S. v. Washington*, 384 F. Supp. 312 (1974); 506 F. Supp. 187 (1980).

26. Jefferson Chapman, Hazel R. Delcourt, and Paul A. Delcourt, "Strawberry Fields, Almost Forever," *Natural History*, September 1989, pp. 50–59. Ragweed pollen, a signal of significant agricultural development, reached levels of 30 to 50 percent in lake sediments 1,500 years ago. Similar levels were reached in other parts of North America during the European expansion. The authors undertook their research in order to learn about the homeland of the Cherokee before the sites were inundated by Tellico Dam.

27. Ronald L. Trosper, "American Indian Relative Ranching Efficiency," *American Economic Review*, 68, no. 4 (September 1978): 503–16.

28. Jack Weatherford, *Indian Givers: How the Indians of the Americas Transformed the World* (New York: Crown, 1988), pp. 65–71.

29. Ibid., pp. 42–45. Recall that mechanized cotton factories happened to be the first industrial sector in Europe. Other industrial materials from the Americas are sisal, rubber, and dyes. Weatherford even suggested that Machu Picchu should be seen as an agricultural station that was built to provide a variety of altitudes and aspects for agricultural research. Chap. 4, "The Food Revolution," pp. 59–78.

30. Ibid., p. 182. Weatherford claimed "From the very first contacts between the Old and New World, European doctors recognized that the Indians held the key to the world's most sophisticated pharmacy" (p. 183). On the dubious side, Indians also provided tobacco and coca.

31. Ibid., p. 130.

32. In 1744, Chief Canassatego asked the colonies to unify so that they could speak with one voice to the Iroquois. In fact, he first proposed the idea of a United States of America. Ibid., p. 135.

11

Forest-based Economic Development in Native American Lands: Two Case Studies

Linda Kruger and Graciela Etchart

Plants ask that we leave some for other creatures,
That we remember seasons to come
And people to come.

—Yakima Nation Cultural Center

WHAT IS ECONOMIC DEVELOPMENT?

The traditional measure of economic development has been growth in per capita real income. In recent years, however, economists have broadened their interpretation of economic development. It is now seen as a multifaceted phenomenon with political, social and economic implications, and which means growth and change, especially changes in values and institutions.[1]

The idea of sustainable development is similar. Sustainable development has been defined as development that meets the needs of the present without compromising the ability of future generations to meet their own needs.[2] When broadly conceived, it addresses the sustainability of economic, social, and environmental systems. "Sustainable development implies using renewable natural resources in a manner which does not eliminate or degrade them, or otherwise diminish their usefulness for future generations."[3] In the case of a forest, sustainability means that a given stock of trees should not decline over time. This may be measured either by volume or area.

The achievement of an ecologically sustainable form of development is the process that seeks to result in a higher standard of living (however interpreted) for human beings by enhancing their capabilities to live well. The process also recognizes that this cannot be achieved at the expense of environmental integrity. Strategies for achieving an ecologically sustainable mode of development would vary according to region, as each would face different conditions and different conceptions of developmental goals.[4]

Accordingly, sustainable development shifts the emphasis in development from quantitative to qualitative considerations, such as community values and relationships, as well as community-based development and local control over resources, self-reliance, personal growth with increased economic capacity, and decentralized forms of government.[5]

ECONOMIC DEVELOPMENT FROM A NATIVE AMERICAN PERSPECTIVE

> Mother Earth was not ours to own but
> was only in our keeping for those yet unborn.
> —Yakima Indian National Cultural Center

Traditionally, Native Americans think that they belong to the land in a spiritual sense much more than the land belongs to them in any material sense.[6] They believe that all aspects of life are sacred. All animate and inanimate beings have their own special qualities and their own inner spiritual force, which must be respected. People are part of this whole, equal or lesser than all other things but not above them. Human existence is not possible without the natural environment because the survival of human beings depends on the survival of the other living things. From this perspective, the harmony of land, water, and air is crucial to the cultural, spiritual, aesthetic, physical, and economic health of the people.

Native peoples perceive themselves as a functional and essential part of the natural elements in their traditionally occupied lands, their holy lands. This value system resulted in the natives' intense attachment to their native soil, a reverent disposition toward habitat and ancestral ways, and a restraint on individual self-seeking in favor of family, kinship, and community.[7] Each native ethnic group has culturally prescribed procedures for using the land, plants, and animals. Maintaining this relationship through the proper stewardship of the natural resources is critical for their persistence as a people.[8] They believe that they have the right to use the land because they have a supernaturally derived responsibility to care for it, and to do so, they must subsist as ethnic groups.

Economic development of resources is not incompatible with the natives' cultural values, but to be acceptable to them, economic development must not violate, but should protect, Indians' identity and the values by which they live, while helping them to make a better economic adjustment to a new social and economic context. Self-determination, internal control of property rights of land and resources, and Indians' involvement in all the stages of development are central to successful economic development in ways that preserve and strengthen cultural identity. "Unless projects for economic development occur on their own terms and in ways that are consonant with their own choices, opposition to economic and political change will preclude any engagement whatsoever in projects of direct change."[9]

Native Americans do have competing demands of conservation and development. They recognize them as conflicting, but they argue that native-controlled development activities are not in conflict with the preservation philosophy because of who is doing the development and how the development is done. If faced with a forced choice situation, they rank in importance cultural resources that could be impacted by a proposed development project. Through this ranking, the probability of the most prized resources being protected is increased and the less special resources are placed at greater risk. Thus, even though all land is sacred, a specific area may be considered as having less sacred value and development may be pursued on it.[10]

The reservations are the last area of the country where Native Americans can practice their culture and exercise their right to self-government in accordance with the values of their people. They can pass and enforce tribal conservation and environmental laws, regulate economic activity, and encourage economic development that is culturally and economically suitable for their reservations. In doing so, they are adapting modern methods to sustain traditional beliefs.

However, they face serious obstacles to the economic development of their reservations. Probably the worst obstacle is the lack of capital. They have little collateral to get loans because their lands are held in trust and they cannot sell them or borrow against them. At the same time, federal funds that have provided some financial relief have been increasingly cut off. The lack of managerial and technical skills within many reservations make them dependent on outside experts that frequently do not share or even understand native beliefs. Finally, the distance to major economic centers and the reservations' poor transportation and communications facilities contribute to their isolation.[11]

In contrast to prior native claims settlements, the settlement of Alaskan natives' claims relied on the creation of corporations instead of reservations. The sections that follow compare these two different approaches to development by native peoples, both of which are based on forest resources. The comparison between the cases is not symmetrical because the available information was not parallel. Nevertheless, the tendencies in both cases are defined and can be compared. In one of them, the natives' involvement in the forest management process ensured the accommodation of their beliefs with Western technology, in line with the concept of sustainable development. In the other, the lack of corporate expertise among the natives, coupled with forced entry into the corporate world, prevented their beliefs from

Figure 11.1
Map of the Yakima Indian Nation

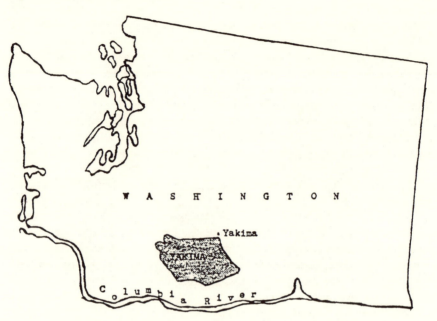

being as easily accommodated in the development process. For these reasons, and others to be explained, the development of the latter approach is
not sustainable.

THE YAKIMA INDIAN NATION OF WASHINGTON STATE

The Nation and Its Government

The American Indians who constitute the Confederated Tribes and Bands
of the Yakima Indian Nation represent fourteen diverse, but culturally related, tribes, bands, and villages living on or near the Yakima Indian Reservation, an area of 1.4 million acres in the south-central portion of the state
of Washington. On June 8, 1855, the Yakimas signed the treaty that established the reservation and created the new political entity, the Yakima Indian
Nation (Figure 11.1).

The northern boundary of the reservation is Ahtanum Ridge, south of the
town of Yakima; on the western side, Pahto or Mt. Adams, the tribe's sacred
mountain, rises to a height of 12,307 feet. Eastward from Mt. Adams lie the
Cascade Mountains. The Yakima River Valley, an important agricultural area,
forms the easternmost boundary, and the southern borderline is provided
by the Horse Heaven–Simcoe Mountains. It is a land rich in timber, fertile

Forest-related Employment and Wages

Forest – Related Indian Employment					Branch of Forestry Wages Only
Branch of Forestry Federal	Tribal	Non-Gov't	Total	Percent	
26	117	26	169	17	$1,794,413
26	148	27	201	*	1,750,938
27	154	25	206	13	1,843,589
28	166	18	212	10	1,635,592
25	164	13	202	9	1,431,511
12	163	16	191	7	1,368,145
15	149	19	183	9	1,326,260
15	104	19	138	9	847,667
10	120	9	139	*	783,692

...ated Tribes and Bands of the Yakima Indian Nation, "Yakima Indian ...st Management Plan: Period 1983–1992," Toppenish, Wash., 1988.

..." through clear communication between the tribe and ...roved communications sought to ensure that the BIA's ...ork was "consistent with the cultural, ecological, and ...of the Yakima Indian Nation as expressed through the ...20

...ispute was related to the BIA trust responsibility and ...tion. The Yakima Tribe continued to influence forest ...funding over half of the forest management budget, ...constituted about 6 percent of the BIA Branch of For-...the tribe continued to expect the bureau to perform ...y in the management of forest resources. The Tribe ...e of the BIA employing tribal members as staff rather ...staff. So, tribal members, employed by the BIA Branch ...responsibility of carrying out the bureau trust respon-...nt of forest resources. Due to a general lack of profes-...rs, the agency's policy became to employ Indians in ...nd, in some cases, classified professional positions as ...e existing professional staff to train and supervise the ...n staff and to monitor and oversee the forest. Table ...st-related Indian employment and wages for the period ...t-related Indian employment has been increasing over

soil, and water. Approximately half of the area is suited for irrigated agricultural purposes or exists in sagebrush-grass cover. Toward the summit of the Cascade Range, the annual available moisture increases and forest vegetation types become the dominant cover. The majority of the reservation's people live in the valley, but as a result of allotment, the Yakimas today are a minority in their own homeland. Of the more than 27,000 people who reside on the reservation, only about 7,000 are Yakimas.[12]

The Treaty of 1855 guaranteed that the reservation would be held for the "exclusive use and benefit" of the Yakimas. It also promised them exclusive fishing rights on the reservation, as well as "at the usual and accustomed places in common with citizens of the Territory." The Indians were guaranteed the right to hunt, gather roots and berries, and pasture their horses and cattle on open, unclaimed land.

The Yakima Indian Nation is governed by the tribal council which was established in 1944. This council is elected by the General Council of the Nation and meets monthly to establish policy and preserve treaty rights. While not in session, three of its members constitute the Executive Committee. Additionally, there are seven committees that report to the tribal council and exert considerable power by overseeing the programs under their jurisdiction. Three of these committees are related to the development of the tribal natural resources. One supervises legislative, timber, grazing, and economic development; one is in charge of land; and a third is responsible for law and order and for fish and wildlife. The Timber Committee and the Natural Resources Division of the tribal government form a joint committee to decide on issues related to the use of the forest.

The Forest

The Yakima's relationship with their land and its resources evolved over a very long period of time and continues to evolve within the framework of new life-styles and changing technology. That evolution and change were sometimes forced on them, but in other instances, the Indians themselves sought new means to reach their own goals. However, whether changes were social or economic, the forest has been integral to the formation of their identity on the reservation. To them, the forest offers hundreds of resources, such as roots, fruits, fibers, animals, fish and other aquatics, birds, minerals, and places of spiritual guidance and strength. The latter is the connecting fiber in traditional Indian life.[13] Preserving and developing the tribal land and its resources is seen as one of the most sacred responsibilities by the tribal government.

The Yakima forest covers an area of about 590,000 acres. Of this total, about 475,000 acres are commercial and the rest are noncommercial. The commercial land is composed of approximately 430,000 acres of tribal land and 50,000 acres in allotments. Noncommercial land includes about 97,000

Table 11.1
Yakima Indian Nation: Timber-related Income

Year (1)	Harvest Volume MBF	Tribal Timber Income ($) (2)	Tribal Income ($)	% of Tribal Income from forest
1974	144,754	10,375,210	10,877,418	95.4
1975	128,510	8,876,415	9,848,507	90.1
1976	120,928	13,525,890	15,367,717	88.0
1977	93,017	13,028,247	13,699,712	95.1
1978	153,377	16,958,834	17,340,638	97.8
1979	135,031	20,611,160	22,653,471	91.0
1980	161,478	15,878,009	19,384,429	81.9
1981	114,693	20,273,450	24,245,017	83.6
1982	57,859	9,081,958	13,393,640	67.8
1983	71,985	9,391,189	NA	
1984	70,236	11,098,667	NA	
1985	70,797	8,898,115	NA	
1986	84,591	14,174,649	NA	
1987	104,916	18,968,694	NA	

NA = Not available

(1) 1974–1976 are calendar years. 1977 timber sales include only January through September. 1978 to present are fiscal years beginning on October 1.

(2) From 1974 to 1982, timber income includes timber-related revenues and fees. From 1983 to present, it includes timber harvests revenue only.

Source: Based on data included in BIA and Confederated Tribes and Bands of the Yakima Indian Nation, "Yakima Indian Reservation Forest Management Plan: Period 1983–1992," Toppenish, Wash., 1988; and Reservation Annual Reports 1982–1991.

acres of grasslands and 14,000 acres of hardwoods and other cover. There are also about 35,000 acres of non-Indian land within the administrative forest boundary. Most of the forests consist of ponderosa pine, Douglas fir, western larch, hemlock, and cedar. The forested area contains a total of 8.5 billion board feet of conifer net sawtimber volume, 9.0 inches DBH (diameter at breast height) and larger.[14]

From an economic perspective, forest income, comprised almost entirely of income from timber harvests that are sold on the open market, has provided a large part of total tribal income. Table 11.1 includes the volume and value in current dollars of timber for the period 1974–82, and the correspondent tribal income. As Table 11.1 shows, since 1974, over 80 percent of the total tribal income has been realized from timber.

Economic Development and the Relationship with the Bureau of Indian Affairs (BIA)

The tribe's involvement with economic development issues has evolved over time. Through the tribal council and an Overall Economic Development

---

and Planning Comm
istration of the fores
timber sales. The re

Since the passing
reservations were n
Secretary of the Int
operations and man
sustained yield."[15,16]
sustained yield agree
of Washington, and
pate. It was in the lat
in the management c
began to discuss timl
actions in considerab
management, bids, a
sustained yield was a
established that "grov
sustained production
stocking."[17]

During the 1970s,
quality, a renewed t
religious/cultural reso
and long-run managen
the primary forest use
of multiple use plann
with other forest uses,
ing, and the harvest of
yield principle. The p
a "disease-insect-free"
tree species. Clear-cu
natural reproduction.[1]

Up to the mid–197(
goals of forest produc
goal of sustained yield
tribe began to put grea
it complained that the
1977, the tribe establi
in the northwestern co
members today and in
consider this area as a
with the overall manag
vironmental and cultur
Timber Program for 19
enues from timber sale

Table 11.2
Yakima Indian Natio

Year	Total Indian Employment within Reservation
1982	1024
1981	*
1980	1563
1979	2061
1978	2232
1977	2892
1976	1950
1975	1540
1974	*

Source: BIA and Confe
Reservation F

Yakima Indian po
the bureau. The i
presales and sales
economic objectiv
Timber Committe

Another issue c
Indian self-detern
management poli
and their employe
estry staff. Howe
its trust responsi
preferred the pra
than adding to tri
of Forestry, had
sibility for manag
sional Indian for
technical position
technicians, usin
nonprofessional l
11.2 summarizes
1974–1982. The

time, but it still remains at less than 20 percent of the total Indian employment within the reservation.

The development trend that emerged in the 1970s became accentuated during the 1980s. The 1982 Branch of Forestry's Program Review stated the importance of receiving tribal input and direction for developing action guidelines that are "totally responsive to tribal desires," thus emphasizing the role of the tribe in the management of the forest.[21]

The 1982–92 Forest Management Plan establishes that management activities will be conducted in such a manner that "will protect the cultural heritage and unique life styles of the Yakima Nation and the Confederated Tribes," while maintaining the economic return to the Indian owners consistent with other goals. The plan objectives require the use of multiple-use management practices that would:

- develop, maintain and enhance commercial forest lands in a perpetually productive state, . . .
- establish and develop a timber sales program and a long-range multiple use forest plan, . . .
- encourage forest development by Indian people, . . . [and]
- preserve the forest in its natural state wherever considered prudent or desirable by the authorized Indian representatives.[22]

The management alternatives must be selected to provide a level of forest production consistent with environmental and silvicultural constraints, and tribal aesthetics, social and cultural desires. Sustained yield is defined as "the highest uniform wood yield that may be sustained under a specified intensity of Management."[23] Silvicultural treatments emphasize the uneven-aged system but allow use of the even-aged system for some forest types or under certain conditions. The plan also provides for the maintenance and improvement of habitats for viable populations of wildlife species and for the perpetuation of plants classified as threatened, endangered or sensitive, and of natural food and medicinal plants.

The land use management plan categorizes units of land, or management areas, by capability and function, and establishes objectives that emphasize the dominant resource present in those areas. The forest acreage by management area and the annual allowable harvest are included in Table 11.3.

As Table 11.3 shows, as much as 25 percent of the forested area is being kept as reserve areas where no harvest is allowed. For specially designated areas, the 1982–92 plan establishes that the cultural value of these sites will take precedence over all other potential uses. These designated sites or zones of traditional significance have been identified as important cultural, historical or educational centers.

This definition is consistent with the resolution of conflict between development and cultural beliefs. Even though the whole forest is special for

Table 11.3
Yakima Indian Nation: Forest Acreage and Total Net Volume

Management area	Forest Acres	Volume MBF	Non-forest Acres	Total area Acres	Annual allowable Harvest (Net AAC MBF)
General forest	256,737	4,242,630	10,001	266,738	105,446
Winter Wildlife Refuge	109,107	1,803,015	56,439	165,546	41,115
Visual Corridors	3,505	57,921	292	3,797	1,461
Reserve Areas 1	123,270	2,350,690	29,992	153,262	-
Totals	492,619	8,454,256	96,724	589,343	148,022

Source: Prepared with information from BIA and Confederated Tribes and Bands of the Yakima Indian Nation, "Yakima Indian Reservation Forest Management Plan: Period 1983–1992," Toppenish, Wash., 1988.

1. Includes major watersheds, primitive areas, alpine areas, tract D recreation area, and special use areas.

the Yakimas, the areas that have particular cultural interest for the tribe have been ranked higher from a cultural perspective and will not be affected by the management of the forest for commercial purposes. The total acreage of these areas, however, is less than 1 percent of the total forest area.

In the case of the Yakima Indian Nation, culture and the appropriate institutional structure provided by the tribal government have not constrained development, but have provided the framework for it. The non-reserved areas of the forest—amounting to 75 percent of the total forested area—have provided, and continue to provide, enough timber income to maintain the stability of the tribal programs over time. In these areas, the conflict between culture and development is not an issue, because there is not such a conflict. However, where the importance of ecological and cultural values is ranked higher—the reserve areas—these values have prevailed over economic profits.

ALASKA NATIVE CORPORATIONS

When you look through the corporate eye, our relationship to the land is altered. We draw our identity as a people from our relationship to the land and to the sea and to the resources. This is a spiritual relationship, a sacred relationship. It is in danger because, from a corporate standpoint, if we are to pursue profit and growth, and this is why profit organizations exist, we would have to assume a position of control over the land and the resources and exploit these resources to achieve economic gain. This is in conflict with our traditional relationship to the land, we were stewards, we were caretakers and where we had respect for the resources that sustained us.[24]

Alaska Native Claims Settlement Act

The 1971 Alaska Native Claims Settlement Act (ANCSA) redefined the lives of most, if not all, of the state's natives.[25] "Congress intended ANCSA to integrate the Natives of Alaska into the institutions of Alaska."[26] Instead of establishing reservations or conveying land to existing tribal entities, ANCSA required the establishment of corporations to manage the 44 million acres of land and just under $1 billion granted Alaska Natives in exchange for extinguishing any claims to other land or resources. This was the first time that private corporations were used to settle native rights actions. Thus, land is owned by the corporations, and not Alaska Natives.

The state was divided into twelve regions. Each region and each village formed a separate corporation. The corporations received land based on native population. They selected land in order to protect subsistence opportunities and historic value and to make money for shareholders from resource wealth of minerals and timber. Cash was distributed to individuals and to village and regional corporations. Sealaska Corporation, for example, is the regional corporation for Southeast Alaska, representing approximately

15,800 Tlingit, Haida, and Tsimshian Indians, 21 percent of all Alaskan Native stockholders. There are twelve village or urban corporations in the Southeast region. For simplicity these are referred to as village corporations. Village corporation stockholders are also Sealaska stockholders. Sealaska stockholders may not be village corporation stockholders, they may be "at-large" members. A list of the Southeast Alaska Native corporations is included in the Appendix. Table 11.4 describes the differences between regional and village corporations.

Corporate Management under ANCSA

Under ANCSA, a native corporation's forests and other undeveloped land was exempted from taxation for twenty years, after which time it would be subject to normal taxes. The act also called for corporate stocks to be held off the market for twenty years after which time they could be freely traded. Natives were concerned about protection of the land base.[27] There was concern that the land could be lost "to bankruptcy, judgements against the corporation, or through the sale of the corporation itself" after 1991.[28] Shareholders' concerns included a fear that there would be a takeover of native lands by outside interests and dispossession of natives.

Native groups pursued congressional help and were successful in achieving amendments to ANCSA in 1987.[29] The amendments prevent corporate stocks from being traded on the open market unless the shareholders vote for the sale of shares; allow land to be placed in a land bank, free from taxation, and protected from adverse possession, bankruptcy proceedings, and involuntary dissolution of the corporation; and permanently exempt undeveloped land from state and local taxes. In addition, after timber is harvested, the land again becomes classified as undeveloped and regains protection from taxes.[30]

Economic Development

Natives, who have historically been dependent on the land for food and other needs, as well as for cultural identity, were given money and land in amounts far greater than they were familiar with managing. Most corporations hired nonnative managers, advisors, and technical and professional staff. The corporate system came from completely outside their culture and experience. For the most part, they simply lacked the training and experience necessary to operate the corporations and the institutional understanding to operate effectively in a market economy.[31] The corporations founded on principles of economics were isolated from native cultural and spiritual values. (As mentioned earlier, this may have been by congressional intent.)[32] Moreover, they received bad advice and made costly mistakes.

Competition developed between corporations for investment and market

Table 11.4
Comparison of Regional and Village Corporations

Regional Corporations	Village Corporations
12 for Natives in Alaska 1 for Natives outside Alaska	208 separate corporations
Sealaska covers all Southeast Alaska	12 village corporations in Southeast Alaska
Shareholders are Natives of the region - no sense of local control	Shareholders are residents of a village or local community provides a sense of local control
Region land allocation 273,000 - 330,000 acres	Land allocation (each corp.) 23,040 acres
Subsurface rights for village corporation lands	No subsurface rights
70 % of revenue from timber and subsurface estate must be distributed among 12 in state regional corporations	No distribution of revenues required
Not less than 50 % of income from distribution and govern- ment settlement money must be distributed to village corps. and at-large shareholders who live outside villages	No distribution required
Provided sufficient capital for investments, corporate operations (Sealaska share $93,162,000.)	Undercapitalized - less than $200,000 over 10 years, while duties required by ANCSA were estimated at $ 70,000/year. Only eight of the 208 were given a chance for success by a '74 Interior Dept. Study.
Greater opportunities for investment	Few business prospects
Developed an infrastructure for business and development	Lack of infrastructure for business and development
Employed Natives with most experience in dominant society	Lack of human resources trained or experience in business
Attracted the best leaders and brought in outsiders	Leadership spread thin

opportunities. They were isolated from centers of commerce and trade, and conflict ensued between the maintenance of subsistence resources and life-styles and the development and extraction of resources. The expansion and, in some cases, introduction of a cash economy and materialistic values led to a dependence on an economy that, in many places, could not be per-petuated.

Shareholders wanted dividends and jobs. Unfortunately, these were usu-ally incompatible goals. In order to turn a profit for shareholders, most money had to be invested away from the rural communities where jobs were needed. If jobs were provided locally, there would be much less profit and little, if any, dividends for shareholders. Shareholders' high expectations of dividends resulted in a conflict between short-term profits and long-term needs.[33]

Approaches by each corporation have been different, based on different cultures, institutions and resources. Some corporations emphasized local employment and community development, while others emphasized profits through outside investments.[34] Many differences led to variable levels of success of native corporations. There are also differences among the indi-vidual shareholders in any one corporation, as some maintain their depen-dence on and connection with the land through a subsistence life-style, while others have moved away from dependence on the land. This has resulted in conflicts between the conservation of subsistence resources and resource development and extraction activities. The conflict occurs mostly in dis-agreement over the degree of development versus conservation that is nec-essary.

Sealaska Timber Corporation

In Southeast Alaska, where most timber assets are located, native cor-porations were allowed to select over 540,000 acres from the Tongass Na-tional Forest under ANCSA. The land entitlement is split almost equally with the village corporations getting 56 percent of the entitlement (area and volume) and Sealaska, the regional corporation, with 44 percent.[35] Sealaska's land is approximately 56 percent Western hemlock, 33 percent Sitka spruce, and 11 percent Western red cedar and Alaska yellow cedar. Of the 200,000 acres of land conveyed as of 1982, 75 percent of the forest was estimated as commercial grade, 11 percent as non-commercial, and 14 percent as non-forest lands (Table 11.5). While most land was conveyed between 1979 and 1981, up to 130,000 acres remain to be conveyed to Sealaska. The estimated value of merchantable timber on the first 130,000 acres was $110 million. The highest-value timber was selected first, however, so the last 130,000 acres will have a lower value.

In 1980 Sealaska Corporation formed Sealaska Timber Corporation (STC), a wholly-owned subsidiary of Sealaska Corporation, to manage and market timber resources from native lands in the region. Seven village corporations

Table 11.5
Sealaska ANCSA Land

Management type	Commercial forest (Acres)	Volume (MMBF)	Non-commerc. forest (Acres)	Total area (Acres) 2
Merchantable timber	130,000	2,618	NE	130,000
Non-merchantable	17,300	NE	58,500	76,800
Stream buffers	1,700	34	NE	NE
Eagle trees	1,000	20	NE	NE
Wildlife corridors	NE	NE	NE	NE
Cultural sites	500	10	1,000	1,500
Reserve areas 1	28,000	540	NE	28,000
Total	178,500	3,222	59,500	236,300

Source: Richard Harris, Sealaska Corporation, phone conversation with author, 1992.
NE = not estimated. All other calculations are estimates.
(1) Reserve areas include major watersheds, high recreation, subsistence, aesthetic and traditional use values.
(2) Nonforest acres have not been calculated.

Table 11.6
Sealaska Corporation: Timber and Total Corporate Revenue (thousand $)

Year 1	Total Corporate Revenue	Volume harvested ANCSA lands (MMBF)	Operating Revenues Nat. Res.	% of Corporation Revenue from Natural Resources
1980	150,775	31.0	10,473	6.9
1981	234,378	46.3	25,445	10.9
1982	234,223	65.5	29,668	12.7
1983	234,853	53.6	12,603	5.4
1984	214,348	21.7	9,383	4.4
1985	237,171	49.6	19,152	8.1
1986	234,881	56.1	22,359	9.5
1987	269,515	101.4	50,771	18.8

Source: Sealaska Annual Reports, 1980–1988.
(1) 1980–1983 are calendar years. 1984 to present are fiscal years ended on March 31.

arranged for STC to manage their timber resources, allowing STC to become the largest exporter of logs in Alaska and fourth largest in North America. Under a corporate reorganization in 1985, STC was split and Sealaska Corporation—Forest Product Group took over responsibility for managing harvest of timber while STC became a marketing agent for forest resources.

Sealaska diversified its holdings and had major investments in seafood operations and construction materials in addition to forest products. As shown in Table 11.6, the revenue from timber sales accounted for only 11 percent of the corporation's 1981 total revenue. While the timber operations only resulted in income of between 9 and 20 percent of its revenues, in the mid–1980s, approximately fifty shareholders had jobs with the timber corporation and indirect employment through contractors added to the jobs and money coming into local communities.

Table 11.7
Estimated Harvests on ANCSA Lands in Southeast Alaska

Fiscal year	Sealaska (MMBF)	Villages (MMBF)	Total (MMBF)
1980	16	55	70
1981	45	77	122
1982	55	155	209
1983	25	207	232
1984	22	180	202
1985	50	214	263
1986	56	243	299
1987	101	234	335

Source: Gunnar Knapp, Native Timber Harvests in Southeast Alaska (Anchorage: Institute of Social and Economic Research, 1989).

Table 11.8
Forest Service Estimates of Harvest of Export Sawlogs and Pulp Logs on Southeast Alaska ANILCA Lands (MMBF).

Fiscal year	Saw logs	Pulp logs	Total
1980	83	62	145
1981	32	35	67
1982	137	22	159
1983	249	43	292
1984	202	56	258
1985	225	47	272
1986	296	NE	296
1987	286	110	396
1988	305	80	385

Source: Gunnar Knapp, Native Timber Harvests in Southeast Alaska (Anchorage: Institute of Social and Economic Research, 1989).
NE = not estimated.

Southeast Alaska Native Corporations' Timber Harvest

As all Native corporations are private entities, information of their operation is proprietary. Consequently, accurate information is hard to get. Estimates of timber volume included in the entitlement varies but is generally accepted to have been between 4.9 and 5.9 billion board feet at conveyance.[36] Since corporations and other private land owners are not required to report harvest data, calculations as to volume in the entitlement and volume harvested are estimates. Tables 11.7 and 11.8 provide information on acreage and harvest from Sealaska and other corporation lands.

In a 1978 report completed for the Forest Service, a rate of 150 million board feet per year was estimated as the maximum sustainable harvest rate for native lands in Southeast Alaska.[37] Harvests on native lands began the following year. Within ten years the harvest rate was up to 400 million board feet per year as the corporations responded to corporate pressure by cutting their timber or selling their timber rights in order to pay debts and dividends. "Some villages . . . found themselves surrounded by clear-cuts on their own land, as trees were harvested faster than they could be replanted."[38] Some corporations logged right across salmon streams, and the long-term costs of the resulting damage may never be known.

While Section 22(k) of ANCSA required that for twelve years these lands be "managed under the principle of sustained yield and under management practices for protection and enhancement of environmental quality no less stringent than such management practices on adjacent national forest land," the requirements were never enforced. Native corporations and agencies interpreted the twelve years to be effective from the 1971 date when the act passed. As conveyance of land did not even begin until eight years later, much land was not conveyed or harvested until more than twelve years after the act's approval.

In addition, the concept of sustained yield is defined in a variety of ways. According to Sealaska's vice president of resources planning and administration, "In regard to Sealaska Corporation's operation our sustained yield concern is ensuring that timber harvest and regeneration occur in a fashion such that second generations of timber will be available for harvest at a future date."[39] This concept of sustained yield is distinctly different from a commonly accepted definition of sustained yield as management that assures continuous nondeclining production and harvest over time.

Since 1983, over half the harvest of timber resources in Southeast Alaska has occurred on native lands. Most village corporations have harvested all their merchantable timber, and Sealaska will complete its logging operations around the year 2000 if harvests continue at current levels.

"We thought we were at the top of a mountain," says Byron Mallott, president of Sealaska, recalling the optimism of five years ago. "In fact, we were at the edge of a cliff and we all walked off together." The value of export quality logs has dropped to less than half its 1980 level. Lower grade pulp logs, which often make up more than half the yield from an acre of forest, are not worth hauling off the hillsides. Several corporations have simply left pulp logs to rot on the ground.

Despite the poor market, logging will continue. Many of the corporations are deeply in debt and can't afford to stop. Since 1980, six village corporations have borrowed more than $30 million to help finance roads, ports, heavy equipment and crew payrolls, according to corporate annual reports. . . . Two banks now hold more than 60,000 acres of Native lands as collateral for loans. . . .

Back in 1980, it was thought that timber investments would begin to pay off in a few years, providing the cash for dividends promised to shareholders. Now the loans are coming due. For many of the corporations, the only way to pay the bills is to log.[40]

An additional incentive to harvest came through tax reform passed in 1986 that allowed native corporations to sell their net operating losses (NOL) until 1991. Losses could be purchased by profitable corporations as a hedge against federal taxes. Native corporations could recover between 24 and 36 cents for each dollar of loss. Soft losses, the difference on paper between the value at time of conveyance and current appraised value, could only be realized by harvesting the timber or selling the stumpage rights without retaining any interest. To take advantage of this opportunity to profit from losses, corporations either sold their stumpage rights or accelerated their harvest. The purchasers of stumpage rights also accelerated harvest in order to realize a return on their investment.

Sealaska Senior Vice-President for Resources Robert Loescher was quoted as follows:

Some village corporations have exhausted their timber supply and are now being criticized for doing so. If those corporations had not harvested their timber, they would not have had the timber depletion losses that made up the vast majority of Net Operating Loss agreements. I believe that the decision to harvest their lands will turn out to be one of the best business moves those corporations ever made. . . .

No Native corporation in Southeast Alaska has enough acreage to manage on an economical sustained yield basis. In Southeast it takes 80 to 100 years for re-growth. Sealaska would have to hold its annual harvest to below 2,500 acres, and village corporations to less than 200 acres annually, in order to maintain a sustained yield timber harvest practice.[41]

Klukwan Village Corporation

Of all village corporations, Klukwan Inc. may be the most financially successful. Ranked by *Alaska Business Monthly* as the seventh largest Alaska-based corporation by revenue and eighth by number of employees for 1990, it is the only village corporation to make the magazine's "Forty-Niners" list of the top forty-nine in-state-based corporations. Of the corporation's 750 employees, 20 percent are shareholders, a percentage higher than the average for all native corporations. Klukwan also provides monthly dividends to its 253 shareholders and has established vocational training programs, training positions in subsidiary companies, and the established Klukwan Heritage Foundation, intended to "promote the cultural maintenance and preservation of their Tlingit Heritage as well as the social welfare of the shareholders."[42]

Klukwan's 1984 Annual Report discusses the strategy taken by the corporation. It defines the forest strictly as a timber resource, an asset to provide economic return.

Timber prices have actually declined over the nearly four years that we have been in operation. Since timber is an asset and all assets should be providing a decent return to the shareholder, it is easy to see why we feel that our timber is not doing its part. We have millions of dollars of timber on the stump and it is actually declining in value with each passing year. Even at an alternative rate of 10 per cent (which is easily obtainable for an investment of this size), we are missing out on millions in earnings as those dollars sit on the stump instead of in the bank. For this reason, we are harvesting significant amounts from Long Island each year to turn our timber asset into assets (primarily cash) which can meet both the immediate and long term needs of our shareholders.[43]

In a unique situation, the Klukwan tribal government already owned the reservation lands of the traditional village of Klukwan, and only village residents were entitled to economic benefits gained from the resources on this land. Special legislation was passed to provide an additional 23,000 acres to benefit shareholders from outside the reservation as well. No land was available in close proximity to the village, so the corporation selected valuable forest land on Long Island, 400 miles to the south. Thus, the village is not dependent on this forest for subsistence or for spiritual and other social and cultural values. These other value needs can be met within forests that are closer. By locating the commercial forest far from the village, the conflict between conservation of subsistence and other values and harvest and development is reduced or eliminated.

Of the various groups of Alaskan Natives, the Tlingit Indians of Klukwan had the most business expertise. Following the establishment of Klukwan Inc., they formed the companies necessary to move the timber from forest to market. Long Island Development was formed to build roads and harvest the trees and a longshoring company was formed which later became West Coast Stevedoring and became established in several ports. After initially depending on Sealaska to market its timber, in 1985 Klukwan Inc. began to do its own marketing. Members of Klukwan's board of directors have business experience and savvy lacking in many other village corporations and the board is unusually active in decision-making.

Klukwan was the first corporation to take advantage of the net operating losses tax legislation and they used the revenues to invest in real estate in an effort to diversify their holdings. Klukwan appears to demonstrate the success of the corporate model as a vehicle for settling aboriginal land claims. (However, there are many variables that worked in Klukwan's favor that were fairly unique and resulted in good fortune that was not shared by other corporations.) While Klukwan and Sealaska are examples of corporate success, ANCSA resulted in impacts to cultural values, traditions and economic devastation for many corporations.

COMPARATIVE ANALYSIS

Native Americans' special attachment to their native soil dictates the proper stewardship of their natural resources, including forests. This is critical to their persistence as a people. In order to be successful, any development alternative has to be consistent with these beliefs and ensure native involvement in the whole development process. This approach is consistent with the idea of sustainable development that suggests that development has to be community-based and environment-oriented and must ensure local control over resources. The Yakima Indian Nation constitutes an example of these ideas put to work, while the Southeast Alaska Native Corporations provide an example of development that does not meet the criteria of sustainable development.

The Yakima Indians have lived in and from their forest for centuries. It provides them with food and employment over time and it is the shelter for their beliefs. Their responsibility for the forest, as well as their cultural attachment, have led them toward a sustainable use of its resources. In contrast, the Alaska Native Corporations were set up to make money for their shareholders through the development of the natural resource assets of their lands. Much of a village corporation's land may be located hundreds of miles away from the village. This makes it easier to view the forest as simply a timber resource to be harvested rather than a collection of values to be managed and preserved. In addition, many shareholders have no historical or spiritual ties to a corporation's lands, and therefore may not feel obliged to stewardship-based management. Shareholders have little influence over the management of the land and its resources. Most of the corporations look to the land simply from a commodity standpoint.

The Yakimas approach management of their forests in a holistic manner over time and space which is consistent with the tribe's heritage. Their management is much more concerned with perpetuation of a variety of forest and resource values important to the Yakima people. The commercial use of the forest has to be within the limits established by the nation's heritage and life-style. In spite of those limits, over the years the forest has provided more than 80 percent of the total tribal income. While the forest will continue to play an important social, cultural and economic role for the Yakimas for years to come, for many Southeast Alaska Corporations the direct economic benefits have been short-term. For Sealaska, timber-related income averaged about 20 percent of the total income over ten years. Much of the cutover forest will regenerate and may be available for future harvest, some eighty or more years in the future, while some of the land may be sold or committed to other purposes.

As a result of the IRA and the BIA's policy, the principle of sustained yield has been incorporated into the Yakima Indian Nation forest management plans since the early 1960s. Timber sales managed according to this

principle add to a substantial amount of the tribe's total income, and consequently, the Yakimas have an incentive to conserve their income source
over time. While it is in the best interest of the Yakima people to manage
their forest under a sustained yield system in order to assure forest resources
in perpetuity, there are many reasons why this approach may not have been
economically feasible or desirable for the Alaska Native Corporations. Native
corporation–owned forests are not managed under sustained yield. Instead,
the forests provide a means to make money to invest in other ventures. The
Alaska Native Corporations were provided several incentives to cut trees at
a rate higher than the sustained yield: (1) to cover harvest and corporate
operating expenses; (2) to make payments on loans and fulfill other financial
obligations; and (3) until 1987, to avoid future taxes. An additional incentive
to accelerate cutting came when laws were passed to allow corporations to
sell their losses. In order to realize a profit from their losses, they had to
harvest or sell stumpage rights by 1991.

The Yakima Tribal Council represents fourteen tribes, bands, and villages,
all united under a single government and sharing the reservation lands.
Native corporations in Alaska are isolated from each other and institutionally
established as competitors. With high harvest costs and trees that grow
slowly, a sustained yield system might have been possible if all the corporations in the Southeast region of the state had joined together. Operating
individually they were unable to pursue sustained yield, and went instead
for a fast-paced liquidation of timber assets.

In the case of the Yakima Indian Nation, it is the tribal government,
together with the BIA through its Branch of Forestry, that defines the forest
management plans, even though the latter organization retains the administration of the timber sales. The Yakima Tribal Council is active in the
definition and the implementation of the whole forest planning process. For
the shareholders of the Alaska Native Corporations, the decision-making
process is in the hands of outsiders, nonnative professional managers who
may not understand natives' values, are motivated by different beliefs, and
will manage the forest as a corporate asset. Shareholders expect dividends
and jobs but few participate in management decision making, such as forest
planning processes.

The federal government holds the Yakima land in trust, and the Indians
cannot borrow capital against it. This prevents them from capitalizing on the
economic value of the standing forest. Native Corporations, on the other
hand, were granted land. The land is not held in trust by the government,
and therefore, corporations can borrow against it. However, by borrowing
against land and resources during times of inflated values, many corporations
obtained money for investments that led to direct losses. While the inability
of borrowing against their land is viewed as working against the Yakimas,
the ability to do so had negative effects for many Alaska Native Corporations.[44]

Table 11.9 summarizes the two different forest management approaches. As can be seen, the Yakimas have been quite successful in utilizing their resources consistent with sustained yield requirements, while the Alaskan corporations have not. The Yakimas have also succeeded in using timber sales to provide a major source of their tribal income (80%), while the Alaskan corporations receive only 20 percent of their income from forest resources.

Neither the Yakimas nor the Alaskan corporations have succeeded in utilizing their timber enterprises to provide any substantial employment opportunities for their tribal members. The Yakimas rely on the BIA, on the basis of its trust responsibilities, to manage their timber. The Alaskan corporations use nontribal corporate management to handle their timber responsibilities. Neither of these entities has more than 20 percent of tribal members as employees.

CONCLUSIONS

Native American philosophy that is reflected in management of their natural resources is consistent with the concept of sustainable development. Native Americans have practiced sustainability for centuries because they believe in their responsibilities toward other beings and "the people to come." For economic development to succeed, it has to be defined and implemented along the lines of their traditional beliefs and must ensure Indians' involvement in the process.

The integration of traditional beliefs with modern technology and philosophy and the active involvement of the tribe in the whole management process proved successful in the case of the Yakima Indian Nation. Conservation and development need not be in conflict, commercial use of resources need not be incompatible with preserving cultural heritage over time. Sustainability has been practiced for centuries and continues to be practiced.

Alaska Native Corporations on the other hand, are private, for-profit businesses whose institutional structure and mode of operation has led to cultural change while corporate decision making remained removed from the influence of cultural values and traditional beliefs. For many Alaska Native Corporations, this conflict was avoided by selecting forest lands far away from their villages. They managed these lands as corporate assets, not recognizing values other than economic values. Lack of consideration of the cultural framework, no direct involvement of the natives in the management process, lack of control by the natives with decisions made by corporate boards of directors, and management based only on economics may lead to depletion of the resource base and, in the most severe cases, to the bankruptcy of the corporation. While the overall success of the corporation as a means to achieve settlement of native claims will be evaluated from political, social, cultural and economic perspectives, what is provided here demonstrates the lack of corporate success in achieving sustainable development.

Table 11.9

Comparative Analysis: Yakima Indian Nation and Southeast Alaska Native Corporation

Issues	Yakima Indian Nation	Southeast Alaska Native Corporations
Population	Reservation: 27,000. Yakimas: 7,000.	15,800.
Organization	14 tribes, bands and villages under one unified tribal government.	12 independent village corporations. 1 regional corporation.
Relations to the land		
. property	Trust. BIA holds responsibility.	Privately owned by the corporations.
. history	Ancestral lands	Ancestral and non-ancestral lands. Some geographically remote from shareholders.
Forest area		
. commercial	About 435,000 acres.	About 178,000 acres.
. reserved	About 150,000 acres, about 25% of forested area.	About 31,200 acres, about 12% of forested area.
Timber-related income as percentage of total tribal income	Above 80 %.	Sealaska Corporation averaged about 20% over 10 years.
Projected annual sales (to maintain income)	About 120,000 MBF.	No goals.
Forest-related employment	Less than 25% of total tribal employment.	50 shareholders out of more than 15,000.
Forest management philosophy/style	Forest as source of multiple values. Multiple use/SY within limits established by Tribe's heritage and lifestyle.	Forest as financial asset. Pure economic incentives. Single use timber.
Development and of forest resources:		
. community-based	Yes	No
. environment-oriented	Yes	No
. local control	Tribal Council involved in policy definitions and management process.	Outside managers. Native involvement in management process only through Corporate Board

Thomas Berger, in his *Village Journey* report, wrote of the Alaska Review Commission, "Perhaps development should be redefined. Consideration should be given to Native ideas of development and to strengthening the Native subsistence economy. Subsistence can be a means of development, of enabling a people to be self-sufficient, of strengthening family and community life. It entails enhancement of an existing economic mode."[45]

The redefinition of development to accommodate Berger's concerns and others is embodied in sustainable development.

ACKNOWLEDGMENTS

The authors want to thank Hazel Umtuch Olney and Lorintha Warwick from the Yakima Indian Nation and Richard Harris from Sealaska Corporation for help in providing background information, and Professors Robert G. Lee, Vicky and Al Borrego, and John Chmelik for their useful comments on the manuscript.

NOTES

1. Jonathan Lemco, "Economic and Political Development in Organizing States," *Journal of Developing Societies*, 4 (1988): 9–21.

2. World Commission on Environment and Development, *Our Common Future* (Bungay, Suffolk, U.K.: Oxford University Press, 1987).

3. R. Goodland and G. Ledec, "Neoclassical Economics and Principles of Sustainable Development," *Ecological Modelling*, 38 (1987).

4. Richard Shearman, "The Meaning and Ethics of Sustainability," *Environmental Management*, 14 (1990): 1–8.

5. William E. Rees, "The Ecology of Sustainable Development," *The Ecologist*, 20 (1990): 18–23.

6. A. David Lester, "The Environment from an Indian Perspective," *EPA Journal*, 12, no. 1 (January/February 1986): 27–28.

7. U.S. Congress, Joint Economic Committee, *Toward Economic Development for Native American Communities: A Compendium of Papers*, submitted to the Subcommittee on Economy in Government (Washington, D.C.: U.S. General Printing Office, 1969).

8. Ibid.

9. Charles C. Geisler, Daniel Usuer, Rayna Green, and Patrick West, eds., *Indian S.I.A.: The Social Impact Assessment of Rapid Resource Development on Native Peoples* (University of Michigan Natural Resources Sociology Research Laboratory Monograph No. 3, 1982), p. 85.

10. Richard W. Stoffle and Michael J. Evans, "Holistic Conservation and Cultural Triage: American Indian Perspectives on Cultural Resources," *Human Organization*, 49 (1990): 91–99.

11. Sharon O'Brien, *American Indian Tribal Governments* (Norman: University of Oklahoma Press, 1989).

12. Ibid.

13. Gary D. Williams and William A. Babcock, *The Yakima Indian Nation Forest Heritage* (Missoula, Mont.: Heritage Research Center, 1983).

14. U.S. Department of Interior, BIA, and Confederate Tribes and Bands of the Yakima Indian Nation, *Yakima Indian Reservation Forest Management Plan* (Toppenish, Wash., 1987).

15. Williams and Babcock, *The Yakima Indian Nation Forest Heritage*, p. 138.

16. The IRA was initially rejected by the Yakima Indian Nation.

17. Williams and Babcock, *The Yakima Indian Nation Forest Heritage*, p. 231.

18. Ibid., p. 276.

19. Ibid., p. 300.

20. Ibid., p. 301.

21. Ibid., p. 313.

22. U.S. Department of Interior, BIA, and Confederate Tribes and Bands of the Yakima Indian Nation, *Yakima Indian Reservation Forest Management Plan*, p. 22.

23. Ibid., Glossary, p. 13.

24. Thomas R. Berger, *Village Journey* (New York: Hill and Wang, 1985).

25. The term *Alaska Native* refers to Alaska's Eskimos, Indians, and Aleuts, who make up 14 percent of the state's population.

26. Berger, *Village Journey*, p. 15.

27. Gary C. Anders and Steve J. Langdon, "Alaska Native Regional Strategies," *Human Organization*, 48 (1989): 162–72.

28. Nicholas E. Flanders, "The Alaska Native Corporation as Conglomerate: The Problem of Profitability," *Human Organization*, 48 (1989): 299–312.

29. Ibid.; Gunnar Knapp, *Native Timber Harvests in Southeast Alaska* (Anchorage: Institute of Social and Economic Research, 1989).

30. Flanders, "Alaska Native Corporation," pp. 299–312. Knapp, *Native Timber Harvests*.

31. Berger, *Village Journey*; Lael Morgan, "Alaska in the '90s: Twenty Years under the Alaska Native Claims Settlement Act, a Milestone in State History," *Alaska Airlines Magazine* (October 1991): 20–25.

32. Berger, *Village Journey*.

33. María Williams and Ross Anderson, "From Villages to Boardrooms," *Seattle Times/Seattle Post Intelligencer*, 22 September 1991.

34. Steven McNabb, "Impacts of Federal Policy Decisions on Alaska Natives," *The Journal of Ethnic Studies*, 18 (1985): 111–26.

35. According to Knapp, "Native Timber Harvests," when conveyances are complete, Sealaska will have received between 270,000 and 340,000 acres, while village corporations will have received 23,000 acres each.

36. Ibid.

37. Ibid.

38. Williams and Anderson, "From Villages to Boardrooms," p. E–2.

39. Richard P. Harris, personal communications, October 1991 and March 1992.

40. Knapp, *Native Timber Harvests*, p. 36.

41. Ibid., p. 38.

42. Rosita Worl, "Klukwan, Inc. A successful village corporation," *Alaska Native Magazine*, 5 (1987): 16–18.

43. Knapp, *Native Timber Harvests*, p. 39.

44. O'Brien, *American Indian Tribal Governments*.

45. Berger, *Village Journey*, p. 47.

APPENDIX: Southeast Alaska Native Corporations

Corporation Type	Village or City	Corporation Name	Number of Shareholders*	Land Entitlement (acres)
Village	Angoon	Kootznoowoo, Inc.	620	23,040
Village	Craig	Shaan-Seet, Inc.	317	23,040
Village	Hoonah	Huna Totem Corp.	870	23,040
Village	Hydaburg	Haida Corp.	563	23,040
Urban	Juneau	Goldbelt, Inc.	2,722	23,040
Village	Kake	Kake Tribal Corp.	558	23,040
Village	Kasaan	Kavilco, Inc.	119	23,040
Village	Klawock	Klawock Heenya Corp.	518	23,040
Village	Klukwan	Klukwan, Inc.	250	23,040
Village	Saxman	Cape Fox Corp.	230	23,040
Urban	Sitka	Shee-Atika, Inc.	1,804	23,040
Village	Yakutat	Yak-Tat-Kwaan, Inc.	392	23,040
Total, village and urban			8,963	276,480
Regional		Sealaska Corporation	15,388	approx. 273,000
Total			15,388	approx. 549,480

Source: Gunnar Knapp, *Native Timber Harvests in Southeast Alaska* (Anchorage: Institute of Social and Economic Research, 1989).
* Village corporation stockholders are also Sealaska stockholders.

Appendix

TITLE III—TRIBAL SELF-GOVERNANCE DEMONSTRATION PROJECT CONTAINED IN PUBLIC LAW 100–472, SEPTEMBER 15, 1988

Section 301. The Secretary of the Interior shall, for a period not to exceed five years following enactment of this title, conduct a research and demonstration project to be known as the Tribal Self-Governance Project according to the provisions of this title.

Section 302. (a) The Secretary shall select twenty tribes to participate in the demonstration project, as follows:

(1) a tribe that successfully completes a Self-Governance Planning Grant, authorized by Conference Report 100–498 to accompany H.J. Res. 395, One Hundredth Congress, first session shall be selected to participate in the demonstration project; and

(2) the Secretary shall select, in such a manner as to achieve geographic representation, the remaining tribal participants from the pool of qualified applicants. In order to be in the pool of qualified applicants—

(A) The governing body of the tribe shall request participation in the demonstration project;

(B) such tribe shall have operated two or more mature contracts; and

(C) such tribe shall have demonstrated for the previous three fiscal years, financial stability and financial management capability as evidenced by such tribe having no significant and material audit exceptions in the required annual audit of such tribe's self-determination contracts.

Section 303. *(a)* The Secretary is directed to negotiate, and to enter into, an annual written funding agreement with the governing body of a participating tribal government which—

(1) shall authorize the tribe to plan, conduct, consolidate, and administer programs, services and functions authorized under the Act of April 16, 1934 (48 Stat. 596), as amended, and the Act of November 2, 1921 (42 Stat. 208);

(2) subject to the terms of the written agreement authorized by this title, shall authorize the tribe to redesign programs, activities, functions or services and to reallocate funds for such programs, activities, functions or services;

(3) shall not include funds provided pursuant to the Tribally Controlled Community College Assistance Act (Public Law 95–471), for elementary and secondary schools under the Indian School Equalization Formula pursuant to title XI of the Education Amendments of 1978 (Public Law 95–561, as amended), or for either the Flathead Agency Irrigation Division or the Flathead Agency Power Division; Provided, That nothing in this section shall affect the contractibility of such divisions under section 102 of this Act;

(4) shall specify the services to be provided, the functions to be performed, and the responsibilities of the tribe and the Secretary pursuant to this agreement;

(5) shall specify the authority of the tribe and the Secretary, and the procedures to be used, to reallocate funds or modify budget allocations within any project year;

(6) shall except as provided in paragraphs (1) and (2), provide for payment by the Secretary to the tribe of funds from one or more programs, services, functions, or activities in an amount equal to that which the tribe would have been eligible to receive under contracts and grants under this Act, including direct program costs and indirect costs, and for funds which are specifically related to the provision by the Secretary of services, and benefits to the tribe and its members; Provided, however, That funds for trust services to individual Indians are available under this written agreement only to the extent that the same services which would have been provided by the Secretary are provided to individual Indians by the tribe;

(7) shall not allow the Secretary to waive, modify or diminish in any way the trust responsibility of the United States with respect to Indian tribes and individual Indians which exists under treaties, Executive orders, and Acts of Congress;

(8) shall allow for retrocession of programs or portions thereof pursuant to section 105(e) of this Act; and

(9) shall be submitted by the Secretary ninety days in advance of the proposed effective date of the agreement of each tribe which is served by the agency which is serving the tribe which is a party to the funding agreement and to the Congress for review by the Select Committee on Indian Affairs of the Senate and the Committee on Interior and Insular Affairs of the House of Representatives.

(b) For the year for which, and to the extent to which, funding is provided to a tribe pursuant to this title, such tribe—

(1) shall not be entitled to contract with the Secretary for such funds

under section 102, except that such tribe shall be eligible for new programs on the same basis as other tribes; and

(2) shall be responsible for the administration of programs, services and activities pursuant to agreements under this title.

(c) At the request of the governing body of the tribe and under the terms of an agreement pursuant to subsection (a), the Secretary shall provide funding to such tribe to implement the agreement.

(d) For the purpose of section 110 of this Act the term *contract* shall also include agreements authorized by this title.

(e) To the extent feasible, the Secretary shall interpret Federal laws and regulations in a manner that will facilitate the agreements authorized by this title.

Section 304. The Secretary shall identify, in the President's annual budget request to the Congress, any funds proposed to be included in the Tribal Self-Governance Project. The use of funds pursuant to this title shall be subject to specific directives or limitations as may be included in applicable appropriations Acts.

Section 305. The Secretary shall submit to the Congress a written report on July 1 and January 1 of each of the five years following the date of enactment of this title on the relative costs and benefits of the Tribal Self-Governance Project. Such report shall be based on mutually determined baseline measurements jointly developed by the Secretary and participating tribes, and shall separately include the views of the tribes.

Section 306. Nothing in this title shall be construed to limit or reduce in any way the services, contracts or funds that any other Indian tribe or tribal organization is eligible to receive under section 102 or any other applicable Federal law and the provisions of section 110 of this Act shall be available to any tribe or Indian organization which alleges that a funding agreement is in violation of this section.

Section 210. Savings Provisions.

Nothing in this Act shall be construed as—

(1) affecting, modifying, diminishing, or otherwise impairing the sovereign immunity from suit enjoyed by an Indian tribe; or

(2) authorizing or requiring the termination of any existing trust responsibility of the United States with respect to Indian people.

Section 211. Severability.

If any provision of this Act or the application thereof to any Indian tribe, entity, person or circumstance is held invalid, neither the remainder of this Act, nor the application of any provisions herein to other Indian tribes, entities, persons, or circumstances, shall be affected thereby.

Selected Bibliography

Barsh, Russel Lawrence, and James Youngblood Henderson. *The Road: Indian Tribes and Political Liberty*. Berkeley: University of California Press, 1980.

Berger, Thomas R. *Village Journey: The Report of the Alaska Native Review Commission*. New York: Hill and Wang, 1985.

Berkhofer, Robert F., Jr. *The White Man's Indian*. New York: Knopf, 1978.

Canby, William C., Jr. *American Indian Law*. St. Paul, Minn.: West Publishing Co., 1988.

Castile, George P., and Robert L. Bee, eds. *State and Reservation*. Albuquerque: University of New Mexico Press, 1992.

Churchill, Ward, ed. *Marxism and Native Americans*. Boston: South End Press, [1982].

Cohen, Fay G. *Treaties on Trial*. Seattle: University of Washington Press, 1982.

Cornell, Stephen. *The Return of the Native: American Indian Political Resurgence*. New York: Oxford University Press, 1988.

Deloria, Vine, Jr. *Behind the Trail of Broken Treaties*. New York: Delacorte Press, 1974.

Deloria, Vine, Jr., and Clifford M. Lytle. *American Indians, American Justice*. Austin: University of Texas Press, 1983.

Herzberg, Hazel. *The Search for an American Indian Identity*. Syracuse: Syracuse University Press, 1971.

Jacobs, Wilbur R. *Dispossessing the American Indian*. Norman: University of Oklahoma Press, 1985.

Lazarus, Edward. *Black Hills/White Justice*. New York: HarperCollins, 1991.

Limerick, Patricia Nelson. *The Legacy of Conquest*. New York: Norton, 1987.

Lyden, Fremont J., and Lyman H. Legters, eds. *Native Americans and Public Policy*. Pittsburgh, Penn.: University of Pittsburgh Press, 1992.

Matthiessen, Peter. *Indian Country*. New York: Viking Press, 1984.

Matthiessen, Peter. *In the Spirit of Crazy Horse*. New York: Viking Press, 1991.

Nabokov, Peter, ed. *Native American Testimony*. New York: Viking Press, 1991.

O'Brien, Sharon, ed. *American Indian Tribal Governments*. Norman: University of Oklahoma Press, 1989.

Olson, James S., and Raymond Wilson. *Native Americans in the Twentieth Century*. Champaign: University of Illinois Press, 1984.

Pevar, Stephen L. *The Rights of Indians and Tribes*. New York: Bantam Books, 1983.

Philp, Kenneth R., ed. *Indian Self-Rule*. Salt Lake City, Utah: Howe Brothers, 1986.

Snipp, C. Matthew. *American Indians: The First of This Land*. New York: Russell Sage Foundation, 1989.

Snipp, C. Matthew, ed. *Public Policy Impacts on American Indian Economic Development*. Albuquerque: University of New Mexico, Institute for Native American Development, 1988.

Sutton, Imre, ed. *Irredeemable America*. Albuquerque: University of New Mexico Press, 1985.

Talbot, Steve. *Roots of Oppression: The American Indian Question*. New York: International Publishers, 1981.

Thornton, Russell. *American Indian Holocaust and Survival*. Norman: University of Oklahoma Press, 1987.

U.S. Department of the Interior. *Report of the Task Force on American Indian Development*. U.S. Department of the Interior, 1986.

Vecsey, Christopher, ed. *Handbook of American Indian Religious Freedom*. New York: Crossroad Publishing Co., 1991.

Wilkinson, Charles F. *American Indians, Time and the Law*. New Haven, Conn.: Yale University Press, 1987.

Wright, Ronald. *Stolen Continents: The Americas through Indian Eyes since 1492*. Boston: Houghton Mifflin, 1992.

Index

About the Editors and Contributors

LYMAN H. LEGTERS is Professor Emeritus at the School of International Studies, University of Washington, and Senior Fellow at the William O. Douglas Institute, Washington.

FREMONT J. LYDEN is Professor Emeritus at the Graduate School of Public Affairs, University of Washington, and board member of the Kluckhohn Research Center. He has written at length on public policy problems. His most recent book, co-edited with Lyman H. Legters, was *Native Americans and Public Policy* (1992).

RUSSEL LAWRENCE BARSH, an attorney who has represented Indian tribes, is affiliated with the Apanuwek Institute of the Mikmaq Research Center, Cape Breton, Nova Scotia.

WARD CHURCHILL (Cree/Cherokee Metis), is Professor of American Indian Studies and Communications in the Center for Studies of Race and Ethnicity in America at the University of Colorado.

STEPHEN CORNELL is Professor of Sociology at the University of California, San Diego.

GRACIELA ETCHART, a doctoral candidate in the Special Individual Ph.D. program at the University of Washington, is on a MacArthur Fellowship for dissertation research in Brazil.

THERESA JULNES is Professor of Public Administration at Portland State University.

JOSEPH P. KALT is Professor of Political Economy in the Kennedy School of Government at Harvard University.

LINDA KRUGER, a graduate student in forestry at the University of Washington, is a research social scientist at the Pacific Northwest Research Station of the U.S. Forest Service.

ERNEST G. MILLER is a Professor in the Graduate School of Public Affairs at the University of Washington.

C. PATRICK MORRIS is Professor of Native American Studies at the University of Washington, Bothell.

JERRY D. STUBBEN, Professor of Political Science, is Chair of the American Indian Studies program at Iowa State University.

RONALD L. TROSPER is a Professor in the School of Forestry and Director of the Native American Forest program at Northern Arizona University.

WILLIAM WILLARD is Professor and Chair of the Department of Comparative American Cultures at Washington State University.